MAN'S EXISTENCE PRECEEDS HIS
ESSENCE

William Barrett is widely known as one of the first philosophers to introduce existentialism to America. Besides a long and distinguished career as a professor of philosophy, he has been editor of *Partisan Review* and the literary critic for *Atlantic Monthly*. Barrett is the author of *The Illusion of Technique* and *The Truants*, among other books.

IRRATIONAL MAN

A Study in Existential Philosophy

WILLIAM BARRETT

DOUBLEDAY ANCHOR BOOKS
DOUBLEDAY & COMPANY, INC.,
GARDEN CITY, NEW YORK

For Jason
whose friendship has meant much

Doubleday & Company, Inc., would like to thank the publishers for their kind permission to reprint quotations from the following books:

A Farewell to Arms, by Ernest Hemingway. Used by permission of the publishers, Charles Scribner's Sons.

The Republic of Silence, by Jean-Paul Sartre. Used by permission of Harcourt, Brace and Company, Inc.

What Is Literature?, by Jean-Paul Sartre. Reprinted by permission of the publishers, Philosophical Library.

A Passage to India, by E. M. Forster. Reprinted by permission of Harcourt, Brace and Company, Inc., New York, and Edward Arnold, Ltd., London.

Landscaped Tables, Landscapes of the Mind, "Stones of Philosophy," by Jean Dubuffet, preface to an exhibition of paintings by Dubuffet at the Pierre Matisse Gallery, February 12, 1952. Used by permission of the Pierre Matisse Gallery.

AUTHOR'S NOTE

I wish to thank Mr. Andrew Chiappe and Miss Catherine Carver for reading the manuscript and making many valuable suggestions for its improvement.

Irrational Man was originally published by Doubleday & Company, Inc. in 1958.

Anchor Books edition: 1962

CONTENTS

"THE PRESENT AGE"

Part One

THE ADVENT OF
EXISTENTIALISM

Chapter One

THE story is told (by Kierkegaard) of the absent-minded
man so abstracted from his own life that he hardly knows
he exists until, one fine morning, he wakes up to find himself dead. It is a story that has a special point today, since
this civilization of ours has at last got its hands on weapons
with which it could easily bring upon itself the fate of
Kierkegaard's hero: we could wake up tomorrow morning
dead—and without ever having touched the roots of our own
existence. There is by this time widespread anxiety and
even panic over the dangers of the atomic age; but the public soul-searching and stocktaking rarely, if ever, go to the
heart of the matter. We do not ask ourselves what the ultimate ideas behind our civilization are that have brought us
into this danger; we do not search for the human face behind the bewildering array of instruments that man has
forged; in a word, we do not dare to be philosophical. Uneasy as we are over the atomic age, on the crucial question
of existence itself we choose to remain as absent-minded as
the man in Kierkegaard's story. One reason we do so lies
in the curiously remote position to which modern society
has relegated philosophy, and which philosophers themselves have been content to accept.

If philosophers are really to deal with the problem of human existence—and no other professional group in society
is likely to take over the job for them—they might very well
begin by asking: How does philosophy itself exist at the

present time? Or, more concretely: How do philosophers exist in the modern world? Nothing very high-flown, metaphysical, or even abstract is intended by this question; and our preliminary answer to it is equally concrete and prosy. Philosophers today exist in the Academy, as members of departments of philosophy in universities, as professional teachers of a more or less theoretical subject known as philosophy. This simple observation, baldly factual and almost statistical, does not seem to take us very deeply into the abstruse problem of existence; but every effort at understanding must take off from our actual situation, the point at which we stand. "Know thyself!" is the command Socrates issued to philosophers at the beginning (or very close to it) of all Western philosophy; and contemporary philosophers might start on the journey of self-knowledge by coming to terms with the somewhat grubby and uninspiring fact of the social status of philosophy as a profession. It is in any case a fact with some interesting ambiguities.

To profess, according to the dictionary, is to confess or declare openly, and therefore publicly; consequently, to acknowledge a calling before the world. So the word bears originally a religious connotation, as when we speak of a profession of faith. But in our present society, with its elaborate subdividing of human functions, a profession is the specialized social task—requiring expertness and know-how —that one performs for pay: it is a living, one's livelihood. Professional people are lawyers, doctors, dentists, engineers —and also professors of philosophy. The profession of the philosopher in the modern world is to be a professor of philosophy; and the realm of Being which the philosopher inhabits as a living individual is no more recondite than a corner within the university.

Not enough has been made of this academic existence of the philosopher, though some contemporary Existentialists have directed searching comment upon it. The price one pays for having a profession is a *déformation professionelle*, as the French put it—a professional deformation. Doctors and engineers tend to see things from the viewpoint of their own specialty, and usually show a very marked blind spot to whatever falls outside this particular province. The more specialized a vision the sharper its focus; but also the more nearly total the blind spot toward all things that lie on the periphery of this focus. As a human being, functioning professionally within the Academy, the philosopher can hardly be expected to escape his own professional deformation, especially since it has become a law of modern society that man is assimilated more and more completely to his social function. And it is just here that a troublesome and profound ambiguity resides for the philosopher today. The profession of philosophy did not always have the narrow and specialized meaning it now has. In ancient Greece it had the very opposite: instead of a specialized theoretical discipline philosophy there was a concrete way of life, a total vision of man and the cosmos in the light of which the individual's whole life was to be lived. These earliest philosophers among the Greeks were seers, poets, almost shamans—as well as the first thinkers. Mythological and intuitive elements permeate their thinking even where we see the first historical efforts toward conceptualization; they traffic with the old gods even while in the process of coining a new significance for them; and everywhere in the fragments of these pre-Socratic Greeks is the sign of a revelation greater than themselves which they are unveiling for the rest of mankind. Even in Plato, where the thought has already become more differentiated and specialized and where the main lines of philosophy as a theoretical discipline are being laid down, the *motive* of philosophy is very different from the cool pursuit of the savant engaged in research. Philosophy is for Plato a passionate way of life; and the imperishable example of Socrates, who lived and died for the philosophic life, was the guiding line of Plato's career for five decades after his master's death. Philosophy is the soul's search for salvation, which means for Plato deliverance from the suffering and evils of the natural world. Even today the motive for an Oriental's taking up the study of philosophy is altogether different from that of a Western student: for the Oriental the only reason for bothering with philosophy is to find release or peace from the torments and perplexities of life. Philosophy can never quite divest itself of these aboriginal claims. They are part of the past, which is never lost, lurking under the veneer of even the most sophisticatedly rational of contemporary philosophies; and even those philosophers who have altogether forsworn the great vision are called upon, particularly by the layman who may not be aware of the historical fate of specialization that has fallen upon philosophy, to give answers to the great questions.

The ancient claims of philosophy are somewhat embarrassing to the contemporary philosopher, who has to justify his existence within the sober community of professional savants and scientists. The modern university is as much an expression of the specialization of the age as is the modern factory. Moreover, the philosopher knows that everything we prize about our modern knowledge, each thing in it that represents an immense stride in certainty and power over what the past called its knowledge, is the result of specialization. Modern science was made possible by the social organization of knowledge. The philosopher today is therefore pressed, and simply by reason of his objective social role in the community, into an imitation of the scientist: he too seeks to perfect the weapons of his knowledge through specialization. Hence the extraordinary preoccupation with technique among modern philosophers, with logical and linguistic analysis, syntax and semantics; and in general with the refining away of all content for the sake of formal subtlety. The movement known as Logical Positivism, in this country (the atmosphere of humanism is probably more dominant in the European universities than here in the United States), actually trafficked upon the *guilt* philosophers felt at not being scientists; that is, at not being researchers producing reliable knowledge in the mode of science. The natural insecurity of philosophers, which in any case lies at the core of their whole uncertain enterprise, was here aggravated beyond measure by the insistence that they transform themselves into scientists.

Specialization is the price we pay for the advancement of knowledge. A price, because the path of specialization

leads away from the ordinary and concrete acts of understanding in terms of which man actually lives his day-to-
day life. It used to be said (I do not know whether this
would still hold today) that if a dozen men were to die the
meaning of Einstein's Theory of Relativity would be lost to
mankind. No mathematician today can embrace the whole
of his subject as did the great Gauss little more than a century ago. The philosopher who has pursued his own specialized path leading away from the urgent and the actual may
claim that his situation parallels that of the scientist, that
his own increasing remoteness from life merely demonstrates
the inexorable law of advancing knowledge. But the cases
are in fact not parallel; for out of the abstractions that only
a handful of experts can understand the physicist is able
to detonate a bomb that alters—and can indeed put an end
to—the life of ordinary mankind. The philosopher has no
such explosive effect upon the life of his time. In fact, if
they were candid, philosophers today would recognize that
they have less and less influence upon the minds around
them. To the degree that their existence has become specialized and academic, their importance beyond the university
cloisters has declined. Their disputes have become disputes
among themselves; and far from gaining the enthusiastic
support needed for a strong popular movement, they now
have little contact with whatever general intellectual elite
still remain here outside the Academy. John Dewey was the
last American philosopher to have any widespread influence
on non-academic life in this country.

Such was the general philosophic situation here when,
after the Second World War, the news of Existentialism
arrived. It was news, which is in itself an unusual thing for
philosophy these days. True, the public interest was not
altogether directed toward the philosophic matters in question. It was news from France, and therefore distinguished
by the particular color and excitement that French intellectual life is able to generate. French Existentialism was
a kind of Bohemian ferment in Paris; it had, as a garnish
for the philosophy, the cult its younger devotees had made

of night-club hangouts, American jazz, special hairdos and style of dress. All this made news for American journalists trying to report on the life that had gone on in Paris during the war and the German Occupation. Moreover, Existentialism was a literary movement as well, and its leaders—Jean-Paul Sartre, Albert Camus, Simone de Beauvoir—were brilliant and engaging writers. Nevertheless, that the American public was curious about the philosophy itself cannot altogether be denied. Perhaps the curiosity consisted in large part of wanting to know what the name, the big word, meant; nothing stirs up popular interest so much as a slogan. But there was also a genuine philosophic curiosity, however inchoate, in all this, for here was a movement that seemed to convey a message and a meaning to a good many people abroad, and Americans wanted to know about it. The desire for meaning still slumbers, though submerged, beneath the extroversion of American life.

The philosophic news from France was only a small detail in the history of the postwar years. French Existentialism, as a cult, is now as dead as last year's fad. Its leaders, to be sure, are still flourishing: Sartre and Simone de Beauvoir are still phenomenally productive, though in the case of Sartre we feel that he has already made at least his penultimate statement, so that now we have his message pretty completely; Albert Camus, the most sensitive and searching of the trio, long ago split off from the group, but has continued his exploration into themes that belonged to the original Existentialist preoccupations. As news and excitement, the movement is altogether dead; and yet it has left its mark on nearly all the writing and thinking of Europe of the last ten years. During the grim decade of the Cold War no intellectual movement of comparable importance appeared. Existentialism is the best in the way of a new and creative movement that these rather uninspired postwar years have been able to turn up. We have to say at least this in a spirit of cool critical assessment, even when we acknowledge all the frivolous and sensational elements that got attached to it.

The important thing, to repeat, was that here was a philosophy that was able to cross the frontier from the Academy into the world at large. This should have been a welcome sign to professional philosophers that ordinary mankind still could hunger and thirst after philosophy if what they were given to bite down on was something that seemed to have a connection with their lives. Instead, the reception given the new movement by philosophers was anything but cordial. Existentialism was rejected, often without very much scrutiny, as sensationalism or mere "psychologizing," a literary attitude, postwar despair, nihilism, or heaven knows what besides. The very themes of Existentialism were something of a scandal to the detached sobriety of Anglo-American philosophy. Such matters as anxiety, death, the conflict between the bogus and the genuine self, the faceless man of the masses, the experience of the death of God are scarcely the themes of analytic philosophy. Yet they are themes of life: People do die, people do struggle all their lives between the demands of real and counterfeit selves, and we do live in an age in which neurotic anxiety has mounted out of all proportion so that even minds inclined to believe that all human problems can be solved by physical techniques begin to label "mental health" as the first of our public problems. The reaction of professional philosophers to Existentialism was merely a symptom of their imprisonment in the narrowness of their own discipline. Never was the professional deformation more in evidence. The divorce of mind from life was something that had happened to philosophers simply in the pursuit of their own specialized problems. Since philosophers are only a tiny fraction of the general population, the matter would not be worth laboring were it not that this divorce of mind from life happens also to be taking place, catastrophically, in modern civilization everywhere. It happens too, as we shall see, to be one of the central themes of existential philosophy—for which we may in time owe it no small debt.

All of this has to be said even when we do concede a certain sensational and youthfully morbid side to French Existentialism. The genius of Sartre—and by this time there can scarcely be doubt that it is real genius—has an undeniably morbid side. But there is no human temperament that does not potentially reveal some truth, and Sartre's morbidity has its own unique and revelatory power. It is true also that a good deal in French Existentialism was the expression of an historical mood—the shambles of defeat after the "phony war" and the experience of utter dereliction under the German Occupation. But are moods of this kind so unimportant and trifling as to be unworthy of the philosopher's consideration? Would it not in fact be a serious and appropriate task for the philosopher to elaborate what is involved in certain basic human moods? We are living in an epoch that has produced two world wars, and these wars were not merely passing incidents but characterize the age down to its marrow; surely a philosophy that has experienced these wars may be said to have some connection with the life of its time. Philosophers who dismissed Existentialism as "merely a mood" or "a postwar mood" betrayed a curious blindness to the concerns of the human spirit, in taking the view that philosophic truth can be found only in those areas of experience in which human moods are *not* present.

Naturally enough, something very deeply American came to the surface in this initial response to Existentialism. Once again the old drama of America confronting Europe was being played out. Existentialism was so definitely a European expression that its very somberness went against the grain of our native youthfulness and optimism. The new philosophy was not a peculiarly French phenomenon, but a creation of the western European continent at the moment in history when all of its horizons—political as well as spiritual—were rapidly shrinking. The American has not yet assimilated psychologically the disappearance of his own geographical frontier, his spiritual horizon is still the limitless play of human possibilities, and as yet he has not lived through the crucial experience of human finitude. (This last is still only an abstract phrase to him.) The expression of themes like those of Existentialism was bound to strike the American as a symptom of despair and defeat, and, generally, of the declining vigor of a senescent civilization. But America, spiritually speaking, is still tied to European civilization, even though the political power lines now run the other way; and these European expressions simply point out the path that America itself will have eventually to tread; when it does it will know at last what the European is talking about.

It is necessary thus to emphasize the European—rather than the specifically French—origins of Existentialism, since in its crucial issues the whole meaning of European civilization (of which we in America are still both descendants and dependents) is radically put in question. Jean-Paul Sartre is not Existentialism—it still seems necessary to make this point for American readers; he does not even represent, as we shall see later, the deepest impulse of this philosophy. Now that French Existentialism as a popular movement (once even something of a popular nuisance) is safely dead, having left a few new reputations surviving in its wake, we can see it much more clearly for what it is—a small branch of a very much larger tree. And the roots of this larger tree reach down into the remotest depths of the Western tradition. Even in the portions of the tree more immediately visible to our contemporary eyes, we have something which is the combined product of many European thinkers, some of them operating in radically different national traditions. Sartre's immediate sources, for example, are German: *Martin Heidegger* (1889–   ) and *Karl Jaspers* (1883–   ), and for his method the great German phenomenologist, *Edmund Husserl* (1859–1938). Heidegger and Jaspers are, strictly speaking, the creators of existential philosophy in this century: they have given it its decisive stamp, brought its problems to new and more precise expression, and in general formed the model around which the thinking of all the other Existentialists revolves. Neither Heidegger nor Jaspers created their philosophies out of whole cloth: the atmosphere of German philosophy during the first part of this century had become quickened by the search for a new "philosophical anthropology"—a new in-

terpretation of man—made necessary by the extraordinary
additions to knowledge in all of the special sciences that
dealt with man. Here particularly the name of *Max Scheler*
(1874–1928), usually not classed as an "existentialist,"
must be mentioned, for his great sensitivity to this new concrete data from psychology and the social sciences, but
most of all for his penetrating grasp of the fact that modern
man had become in his very essence problematic. Both
Scheler and Heidegger owe a great debt to Husserl, yet
the relation of the latter to Existentialism is extremely paradoxical. By temperament Husserl was the anti-modernist
par excellence among modern philosophers; he was a passionate exponent of classical rationalism, whose single and
exalted aim was to ground the rationality of man upon a
more adequate and comprehensive basis than the past had
achieved. Yet by insisting that the philosopher must cast
aside preconceptions in attending to the actual concrete
data of experience, Husserl flung wide the doors of philosophy to the rich existential content that his more radical followers were to quarry. In his last writings Husserl's thought
even turns slowly and haltingly in the direction of Heidegger's themes. The great rationalist is dragged slowly to
earth.

But what lifted Heidegger and Jaspers above the level of
their contemporary philosophic atmosphere and impelled
them to give a new voice to the intellectual consciousness
of the age was their decisive relation to two older nineteenth-century thinkers: *Sören Kierkegaard* (1813–1855)
and *Friedrich Nietzsche* (1844–1900). Jaspers has been
the more outspoken in acknowledging this filial relation-
ship: the philosopher, he says, who has really *experienced*
the thought of Kierkegaard and Nietzsche can never again
philosophize in the traditional mode of academic philosophy. Neither Kierkegaard nor Nietzsche was an academic
philosopher; Nietzsche, for seven years a professor of Greek
at Basel in Switzerland, did his most radical philosophizing
after he had fled from the world of the university and its
sober community of scholars; Kierkegaard never held an
academic chair. Neither developed a system; both in fact

gibed at systematizers and even the possibilities of a philosophic system; and while they proliferated in ideas that
were far in advance of their time and could be spelled out
only by the following century, these ideas were not the
stock themes of academic philosophy. Ideas are not even
the real subject matter of these philosophers—and this in
itself is something of a revolution in Western philosophy:
their central subject is the unique experience of the single
one, the individual, who chooses to place himself on trial
before the gravest question of his civilization. For both
Kierkegaard and Nietzsche this gravest question is Christianity, though they were driven to opposite positions in
regard to it. Kierkegaard set himself the task of determin-
ing whether Christianity can still be lived or whether a civilization still nominally Christian must finally confess spiritual bankruptcy; and all his ideas were simply sparks thrown
off in the fiery process of seeking to realize the truth of
Christ in his own life. Nietzsche begins with the confession
of bankruptcy: God is dead, says Nietzsche, and European
man if he were more honest, courageous, and had keener
eyes for what went on in the depths of his own soul would
know that this death has taken place there, despite the lip
service still paid to the old formulae and ideals of religion.
Nietzsche experimented with his own life to be able to answer the question: What next? What happens to the race
when at long last it has severed the umbilical cord that
bound it for millennia to the gods and a transcendent
world beyond this earthly world? He placed his own life
on trial in order to experience this death of God to its
depths. More than thinkers, Kierkegaard and Nietzsche
were witnesses—witnesses who suffered for their time what
the time itself would not acknowledge as its own secret
wound. No concept or system of concepts lies at the center
of either of their philosophies, but rather the individual human personality itself struggling for self-realization. No
wonder both are among the greatest of intuitive psychologists.

Though Kierkegaard was a Dane, intellectual Denmark
in his time was a cultural province of Germany, and his

thought, nourished almost completely by German sources, belongs ultimately within the wider tradition of German philosophy. Modern existential philosophy is thus by and large a creation of the German genius. It rises out of that old strain of the Germanic mind which, since Meister Eckhart at the end of the Middle Ages, has sought to give voice to the deepest inwardness of European man. But this voice is also a thoroughly modern one and speaks neither with the serene mysticism of Eckhart nor with the intellectual intoxication and dreaminess of German idealism. Here introversion has come face to face with its other, the concrete actualities of life before which the older German philosophy had remained in wool-gathering abstraction; face to face with historical crisis; with time, death, and personal anxiety.

Yet modern Existentialism is not of exclusively German provenance; rather it is a total European creation, perhaps the last philosophic legacy of Europe to America or whatever other civilization is now on its way to supplant Europe. The number of European thinkers of widely varying racial and national traditions who have collaborated in the fabrication of existential philosophy is much larger than the public, still somewhat bedazzled by French Existentialism, imagines. The picture of French Existentialism itself is not complete without the figure of *Gabriel Marcel* (1889–), Sartre's extreme opposite and trenchant critic, a devout Catholic whose philosophic sources are not German at all, but are surprisingly enough the American idealist Josiah Royce and the French intuitionist Henri Bergson. According to the record he has left in his *Metaphysical Journal,* Marcel's existentialism developed out of purely personal experience, and perhaps that is its greatest significance for us, whatever final value his philosophic formulations may have. The intimacy and concreteness of personal feeling taught Marcel the incompleteness of all philosophies that deal purely in intellectual abstractions. But the door that opened upon this experience was Bergson's doctrine of intuition; and the figure of *Henri Bergson* (1859–1941) cannot really be omitted from any historical sketch of modern existential philosophy. Without Bergson the whole atmosphere in which Existentialists have philosophized would not have been what it was. He was the first to insist on the insufficiency of the abstract intelligence to grasp the richness of experience, on the urgent and irreducible reality of time, and—perhaps in the long run the most significant insight of all—on the inner depth of the psychic life which cannot be measured by the quantitative methods of the physical sciences; and for making all of these points the Existentialists stand greatly in his debt. Yet, from the existential point of view, there is a curious incompleteness about Bergson's thinking, as if he never came really to grips with the central subject, Man, but remained perpetually dodging and tacking about on its periphery. Certain premises of Bergson's thought—which remain, to be sure, little more than premises—are more radical than any the Existentialists have yet explored. Bergson's reputation except in France has greatly fallen off, but he is due for a revival, at which time hindsight will enable us to see that his philosophy contains much more than it seemed to, even at the height of his fame.

The Russians (White Russians, of course) have contributed three typical and interesting figures to Existentialism: *Vladimir Solovev* (1853–1900), *Leon Shestov* (1868–1938), and *Nikolai Berdyaev* (1874–1948), of whom only the last seems to be known in this country. These men are all spiritual children of Dostoevski, and they bring a peculiarly Russian vision to Existentialism: total, extreme, and apocalyptic. Solovev, primarily a theologian and religious writer, belonged to the first generation that felt the impact of Dostoevski as both prophet and novelist, and he develops the typically Dostoevskian position that there can be no compromise between the spirit of rationalism and the spirit of religion. Both Berdyaev and Shestov were Russian *émigrés*, cosmopolitans of the spirit, but nevertheless remained Russian to the core; and their writings, like those of the great Russian novelists of the nineteenth century, can show us what the mind of western Europe, the heir of classicism and rationalism, looks like to an outsider—particularly to a Russian outsider who will be satisfied with no philosophic answers that fall short of the total and passionate feelings of his own humanity.

Modern Spain has contributed two figures to existential philosophy, in *Miguel de Unamuno* (1864–1936) and *José Ortega y Gasset* (1883–1955). Unamuno, a poet first and last, wrote one of the most moving and genuine philosophic books of the whole movement; his *Tragic Sense of Life* is a work that fulfills, though in an anti-Nietzschean sense, Nietzsche's command to remain true to the earth. Unamuno had read Kierkegaard, but his thought is an expression of his own personal passion and of the Basque earth from which he sprang. Ortega, a cooler and more cosmopolitan figure, is best known in this country as the social critic of *The Revolt of the Masses*. All the basic premises of Ortega's thought derive from modern German philosophy: so far as he philosophizes, his mind is Germanic; but he was able to translate German philosophy into the language of the people, without pedantry and jargon, and particularly into the simplicity of an altogether alien language, Spanish, so that the translation itself becomes an act of creative thought. Ortega loves to hide the profundity of his thought behind the simple and casual language of a journalist or belletrist.

On the outer edge of the German tradition moves the remarkable figure of *Martin Buber* (1878–   ), a Jew whose culture is altogether Germanic but whose thought after many peregrinations has succeeded in rediscovering and anchoring itself profoundly to its Biblical and Hebraic inheritance. Buber is one of the few thinkers who has succeeded in the desperate modern search for roots, a fact with which his work continuously impresses us. The image of Biblical man moves like a shadow behind everything he writes. His thinking has the narrowness and concrete power, often the stubborn obstinacy, of Hebraism. At first glance his contribution would seem to be the slenderest of all the Existentialists, to be summed up in the title of his most moving book, *I and Thou*. It is as if Buber had sought to recast Kierkegaard's dictum, "Purity of heart is to will one thing," into: Depth of mind is to think one thought. But this one thought—that meaning in life happens in the area between person and person in that situation of contact when one says *I* to the other's *Thou*—is worth a lifetime's digging. In any case Buber is a necessary corrective to more ambitious systematizers like Heidegger and Sartre.

Thus we see that Existentialism numbers among its most powerful representatives Jews, Catholics, Protestants —as well as atheists. Contrary to the first facile journalistic reactions, the seriousness of existential thought does not arise merely out of the despair of a world from which God has departed. Such a generalization was prompted largely by the identification of existential philosophy with the school of Sartre. It should appear, from the foregoing sketch, how tiny a fragment of Existentialism the Sartrian school really does represent. So far as the central impulses of existential thought are concerned, it does not altogether matter, at least in one sense, in what religious sect a man finally finds his home. Nor is it mere heterogenous lumping-together to put Catholics, Jews, Protestants, and atheists under the rubric of one philosophy. This philosophy, as a particular mode of human thought, is single even though its practitioners wind up in different religious camps. What is common, and central, to all these philosophers is that the meaning of religion, and religious faith, is recast in relation to the individual. Each has put religion itself radically in question, and it is only to be expected that the faith, or the denial of faith, that emerges in their thought should be somewhat disconcerting to those who have followed the more public and external paths into a church. Unamuno seemed always on the verge of excommunication by the Spanish bishops; Buber is a prophet with not very much honor in his native land of Israel; and Kierkegaard fought the last battle of his life against the ordained hierarchy of the Danish Church. The atheist sect, on the other hand, sniffs the taint of heresy in Heidegger, whose thought, which he himself calls in one place a "waiting for god," has been criticized by one American philosopher as open-

ing the back door to theology. It is evident that anyone
who has passed through the depths of modern experience
and strives to place religion in relation to that experience is
bound to acquire the label of heretic.

Modern experience—an ambiguous enough term, to be
sure, and one that will require subsequent definition—is the
bond among these philosophers. The roster of names we
have given is hardly complete, but surely sufficient to indicate that Existentialism is not a passing fad or a mere
philosophic mood of the postwar period but a major movement of human thought that lies directly in the main
stream of modern history. Over the past hundred years the
development of philosophy has shown a remarkable en-
largement of content, a progressive orientation toward the
immediate and qualitative, the existent and the actual—toward "concreteness and adequacy," to use the words that
A. N. Whitehead borrowed from William James. Philosophers can no longer attempt, as the British empiricists
Locke and Hume attempted, to construct human experience
out of simple ideas and elementary sensations. The psychic
life of man is not a mosaic of such mental atoms, and philosophers were able to cling to this belief so long only because they had put their own abstractions in place of
concrete experience. Thus Whitehead himself, who as a
Platonist can scarcely be lumped with the Existentialists,
nevertheless shares in this general existential trend within
modern philosophy when he describes philosophy itself as
"the critique of abstractions"—the endless effort to drag the
balloon of the mind back to the earth of actual experience.

Of all the non-European philosophers, William James
probably best deserves to be labeled an Existentialist. Indeed, at this late date, we may very well wonder whether
it would not be more accurate to call James an Existentialist
than a Pragmatist. What remains of American Pragmatism
today is forced to think of him as the black sheep of
the movement. Pragmatists nowadays acknowledge James's
genius but are embarrassed by his extremes: by the una-
shamedly personal tone of his philosophizing, his willing-
ness to give psychology the final voice over logic where the

two seem in conflict, and his belief in the revelatory value of religious experience. There are pages in James that could have been written by Kierkegaard, and the Epilogue to *Varieties of Religious Experience* puts the case for the primacy of personal experience over abstraction as strongly as any of the Existentialists has ever done. James's vituperation of rationalism is so passionate that latter-day Pragmatists see their own residual rationalism of scientific method thereby put in question. And it is not merely a matter of tone, but of principle, that places James among the Existentialists: he plumped for a world which contained contingency, discontinuity, and in which the centers of experience were irreducibly plural and personal, as against a "block" universe that could be enclosed in a single rational system.

Pragmatism meant something more and different for James than it did for Charles Sanders Peirce or John Dewey. The contrast between James and Dewey, particularly, sheds light on the precise point at which Pragmatism, in the strict sense, ends and Existentialism begins. A comparison between the earlier and the later writings of Dewey is almost equally illuminating on the same point. Dewey is moving in the general existential direction of modern philosophy with his insistence that the modern philosopher must break with the whole classical tradition of thought. He sees the "negative" and destructive side of philosophy (with which Existentialism has been so heavily taxed by its critics): every thinker, Dewey tells us, puts some portion of the stable world in danger as soon as he begins to think. The genial inspiration that lies behind his whole rather gangling and loose-jointed philosophy is the belief that in all departments of human experience things do not fall from heaven but grow up out of the earth. Thinking itself is only the halting and fumbling effort of a thoroughly biological creature to cope with his environment. The image of man as an earth-bound and time-bound creature permeates Dewey's writings as it does that of the Existentialists—up to a point. Beyond that point he moves in a direction that is the very opposite of Existentialism. What Dewey never calls into

question is the thing he labels Intelligence, which in his last
writings came to mean simply Scientific Method. Dewey
places the human person securely within his biological and
social context, but he never goes past this context into that
deepest center of the human person where fear and trembling start. Any examination of inner experience—really
inner experience—would have seemed to Dewey to take the
philosopher too far away from nature in the direction of the
theological. We have to remind ourselves here of the provincial and overtheologized atmosphere of the America in
which Dewey started his work, and against which he had
to struggle so hard to establish the validity of a secular intelligence. Given Dewey's emphasis upon the biological and
sociological contexts as ultimate, however, together with his
interpretation of human thought as basically an effort to
transform the environment, we end with the picture of man
as essentially *homo faber*, the technological animal. This belief in technique is still a supreme article of the American
faith. Dewey grew up in a period in which America was
still wrestling with its frontier, and the mood of his writings
is unshaken optimism at the expansion of our technical mastery over nature. Ultimately, the difference between Dewey
and the Existentialists is the difference between America
and Europe. The philosopher cannot seriously put to himself questions that his civilization has not lived.

That is why we propose to limit the scope of our subject
to Europe and consider Existentialism as a distinctly European product of this period: in fact, as the philosophy of
Europe in this century. In the broadest sense of the term,
no doubt, all modern thought has been touched by a
greater existential emphasis than was the philosophy of the
earlier modern period. This is simply the result of the
stepped-up secularization of Western civilization, in the
course of which man has inevitably become more attached
to the promises of this earth than to the goal of a transcendent realm beyond nature. But while it is important to call
attention at the outset to this broad sense of the word "existential," to carry this meaning through in detail would inevitably dilute the specific substance of Existentialism. It is

Europe that has been in crisis, and it is European thinkers who have brought the existential problems to a focal expression, who have in fact dared to raise the ultimate questions. The significance of this philosophy is another matter, however, and can hardly be confined to its place of origin. Its significance is for the world and for this epoch of the world.

The reader may very well ask why, in view of this broader existential trend within modern philosophy, Existentialism should first have been greeted by professional philosophers in this country as an eccentric and sensational kind of tempest in a teapot. We should point out that Anglo-American philosophy is dominated by an altogether different and alien mode of thought—variously called analytic philosophy, Logical Positivism, or sometimes merely "scientific philosophy." No doubt, Positivism has also good claims to being the philosophy of this time: it takes as its central fact what is undoubtedly the central fact distinguishing our civilization from all others—science; but it goes on from this to take science as the ultimate ruler of human life, which it never has been and psychologically never can be. Positivist man is a curious creature who dwells in the tiny island of light composed of what he finds scientifically "meaningful," while the whole surrounding area in which ordinary men live from day to day and have their dealings with other men is consigned to the outer darkness of the "meaningless." Positivism has simply accepted the fractured being of modern man and erected a philosophy to intensify it. Existentialism, whether successfully or not, has attempted instead to gather all the elements of human reality into a total picture of man. Positivist man and Existentialist man are no doubt offspring of the same parent epoch, but, somewhat as Cain and Abel were, the brothers are divided unalterably by temperament and the initial choice they make of their own being. Of course there is on the contemporary scene a more powerful claimant to philosophic mastery than either of them: Marxism. Marxist man is a creature of technics, a busy and ingenious animal, with secular religious faith in History, of which he is the chosen collaborator. Like Positivism, Marxism has no philosophical categories for the unique facts of human personality, and in the natural course of things manages to collectivize this human personality out of existence (except where a single personality attains power, and then his personal paranoia plays havoc with the lives of two hundred million people). Both Marxism and Positivism are, intellectually speaking, relics of the nineteenth-century Enlightenment that have not yet come to terms with the shadow side of human life as grasped even by some of the nineteenth-century thinkers themselves. The Marxist and Positivist picture of man, consequently, is thin and oversimplified. Existential philosophy, as a revolt against such oversimplification, attempts to grasp the image of the whole man, even where this involves bringing to consciousness all that is dark and questionable in his existence. And in just this respect it is a much more authentic expression of our own contemporary experience.

In proof of this we turn now to look at the historical characteristics of the time that has engendered this philosophy.

THE ENCOUNTER WITH
NOTHINGNESS

Chapter Two

No AGE has ever been so self-conscious as ours. At any rate, the quantity of journalism the modern age has turned out in the process of its own self-analysis already overflows our archives and, were it not that most of it is doomed to perish, would be a dull burden to hand down to our descendants. The task still goes on, as indeed it must, for the last word has not been spoken, and modern man seems even further from understanding himself than when he first began to question his own identity. Of documentation of external facts we have had enough and to spare, more than the squirrellike scholars will ever be able to piece together into a single whole, enough to keep the busy popularizers spouting in bright-eyed knowledgeability the rest of their days; but of the inner facts—of what goes on at the center where the forces of our fate first announce themselves—we are still pretty much in ignorance, and most of the contemporary world is caught up in an unconscious and gigantic conspiracy to run away from these facts. Hence the necessity of returning to a subject that only appears to be well worn. With civilizations, as with individuals, the outer fact is often merely the explosion resulting from accumulated inner tension, the signs of which were plentifully present, though none of the persons concerned chose to heed them.

1. THE DECLINE OF RELIGION

The central fact of modern history in the West—by which
we mean the long period from the end of the Middle Ages
to the present—is unquestionably the decline of religion. No
doubt, the Churches are still very powerful organizations;
there are millions of churchgoers all over the world; and
even the purely intellectual possibilities of religious belief
look better to churchmen now than in the bleak days of
self-confident nineteenth-century materialism. A few years
ago there was even considerable talk about a "religious revival," and some popular and patriotic periodicals such as
Life magazine gave a great deal of space to it; but the talk
has by now pretty much died down, the movement, if any,
subsided, and the American public buys more automobiles
and television sets than ever before. When *Life* magazine
promotes a revival of religion, one is only too painfully
aware from the nature of this publication that religion is
considered as being in the national interest; one could
scarcely have a clearer indication of the broader historical
fact that in the modern world the nation-state, a thoroughly
secular institution, outranks any church.

The decline of religion in modern times means simply
that religion is no longer the uncontested center and ruler
of man's life, and that the Church is no longer the final and
unquestioned home and asylum of his being. The deepest
significance of this change does not even appear principally
at the purely intellectual level, in loss of belief, though this
loss due to the critical inroads of science has been a major
historical cause of the decline. The waning of religion is a
much more concrete and complex fact than a mere change
in conscious outlook; it penetrates the deepest strata of
man's total psychic life. It is indeed one of the major stages
in man's psychic evolution—as Nietzsche, almost alone
among nineteenth-century philosophers, was to see. Religion to medieval man was not so much a theological system
as a solid psychological matrix surrounding the individual's
life from birth to death, sanctifying and enclosing all its or-

dinary and extraordinary occasions in sacrament and ritual. The loss of the Church was the loss of a whole system of symbols, images, dogmas, and rites which had the psychological validity of immediate experience, and within which hitherto the whole psychic life of Western man had been safely contained. In losing religion, man lost the concrete connection with a transcendent realm of being; he was set free to deal with this world in all its brute objectivity. But he was bound to feel homeless in such a world, which no longer answered the needs of his spirit. A home is the accepted framework which habitually contains our life. To lose one's psychic container is to be cast adrift, to become a wanderer upon the face of the earth. Henceforth, in seeking his own human completeness man would have to do for himself what he once had done for him, unconsciously, by the Church, through the medium of its sacramental life. Naturally enough, man's feeling of homelessness did not make itself felt for some time; the Renaissance man was still enthralled by a new and powerful vision of mastery over the whole earth.

No believer, no matter how sincere, could possibly write the *Divine Comedy* today, even if he possessed a talent equal to Dante's. Visions and symbols do not have the immediate and overwhelming reality for us that they had for the medieval poet. In the *Divine Comedy* the whole of nature is merely a canvas upon which the religious symbol and image are painted. Western man has spent more than five hundred years—half a millennium—in stripping nature of these projections and turning it into a realm of neutral objects which his science may control. Thus it could hardly be expected that the religious image would have the same force for us as it did for Dante. This is simply a psychic fact within human history; psychic facts have just as much historical validity as the facts that we now, unlike the man of Dante's time, travel in airplanes and work in factories regulated by computing machines. A great work of art can never be repeated—the history of art shows us time and again that literal imitation leads to pastiche—because it springs from the human soul, which evolves like everything else in nature. This point must be insisted upon, contrary to the view of some of our more enthusiastic medievalists who picture the psychic containment of medieval man as a situation of human completeness to which we must return. History has never allowed man to return to the past in any total sense. And our psychological problems cannot be solved by a regression to a past state in which they had not yet been brought into being. On the other hand, enlightened and progressive thinkers are equally blind when they fail to recognize that every major step forward by mankind entails some loss, the sacrifice of an older security and the creation and heightening of new tensions. (We should bear this in mind against some of the criticisms of Existentialism as a philosophy that has unbearably heightened human tensions: it did not create those tensions, which were already at work in the soul of modern man, but simply sought to give them philosophic expression, rather than evading them by pretending they were not there.)

It is far from true that the passage from the Middle Ages to modern times is the substitution of a rational for a religious outlook; on the contrary, the whole of medieval philosophy—as Whitehead has very aptly remarked—is one of "unbounded rationalism" in comparison with modern thought. Certainly, the difference between a St. Thomas Aquinas in the thirteenth century and a Kant at the end of the eighteenth century is conclusive on this point: For Aquinas the whole natural world, and particularly this natural world as it opens toward God as First Cause, was transparently accessible to human reason; while to Kant, writing at the bitter end of the century of Enlightenment, the limits of human reason had very radically shrunk. (Indeed, as we shall see later, the very meaning of human reason became altered in Kant.) But this "unbounded rationalism" of the medieval philosopher is altogether different from the untrammeled use later thinkers made of human reason, applying it like an acid solvent to all things human or divine. The rationalism of the medieval philosophers was contained by the mysteries of faith and dogma, which were altogether beyond the grasp of human reason, but were nevertheless powerfully real and meaningful to man as symbols that kept the vital circuit open between reason and emotion, between the rational and non-rational in the human psyche. Hence, this rationalism of the medieval philosophers does not end with the attenuated, bleak, or grim picture of man we find in the modern rationalists. Here, once again, the condition under which the philosopher creates his philosophy, like that under which the poet creates his poetry, has to do with deeper levels of his being—deeper than the merely conscious level of having or not having a rational point of view. We could not expect to produce a St. Thomas Aquinas, any more than a Dante, today. The total psychic condition of man—of which after all thinking is one of the manifestations—has evolved too radically. Which may be why present-day Thomists have on the whole remained singularly unconvincing to their contemporaries.

At the gateway that leads from the Middle Ages into the modern world stand Science (which later became the spirit of the Enlightenment), Protestantism, and Capitalism. At first glance, the spirit of Protestantism would seem to have very little to do with that of the New Science, since in matters religious Protestantism placed all the weight of its emphasis upon the irrational datum of faith, as against the imposing rational structures of medieval theology, and there is Luther's famous curse upon "the whore, Reason." In secular matters, however—and particularly in its relation toward nature—Protestantism fitted in very well with the New Science. By stripping away the wealth of images and symbols from medieval Christianity, Protestantism unveiled nature as a realm of objects hostile to the spirit and to be conquered by puritan zeal and industry. Thus Protestantism, like science, helped carry forward that immense project of modern man: the despiritualization of nature, the emptying of it of all the symbolic images projected upon it by the human psyche. With Protestantism begins that long modern struggle, which reaches its culmination in the twentieth century, to strip man naked. To be sure, in all of this the aim was progress, and Protestantism did succeed in raising the religious consciousness to a higher level of individual

sincerity, soul-searching, and strenuous inwardness. Man
was impoverished in order to come face to face with his
God and the severe and inexplicable demands of his faith;
but in the process he was stripped of all the mediating rites
and dogmas that could make this confrontation less dangerous to his psychic balance. Protestantism achieved a
heightening of the religious consciousness, but at the same
time severed this consciousness from the deep unconscious
life of our total human nature. In this respect, its historical
thrust runs parallel to that of the New Science and capitalism, since science was making the mythical and symbolic
picture of nature disappear before the success of its own
rational explanations, and capitalism was opening up the
whole world as a field of operations for rationally planned
enterprise.

Faith, for Protestantism, is nevertheless the irrational and
numinous center of religion; Luther was saturated with the
feeling of St. Paul that man of himself can do nothing and
only God working in us can bring salvation. Here the inflation of human consciousness is radically denied, and the
conscious mind is recognized as the mere instrument and
plaything of a much greater unconscious force. Faith is an
abyss that engulfs the rational nature of man. The Protestant doctrine of Original Sin is in all its severity a kind of
compensatory recognition of those depths below the level
of consciousness where the earnest soul demands to inter-
rogate itself—except that those depths are cast into the outer
darkness of depravity. So long as faith retained its intensity,
however, the irrational elements of human nature were accorded recognition and a central place in the total human
economy. But as the modern world moves onward, it becomes more and more secularized in every department of
life; faith consequently becomes attenuated, and Protestant
man begins to look more and more like a gaunt skeleton, a
sculpture by Giacometti. A secular civilization leaves him
more starkly naked than the iconoclasm of the Reformation
had ever dreamed. The more severely he struggles to hold
on to the primal face-to-face relation with God, the more
tenuous this becomes, until in the end the relation to God

Himself threatens to become a relation to Nothingness. In
this sense Kierkegaard, in the middle of the nineteenth century, was the reckoning point of the whole Protestant Reformation that began three centuries earlier: He sees faith
for the uncompromising and desperate wager it is, if one
takes it in all its Protestant strictness; and he cannot say,
like his Catholic counterpart Pascal, "Stupefy yourself, take
holy water, receive the sacraments, and in the end all shall
be well"—for Protestant man has forsworn the sacraments
and natural symbols of the soul as the snares and pomp of
the devil. Some of Kierkegaard's books, such as *The Sickness Unto Death* and *The Concept of Dread,* are still frightening to our contemporaries and so are excused or merely
passed over as the personal outpourings of a very melancholy temperament; yet they are the truthful record of
what the Protestant soul must experience on the brink of
the great Void. Protestant man is the beginning of the
West's fateful encounter with Nothingness—an encounter
that was long overdue and is perhaps only now in the twentieth century reaching its culmination.

2. THE RATIONAL ORDERING OF
SOCIETY

Naturally, none of this was perceived at its beginning. In
human history, as in the individual human life, the significance of the small beginnings is perceived at last only in
their end. In its secular ethic, Protestantism was much in
accord with the spirit of capitalism, as modern historians
have repeatedly shown. For several centuries the two went
hand in hand, ravaging and rebuilding the globe, conquering new continents and territories, and in general seeming
triumphantly to prove that this earth is itself the promised
land where zeal and industry really pay off. Even in the
midst of the nineteenth century, when capitalism had also
succeeded in erecting the worst slums in human history, the
Englishman Macaulay could comment smugly upon the
fact that the Protestant nations are the most energetic and

prosperous and suggest that this may very well be a sign of
the superiority of their religion. The great German sociolo-
gist, Max Weber, has provided one of the chief keys to the
whole of modern history by describing its central process
as the ever-increasing rational organization of human life.
It is in this light too that the historical rise of capitalism
must be understood: the capitalist emerges from feudal society as the enterprising and calculating mind who must
organize production rationally to show a favorable balance
of profits over costs. Where feudalism is concrete and organic, with man dominated by the image of the land, capitalism is abstract and calculating in spirit, and severs man
from the earth. In capitalism, everything follows from this
necessity of rationally organizing economic enterprise in the
interests of efficiency: the collectivization of labor in factories and the consequent subdivision of human function;
the accumulation of masses of the population in cities, with
the inevitable increase in the technical control of life that
this makes necessary; and the attempt rationally to control
public demand by elaborate and fantastic advertising, mass
pressure, and even planned sociological research. The process of rationalizing economic enterprise thus knows no limits
and comes to cover the whole of society's life. That capitalism has given way in our time, over large areas of the
earth, to a form of total collectivization that has been taken
over by the State does not alter the fundamental human
issues involved. The collectivization becomes all the more
drastic when a *mystique* of the State, backed by brutal regi-
mentation by the police, is added to it. Collectivized man,
whether communist or capitalist, is still only an abstract
fragment of man.

We are so used to the fact that we forget it or fail to
perceive that the man of the present day lives on a level of
abstraction altogether beyond the man of the past. When
the contemporary man in the street with only an ordinary
education quickly solves an elementary problem in arithmetic, he is doing something which for a medieval mathematician—an expert—would have required hours. No doubt,
the medieval man would have produced along with his cal-

culation a rigorous proof of the whole process; it does not matter that the modern man does not *know* what he is doing, so long as he can manipulate abstractions easily and efficiently. The ordinary man today answers complicated questionnaires, fills out tax forms, performs elaborate calculations, which the medieval man was never called upon to do—and all this merely in the normal routine of being a responsible citizen within a mass society. Every step forward in mechanical technique is a step in the direction of abstraction. This capacity for living easily and familiarly at an extraordinary level of abstraction is the source of modern man's power. With it he has transformed the planet, annihilated space, and trebled the world's population. But it is also a power which has, like everything human, its negative side, in the desolating sense of rootlessness, vacuity, and the lack of concrete feeling that assails modern man in his moments of real anxiety.

The sheer economic power of modern society is attended by the same human ambiguities. The rational ordering of production makes possible a material level of prosperity beyond anything known by the past. Not only can the material wants of the masses be satisfied to a degree greater than ever before, but technology is fertile enough to generate new wants that it can also satisfy. Automobiles, radio, and now television become actual needs for great numbers of people. All of this makes for an extraordinary *externalization* of life in our time. The tempo of living is heightened, but a greed for novelties sets in. The machinery of communication makes possible the almost instantaneous conveying of news from one point on the globe to another. People read three or four editions of a daily paper, hear the news on the radio, or see tomorrow morning's news on their television screen at night. Journalism has become a great god of the period, and gods have a way of ruthlessly and demonically taking over their servitors. In thus becoming a state of mind—as Kierkegaard prophesied it would do, writing with amazing clairvoyance more than a century ago—journalism enables people to deal with life more and more at second hand. Information usually consists of half-

truths, and "knowledgeability" becomes a substitute for
real knowledge. Moreover, popular journalism has by now
extended its operations into what were previously considered the strongholds of culture—religion, art, philosophy.
Everyman walks around with a pocket digest of culture in
his head. The more competent and streamlined journalism
becomes, the greater its threat to the public mind—particularly in a country like the United States. It becomes more
and more difficult to distinguish the secondhand from the
real thing, until most people end by forgetting there is such
a distinction. The very success of technique engenders a
whole style of life for the period, which subsists purely on
externals. What lies behind those externals—the human person, in its uniqueness and its totality—dwindles to a shadow
and a ghost.

In his *Man in the Modern Age* Karl Jaspers has diagnosed
all these depersonalizing forces within modern society so
completely that they hardly need pointing out here. Jaspers
sees the historical meaning of existential philosophy as a
struggle to awaken in the individual the possibilities of an
authentic and genuine life, in the face of the great modern
drift toward a standardized mass society. Jaspers wrote his
book in 1930, three years before Hitler came to power and
precisely at the end of a postwar decade in Germany of
great intellectual brilliance and greater economic bankruptcy under the Weimar Republic. The book is thus saturated from beginning to end with the dual feeling of the
great threat and the great promise of modern life. Jaspers
was one of that generation of Europeans for whom the outbreak of the First World War, coming in the first years of
their mature life, marked a turning point in their whole way
of looking at Europe and its civilization. August 1914 is
the axial date in modern Western history, and once past it
we are directly confronted with the present-day world. The
sense of power over the material universe with which modern man emerged, as we have seen, from the Middle Ages,
changed on that date into its opposite: a sense of weakness
and dereliction before the whirlwind that man is able to
unleash but not to control. That feeling of danger has per-

sisted and grown stronger, and our generation knows it as an uncanny awareness of the explosive quality of man's secular powers—and now, alas, with the possession of atomic weapons, the word must be taken literally. This awareness is a far cry from that sense of intoxication and power with which the Renaissance and the Enlightenment sought to banish the darkness of the Middle Ages and to turn their energies confidently to the conquest of nature; a far cry from early Protestantism's conviction of the sincerity of its own conscience and the absolute value of its secular ethic; a far cry from the sense of triumph with which capitalism pointed to the material prosperity of bourgeois civilization as its justification and end. Jaspers is a Protestant who sees in Protestantism no final resolution for the tensions of the human soul; a bourgeois who has lived through a period in which all the stable fabric and norms of bourgeois life have been dissolved; and a man of the Enlightenment, a professor, who philosophizes in order to illumine human existence, but who sees this illumination as a tiny and flickering light set against the encompassing darkness of the forces of night.

The First World War was the beginning of the end of the bourgeois civilization of Europe. Of course, ends often take long in being accomplished, and capitalism is still hanging on by the skin of its teeth in the Western countries. Our point here, however, has to do not with the mere economic organization of society, but with the concrete and total fact of the civilization itself, with all its values and attitudes, unspoken and spoken. It would be superficial to take the outbreak of that war, as Marxists do, as signifying merely the bankruptcy of capitalism, its inability to function further without crisis and bloodshed. August 1914 was a much more total *human* debacle than that, and the words that catch it are those of the novelist Henry James, exclaiming with shocked horror, "To have to take it all now for what the treacherous years were all the while making for and *meaning* is too tragic for any words." As an American, James had experienced to the full the enchantment and refinement of European civilization; it had been a central theme in nearly all his writing, and here in this momentary outburst there rises to his mind the awful vision of all Europe's elegance and beauty being mere gaudy decoration over the face of a human abyss. August 1914 was a debacle for European man as a whole and not merely for the wicked conspiracy of financiers, militarists, and politicians. The period from 1870 to 1914 has been aptly described by one historian as the generation of materialism: the principal countries of Europe had become unified as nations, prosperity was in the air, and the bourgeois contemplated with self-satisfaction an epoch of vast material progress and political stability. August 1914 shattered the foundations of that human world. It revealed that the apparent stability, security, and material progress of society had rested, like everything human, upon the void. European man came face to face with himself as a stranger. When he ceased to be contained and sheltered within a stable social and political environment, he saw that his rational and enlightened philosophy could no longer console him with the assurance that it satisfactorily answered the question What is man?

Existential philosophy (like much of modern art) is thus a product of bourgeois society in a state of dissolution. Marxists have labored this point but without really understanding it; nevertheless, it remains true. The dissolution is a fact, but neither Existentialism nor modern art produced it. Nor is "dissolution" synonymous with "decadence." A society coming apart at top and bottom, or passing over into another form, contains just as many possibilities for revelation as a society running along smoothly in its own rut. The individual is thrust out of the sheltered nest that society has provided. He can no longer hide his nakedness by the old disguises. He learns how much of what he has taken for granted was by its own nature neither eternal nor necessary but thoroughly temporal and contingent. He learns that the solitude of the self is an irreducible dimension of human life no matter how completely that self had seemed to be contained in its social milieu. In the end, he sees each man as solitary and unsheltered before his own death. Admittedly, these are painful truths, but the most basic things

are always learned with pain, since our inertia and complacent love of comfort prevent us from learning them until
they are forced upon us. It appears that man is willing to
learn about himself only after some disaster; after war, economic crisis, and political upheaval have taught him how
flimsy is that human world in which he thought himself so
securely grounded. What he learns has always been there,
lying concealed beneath the surface of even the best-
functioning societies; it is no less true for having come out
of a period of chaos and disaster. But so long as man does
not have to face up to such a truth, he will not do so.

Thus with the modern period, man—to recapitulate—has
entered upon a secular phase of his history. He entered it
with exuberance over the prospect of increased power he
would have over the world around him. But in this world,
in which his dreams of power were often more than fulfilled, he found himself for the first time *homeless*. Science
stripped nature of its human forms and presented man with
a universe that was neutral, alien, in its vastness and force,
to his human purposes. Religion, before this phase set in,
had been a structure that encompassed man's life, provid-
ing him with a system of images and symbols by which he
could express his own aspirations toward psychic wholeness. With the loss of this containing framework man became not only a dispossessed but a fragmentary being.

In society, as in the spiritual world, secular goals have
come to predominate; the rational organization of the economy has increased human power over nature, and politically also society has become more rational, utilitarian,
democratic, with a resulting material wealth and progress.
The men of the Enlightenment foresaw no end to this triumphant expansion of reason into all the areas of social life.
But here too reason has foundered upon its opposite, upon
the surd and unpredictable realities—wars, economic crises
and dislocations, political upheavals among the masses.
Moreover, man's feeling of homelessness, of alienation has
been intensified in the midst of a bureaucratized, impersonal mass society. He has come to feel himself an outsider

even within his own human society. He is trebly alienated: a stranger to God, to nature, and to the gigantic social apparatus that supplies his material wants.

But the worst and final form of alienation, toward which indeed the others tend, is man's alienation from his own self. In a society that requires of man only that he perform competently his own particular social function, man becomes identified with this function, and the rest of his being is allowed to subsist as best it can—usually to be dropped below the surface of consciousness and forgotten.

3. SCIENCE AND FINITUDE

The foregoing, all matters of historical fact, have also become the themes of existential philosophy. This philosophy embodies the self-questioning of the time, seeking to reorient itself to its own historical destiny. Indeed, the whole problematic of Existentialism unfolds from this historical situation. Alienation and estrangement; a sense of the basic fragility and contingency of human life; the impotence of reason confronted with the depths of existence; the threat of Nothingness, and the solitary and unsheltered condition of the individual before this threat. One can scarcely subordinate these problems logically one to another; each participates in all the others, and they all circulate around a common center. A single atmosphere pervades them all like a chilly wind: the radical feeling of human finitude. The limitless horizons into which man looked at the time of the Renaissance have at last contracted. Oddly enough, man's discovery that he himself is finite through and through—is so, one might say, from the inside out—comes at a time when there seem no longer to be any limits to his technological conquest of nature. But the truth about man is never to be found in one quality that opposes another, but in both qualities at once; and so his weakness is only one side of the coin, his power the other. A recognition of limits, of boundaries, may be the only thing that prevents power from dizzy collapse.

But, it might be argued, what makes Western civilization unique is its possession of science, and in science we find uniform and continuous progress without limits. Research goes on, its results are rich and positive, and these are brought together in ever wider and more inclusive systems. There would seem, in this process, to be no contracting of horizons either in fact or in possibility. In a certain sense this is true, and yet science in the twentieth century has come up with answers which make the ambitions of rationalism seem overweening, and which themselves suggest that man must redefine his traditional concept of reason. It would be unlikely if this were otherwise, for scientists too are men and therefore participate in the collective psyche as well as help fashion it. Religion, social forms, science, and art are modes in which man exists; and the more we come to recognize the temporal being of man the more we must recognize a unity within and behind all these modes in which that temporal existence finds its expression.

Science too—and within its own authentic sphere—has come up against the fact of human finitude. That this has happened within science itself, and not in the philosophizing about science, makes the discovery more authentic and momentous. The anthropological sciences, and particularly modern depth psychology, have shown us that human reason is the long historical fabrication of a creature, man, whose psychic roots still extend downward into the primeval soil. These discoveries of the irrational, however, lie outside reason itself; they are stubborn obstacles to the use of reason in our lives, but obstacles which the confirmed rationalist might still hope to circumvent by a cleverer use of that very tool, reason. The more decisive limitations are those that have shown up *within* the workings of reason, in the more rigorous sciences of physics and mathematics. The most advanced of Western sciences, physics and mathematics, have in our time become paradoxical: that is, they have arrived at the state where they breed paradoxes for reason itself. More than a hundred and fifty years ago the philosopher Kant attempted to show that there were ineluctable limits to reason; but the Western mind, positivistic to the core, could be expected to take such a conclusion seriously only when it showed up in the findings of science. Science has in this century, with the discoveries of Heisenberg in physics, and Godel in mathematics, at last caught up with Kant.

Heisenberg's Principle of Indeterminacy shows that there are essential limits to our ability to know and predict physical states of affairs, and opens up to us a glimpse of a nature that may at bottom be irrational and chaotic—at any rate, our knowledge of it is limited so that we cannot know this not to be the case. This finding marks an end to the old dream of physicists who, motivated by a thoroughly rational prejudice, thought that reality must be predictable through and through. The figure of the Laplacian Demon was a very striking symbol of this: Imagine, says Laplace, a Being who knows the position and momentum of every particle in the universe, together with the laws of motion governing such particles; such a Being would be able to predict all subsequent states of the universe. Physicists can no longer operate on such cryptotheological faiths, but must take their predictability only where and to the extent that it exhibits itself in experience.

The situation in physics is made more paradoxical by Bohr's Principle of Complementarity, according to which the electron must be regarded both as a wave and as a particle, according to its context. The application of these contradictory designations would have seemed thoroughly illogical to a nineteenth-century physicist. Indeed, some physicists have suggested a new form of logic, from which the classic law of the Excluded Middle (either A or not A) would be dropped; and when new forms of logic are being constructed, one can only conclude that the nature of what is and what is not rational stands open to doubt. In practice, the Principle of Complementarity sets a rigorous limit upon the observations of physics: As one physicist, Von Pauli, puts it, *"I can choose to observe one experimental set-up, A, and ruin B, or choose to observe B and ruin A. I cannot choose not to ruin one of them."* Here the language is perfectly appropriate to the pathos of knowledge in every area in life: we know one thing at the cost of not knowing something else, and it is simply not the case that we can choose to know everything at once. What is remarkable is that here, at the very farthest reaches of precise experimentation, in the most rigorous of the natural sciences, the ordinary and banal fact of our human limitations emerges.

Godel's findings seem to have even more far-reaching consequences, when one considers that in the Western tradition, from the Pythagoreans and Plato onward, mathematics as the very model of intelligibility has been the central citadel of rationalism. Now it turns out that even in his most precise science—in the province where his reason had seemed omnipotent—man cannot escape his essential finitude: every system of mathematics that he constructs is doomed to incompleteness. Godel has shown that mathematics contains insoluble problems, and hence can never be formalized in any complete system. This means, in other words, that mathematics can never be turned over to a giant computing machine; it will always be unfinished, and therefore mathematicians—the human beings who construct mathematics—will always be in business. The human element here rises above the machine: mathematics is unfinished as is any human life.

But since mathematics can never be completed, it might be argued that Godel's finding shows us that there are no limits to mathematical knowledge. True, in one sense; but in another sense it sets a more drastic limitation upon mathematical knowledge, since mathematicians now know they can never, formally speaking, reach rock bottom; in fact, there is no rock bottom, since mathematics has no self-subsistent reality independent of the human activity that mathematicians carry on. And if human reason can never reach rock bottom (complete systematization) in mathematics, it is not likely to reach it anywhere else. There is no System possible for human existence, Kierkegaard said a century ago, differing with Hegel, who wished to enclose reality within a completely rational structure; the System is impossible for mathematics, Godel tells us today. In practice, the fact that there is no rock bottom means that the

mathematician can never prove the consistency of mathematics except by using means that are shakier than the system he is trying to prove consistent. Mathematics thus
cannot escape finally the uncertainty that attaches to any
human enterprise.

The situation is all the more vexing since mathematicians
in the last half century have come up with some very troublesome paradoxes. Mathematics is like a ship in mid-ocean
that has sprung certain leaks (paradoxes); the leaks have
been temporarily plugged, but our reason can never guarantee that the ship will not spring others. This human insecurity in what had been the most secure of the disciplines
of rationality marks a new turn in Western thinking. When
the mathematician Hermann Weyl exclaims, "We have
tried to storm Heaven, and we have only succeeded in pil-
ing up the tower of Babel," he is giving passionate expression to the collapse of human *hubris;* and we can be sure
that mathematics has at last been returned to its rightful
status as an activity or mode of being of finite man.

The concurrence of these various discoveries in time is
extraordinary. Heidegger published his *Being and Time,* a
somber and rigorous meditation on human finitude, in 1927.
In the same year Heisenberg gave to the world his Principle
of Indeterminacy. In 1929 the mathematician Skolem published a theorem which some mathematicians now think almost as remarkable as Godel's: that even the elementary
number system cannot be categorically formalized. In 1931
appeared Godel's epoch-making discovery. When events
run parallel this way, when they occur so close together in
time, but independently of each other and in diverse fields,
we are tempted to conclude that they are not mere "meaningless" coincidences but very meaningful symptoms. The
whole mind of the time seems to be inclining in one direction.

What emerges from these separate strands of history is
an image of man himself that bears a new, stark, more
nearly naked, and more questionable aspect. The contrac-
tion of man's horizons amounts to a denudation, a stripping
down, of this being who has now to confront himself at the

center of all his horizons. The labor of modern culture, wherever it has been authentic, has been a labor of denudation. A return to the sources; "to the things themselves," as Husserl puts it; toward a new truthfulness, the casting away of ready-made presuppositions and empty forms—these are some of the slogans under which this phase in history has presented itself. Naturally enough, much of this stripping down must appear as the work of destruction, as revolutionary or even "negative": a being who has become thoroughly questionable to himself must also find questionable his relation to the total past which in a sense he represents.

This apparent "coincidence" of historical forces becomes even more remarkable and meaningful when we consider modern art. What man has experienced historically with the changes in religion, in social and economic forms, and now in modern science as well—all of this experience is revealed to us, in a more striking and more human way, through art. Art is the collective dream of a period, a dream in which, if we have eyes to see, we can trace the physiognomy of the time most clearly. A brief glance at modern art may serve to make plain that the spiritual features of modernity which we have been anatomizing in this chapter have not been bare and empty abstractions, but a living human drama in which we have all been deeply involved, but which the artist has the clearest eyes to see.

THE TESTIMONY OF MODERN
ART

Chapter Three

> Now that my ladder's gone,
> I must lie down where all ladders start,
> In the foul rag-and-bone shop of the heart.
> W. B. YEATS

ANYONE who attempts to gain a unified understanding of modern art as a whole is bound to suffer the uncomfortable sensation of having fallen into a thicket of brambles. We ourselves are involved in the subject, and we can hardly achieve the detachment of the historian a few centuries hence. Modern art still provokes violent controversy, even after it has been on the scene a good half century and names like Picasso and Joyce have become almost household words. The Philistine still finds it shocking, scandalous, and foolish; and there is always a case to be made for the Philistine, and surely for the Philistine in ourselves without whom we could not carry on the drab business of ordinary living. Indeed, from the point of view we are taking here, the Philistine attitude, particularly in its irritation, may be just as revelatory historically as any other. But it is a case not only of the Philistine; sensitive observers still exist—directors of museums, connoisseurs, and historians—who find in modern art a disastrous falling away from the excellence of the art of the past. In a sense, all this controversy is pointless; so much of it has to do with the eventual historical rating of our own period, which is something we cannot even foresee. The century from Manet to Matisse may figure in future art histories as a period of impoverishment and decline, whose works cannot stand beside those of the old masters; or it may figure as a period of such abundant creativity that it can be matched only by the Renaissance during the fifteenth century. My own personal prejudice is toward the latter judgment, but I have no way of proving it; and such speculation, in any case, does not enter into my own experience of this art. We have simply got to give up the attempt to assess ourselves for posterity; the men of the future will form their own opinions without our help. What we so self-consciously call "modern art," after all, is nothing more nor less than the art of this time, *our* art; there is no other today. If we could have a different art, or a better, we would have it. As it is, we are lucky in this period to have any art at all. The Philistine rebukes the artist for being willful, as if all of modern art were a deliberate conspiracy against him, the viewer; the artist can hardly hope to make this man understand that art is not a mere matter of conscious will and conscious contrivance, and that the artist, by changing his ideas (even by adopting the Philistine's), will not become a different person living at a different time and place. In the end the only authentic art is that which has about it the power of inevitability.

Nevertheless, the controversy, irritation, and bafflement to which modern art gives rise does provide us a very effective handle with which to take hold of it. Irritation usually arises when something touches a sore spot in ourselves, which most of the time we would like desperately to hide; rarely if ever does the fault lie totally with the provoking object. Modern art touches a sore spot, or several sore spots, in the ordinary citizen of which he is totally unaware. The more irritated he becomes at modern art the more he betrays the fact that he himself, and his civilization, are implicated in what the artist shows him. The ordinary citizen objects to modern art because it is difficult and obscure. Is it so certain that the world the ordinary citizen takes for granted, the values upon which his civilization rests are so clear, either to him or in themselves? Sometimes the artist's image is very clear (in general, modern art is *simpler* than academic art), but it goes against the grain of the ordinary man because secretly he understands its intent all too well; and besides, he has already limited "understanding" to the habitual pigeonholes into which he slips every experience. The ordinary man is uncomfortable, angry, or derisive before the dislocation of forms in modern art, before its bold distortions, or arbitrary manipulations of objects. The painter puts three or more eyes in the face, or several noses, or twists and elongates the body at the expense of photographic resemblance in order to build up his own inner image. Has the contrary attitude of strict and literal attachment to objects succeeded in resolving all the anxieties of the ordinary man, and has not in fact the rampant extroversion of modern civilization brought it to the brink of the abyss? Finally, the ordinary man—and in this respect the ordinary man is joined by the learned and sensitive traditionalist in art—objects to the content of modern art: it is too bare and bleak, too negative or "nihilistic," too shocking or scandalous; it dishes out unpalatable truths. But have the traditional ideals worked so well in this century that we can afford to neglect the unpalatable truths about human life that those ideals have chosen to ignore? Does the aesthete who extols the greatness of the past as an argument against modern art have any idea of how pallid his own response to, say, the Virgin of Chartres appears beside the medieval man's response? Or that his own aestheticism, however cultured, is in fact a form of sentimentality—since sentimentality, at bottom, is nothing but false feeling, feeling that is untrue to its object, whether by being excessive or watered down?

In a famous passage in *A Farewell to Arms* Ernest Hemingway writes:

I was always embarrassed by the words sacred, glorious, and sacrifice and the expression in vain. We had heard them, sometimes standing in the rain almost out of ear-

shot, so that only the shouted words came through, and
had read them, on proclamations that were slapped up
by billposters over other proclamations, now for a long
time, and I had seen nothing sacred, and the things that
were glorious had no glory and the sacrifices were like
the stockyards at Chicago if nothing was done with the
meat except to bury it. There were many words that you
could not stand to hear and finally only the names of
places had dignity. Certain numbers were the same way
and certain dates and these with the names of places
were all you could say and have them mean anything.
Abstract words such as glory, honor, courage, or hallow
were obscene beside the concrete names of villages, the
numbers of roads, the names of rivers, the numbers of
regiments and the dates.

For a whole generation that was the great statement of protest against the butchery of the First World War. But it
has a greater historical significance than that: it can be
taken as a kind of manifesto of modern art and literature,
an incitement to break through empty abstractions of whatever kind, to destroy sentimentality even if the real feelings exposed should appear humble and impoverished—the
names of places and dates; and even if in stripping himself
naked the artist seems to be left with Nothing. Modern art
thus begins, and sometimes ends, as a confession of spiritual poverty. That is its greatness and its triumph, but also
the needle it jabs into the Philistine's sore spot, for the last
thing he wants to be reminded of is his spiritual poverty.
In fact, his greatest poverty is not to know how impoverished he is, and so long as he mouths the empty ideals or
religious phrases of the past he is but as tinkling brass. In
matters of the spirit, poverty and riches are sometimes
closer than identical twins: the man who struts with borrowed feathers may be poor as a church mouse within,
while a work that seems stark and bleak can, if genuine,
speak with all the inexhaustible richness of the world. The
triumph of Hemingway's style is its ability to break through
abstractions to see what it is one really senses and feels.

When the modern sculptor disdains the pomp of marble
and uses industrial materials, steel wire, or bolts, or even
rejected materials like old board, rope, or nails, he is perhaps showing himself to be impoverished next to the heroic
grandeur of a Michelangelo, but he is also bringing us back
to the inexhaustible brute world that surrounds us. Sometimes the confession of poverty takes a violent and aggressive tone, as when the Dadaists drew a mustache on the
Mona Lisa. Dada itself, like Hemingway, came out of the
revolt against the First World War, and despite its clown-
ing must now be regarded as one of the *valid* eruptions of
the irrational in this century. The generation of the First
World War could hardly be expected to view Western culture as sacrosanct, since they perceived—and rightly—that
it was bound up with the civilization that had ended in
that ghastly butchery. Better then to reject the trappings
of that culture, even art itself, if that would leave one a
little more honest in one's nakedness. To discover one's own
spiritual poverty is to achieve a positive conquest by the
spirit.

Modern art has been an immense movement toward the
destruction of forms—of received and traditional forms. The
positive side of this has been an immense expansion of the
possibilities of art and an almost greedy acquisition of new
forms from all over the globe. Around 1900 French painters
became interested in African sculpture. (The introduction
of Japanese prints into Europe in the nineteenth century
had already brought with it a profound shift in the sensibility of Western painters.) And these borrowings were
only the beginning: by now we have become accustomed
to painters and sculptors drawing their forms from Oriental
and primitive art of every culture. This century in art,
André Malraux has said, will go down in history not as the
period of abstract art but as the period in which all the art
of the past, and from every quarter of the globe, became
available to the painter and sculptor, and through them became a part of our modern taste. Certainly, we can no
longer look upon the canon of Western art—Greco-Roman
art as revived, extended, and graced by the Renaissance—

as *the* tradition in art, or even any longer as distinctly and uniquely *ours*. That canon is in fact only one tradition among many, and indeed in its strict adherence to representational form is rather the exception in the whole gallery of *human* art. Such an extension of the resources of the past, for the modern artist, implies a different and more comprehensive understanding of the term "human" itself: a Sumerian figure of a fertility goddess is as "human" to us as a Greek Aphrodite. When the sensibility of an age can accommodate the alien "inhuman" forms of primitive art side by side with the classic "human" figures of Greece or the Renaissance, it should be obvious that the attitude toward man that we call classical humanism—which is the intellectual expression of the spirit that informs the classical canon of Western art—has also gone by the boards. This is an historical fact the most immediate evidence of which is the whole body of modern art itself. Even if existential philosophy had not been formulated, we would know from modern art that a new and radical conception of man was at work in this period.

It would be a mistake to construe this breaking out on the part of Western artists from the confinement of what had been their tradition as mere expansion or a spiritually imperialistic act of acquisition. It is not simply an external and quantitative change in the number of forms the artist can assimilate, it is also, and more profoundly, an internal and qualitative change in the spirit with which the artist appropriates these forms. This breaking out of the tradition is in fact also a breakdown within the Western tradition. On this point the artistic conservative who rejects modern art, seeing it as a scandal and a departure from the tradition, sees rightly, however he may turn what he sees to his own purposes. That Western painters and sculptors have in this century gone outside their own tradition to nourish themselves on the art of the rest of the world—Oriental, African, Melanesian—signifies that what we have known as *the* tradition is no longer able to nourish its most creative members: the confining mold of this tradition has broken, under pressures both from within and without. It would be possible to avoid this painful conclusion, and to dismiss this group of artists as mere irresponsibles, and skillful renegades from the tradition, if there were any artists of comparable achievement whose work the anti-modernist could set over against theirs. But what is equally sure—and this negative evidence is strong or even stronger on the side of the moderns—is that the academic art of this period is as dead as mutton. It excites no one, depresses no one, and does not even really soothe anyone. It simply does not live; it is outside the time.

If we turn to the internal and formal characteristics of modern art, without reference to its external inspirations in African or primitive or Oriental art, we find the same indications of a radical transformation of the Western spirit. Cubism is the classicism of modern art: that is, the one formally perfected style which modern art has elaborated and from which all modern abstract art that is valid has derived. A great deal of nonsense has been written about the creation of Cubism, connecting it with relativity physics, psychoanalysis, and heaven knows how many other complex and remote things. The fact is that the painters who created Cubism were creating paintings and nothing else—certainly they were not dealing in ideologies. Cubism evolved in a succession of perfectly logical steps out of previous stages of painting, out of the Impressionists and Cézanne, and it raised a series of pictorial problems that had to be solved within the medium of painting and by painters working strictly as painters—that is, upon the visual image as such.

Yet a great formal style in painting has never been created that did not draw upon the depths of the human spirit, and that did not, in its newness, express a fresh mutation of the human spirit. Cubism achieved a radical flattening of space by insisting on the two-dimensional fact of the canvas. This flattening out of space would seem not to be a negligible fact historically if we reflect that when, once before in history, such a development occurred but in the opposite direction—when the flatness of the Gothic or primitive painters passed over into the solidity, perspective, and three-dimensional style of early Renaissance painting—it was a mark that man was turning outward, into space, after the long period of introspection of the Middle Ages. Western man moved out into space in his painting, in the fourteenth century, before he set forth into actual physical space in the age of exploration that was to follow. Thus painting was prophetic of the new turn of the human spirit which was eventually to find expression in the conquest of the whole globe. Have we the right, then, to suggest that the flattening of painting in our own century portends a turning inward of the human spirit, or at any rate a turning away from that outer world of space which has hitherto been the ultimate arena of Western man's extroversion? With Cubism begins that process of detachment from the object which has become the hallmark of modern art. Even though Cubism is a classical and formal style, the artist nevertheless asserts his own subjectivity by the freedom with which he cuts up and dislocates objects—bottles, pitchers, guitars—as it pleases him for the sake of the picture, which is now no longer held up to us as a representation of those objects but as a visual image with its own independent value alongside that of nature. The subjectivity that is generally present in modern art is a psychological compensation for, sometimes a violent revolt against, the gigantic externalization of life within modern society. The world pictured by the modern artist is, like the world meditated upon by the existential philosopher, a world where man is a stranger.

When mankind no longer lives spontaneously turned toward God or the supersensible world—when, to echo the words of Yeats, the ladder is gone by which we would climb to a higher reality—the artist too must stand face to face with a flat and inexplicable world. This shows itself even in the formal structures of modern art. Where the movement of the spirit is no longer vertical but only horizontal, the climactic elements in art are in general leveled out, flattened. The flattening of pictorial space that is achieved in Cubism is not an isolated fact, true only of painting, but is paralleled by similar changes in literary techniques. There is a general process of flattening, three chief aspects of which may be noted:

(1) *The flattening out of all planes* upon the plane of the picture. Near and far are pushed together. So in certain works of modern literature time, instead of space, is flattened out upon one plane. Past and present are represented as occurring simultaneously, upon a single plane of time. James Joyce's *Ulysses,* T. S. Eliot's *The Waste Land,* and Ezra Pound's *Cantos* are examples; and perhaps the most powerful use of the device was made by Faulkner in his early novel *The Sound and the Fury.*

(2) More important perhaps is *the flattening out of climaxes,* which occurs both in painting and literature. In traditional Western painting there is a central subject, located at or near the center of the picture, and the surrounding space in the picture is subordinate to this. In a portrait the figure is placed near the center, and the background becomes secondary to it, something to be blended as harmoniously as possible with the figure. Cubism abolished this idea of the pictorial climax: the whole space of the picture became of equal importance. Negative spaces (in which there are no objects) are as important as positive spaces (the contours of physical objects). If a human figure is treated, it may be broken up and distributed over various parts of the canvas. Formally speaking, the spirit of this art is anticlimactic.

When we turn to observe this same deflation or flattening of climaxes in literature, the broader human and philosophic questions involved become much clearer. The classical tradition in literature, deriving from Aristotle's *Poetics,* tells us that a drama (and consequently any other literary work) must have a beginning, middle, and end. The action begins at a certain point, rises toward a climax, and then falls to a denouement. One can diagram a classical plot of this kind by means of a triangle whose apex represents the climax with which everything in the play has some logical and necessary connection. The author subordinates himself to the requirements of logic, necessity, probability. His structure must be an intelligible whole in which each part develops logically out of what went before. If our existence itself is never quite like this, no matter; art is a selection from life, and the poet is required to be selective. However, it is important to note that this canon of intelligible literary structure—beginning, middle, and end, with a well-defined climax—arose in a culture in which the universe too was believed to be an ordered structure, a rational and intelligible whole.

What happens if we try to apply this classical Aristotelian canon to a modern work like Joyce's *Ulysses*, 734 pages of power and dullness, beauty and sordidness, comedy and pathos, where the movement is always horizontal, never ascending toward any crisis, and where we detect not the shadow of anything like a climax, in the traditional sense of that term? If Joyce's had been a disordered mind, we could dismiss all this as a sprawling chaos; but he was in fact an artist in superb control of his material, so that the disorder has to be attributed to his material, to life itself. It is, in fact, the banal gritty thing that we live that Joyce gives us, in comparison with which most other fiction is indeed fiction. This world is dense, opaque, unintelligible; that is the datum from which the modern artist always starts. The formal dictates of the well-made play or the well-made novel, which were the logical outcome of thoroughly rational preconceptions about reality, we can no longer hold to when we become attentive "to the things themselves," to the facts, to existence in the mode in which we do exist. If our epoch still held to the idea, as Western man once did, that the whole of reality is a system in which each detail providentially and rationally is subordinated to others and ultimately to the whole itself, we could demand of the artist that his form imitate this idea of reality, and give us coherence, logic, and the picture of a world with no loose ends. But to make such a demand nowadays is worse than an impertinence: it is a travesty upon the historical being of the artist.

Even where the writer has more of a story, in the traditional sense, to tell, he may prefer not to tell it in the tradi-

tional way. In *The Sound and the Fury* Faulkner has much
more of a novelistic narrative than Joyce in *Ulysses*—the decline of a family, a suicide, the elopement of a girl, and so
on—but he chooses not to present these events in the form
of the well-made novel. And the choice is wise, for the
power of the novel is increased immeasurably thereby. The
brute, irrational, given quality of the world comes through
so strongly in Faulkner's peculiar technique that he actually shows, and does not merely state, the meaning of the
quotation from which his title is derived:

> [Life] *is a tale,*
> *Told by an idiot, full of sound and fury,*
> *Signifying nothing.*

Shakespeare places these lines in the context of a fairly
well-made tragedy in which evil is destroyed and good triumphs; but Faulkner shows us the world of which Shakespeare's statement would be true: a world opaque, dense,
and irrational, that could not have existed for Shakespeare,
close as he was still to medieval Christianity. Even where
a purposeful human action is planned, in the novel, and the
necessary steps taken to carry it through—as in the section
on the day Quentin Compson commits suicide—what really
happens has little to do with the traditional order, logic,
sequence of events that normally accompany such an action. The day described shows us not the abstraction
"Quentin Compson commits suicide" but, as the author
turns his own and his reader's eye "to the things themselves," a process far more concrete and contingent: a spar-
row chirps at the window, a watch breaks, the hero gets
entangled in a perfectly absurd melee with a little runaway
girl, there is a fist fight, etc.; and underneath all this is, but
never mentioned, the slow blind surge moving forward like
an underground river toward the sea, of a man's going to
his death. This section, and the book itself, is a master-
piece, perhaps as great as anything yet written by an
American; and is to be recommended to anyone who
wants to know the concrete feel of that world with which
in his thinking the existential philosopher has to deal.

In the course of the brute random flow of detail that is that last day of his life, Quentin Compson breaks the crystal of his watch. He twists off the two hands and thereafter, throughout the day, the watch continues to tick loudly but cannot, with its faceless dial, indicate the time. Faulkner could not have hit on a better image to convey the sense of time which permeates the whole book. The normal reckonable sequence of time—one moment after another—has been broken, has disappeared; but as the watch pounds on, time is all the more urgent and real for Quentin Compson. He cannot escape time, he is in it, it is the time of his fate and his decision; and the watch has no hands to reassure him of that normal, calculable progression of minutes and hours in which our ordinary day-to-day life is passed. Time is no longer a reckonable sequence, then, for him, but an inexhaustible inescapable presence. We are close here—as we shall see later—to the thought of Heidegger. (Faulkner certainly never read Heidegger; he may never even have heard of him. So much the better; for the testimony of the artist, the poet, is all the more valid when it is not contaminated by any intellectual preconceptions.) Real time, the time that makes up the dramatic substance of our life, is something deeper and more primordial than watches, clocks, and calendars. Time is the dense medium in which Faulkner's characters move about as if dragging their feet through water: it is their substance or Being, as Heidegger would put it. The abolition of clock time does not mean a retreat into the world of the timeless; quite the contrary: the timeless world, the eternal, has disappeared from the horizon of the modern writer as it has from the horizon of modern Existentialists like Sartre and Heidegger, and from the horizon of our own everyday life; and time thereby becomes all the more inexorable and absolute a reality. The temporal is the horizon of modern man, as the eternal was the horizon of the man of the Middle Ages. That modern writers have been so preoccupied with the reality of time, handling it with radically new techniques and from radically new points of view, is evidence that the philosophers in our age who have attempted a new understanding of

time are responding to the same hidden historical concerns, and are not merely elaborating some new conceptual
novelty out of their heads.

These details about art, it should be apparent to the
reader, are not dragged in by the heels. Nor are they the
elaborate constructions which it has become the critical
fashion in this country to force upon works of art. On the
contrary, the features we have mentioned lie open and accessible—on the very surface, so to speak, of the works of
art themselves; and to see them requires only that we take
art seriously, which means to take it as a revelation: a revelation of its time and of the being of man, and of the two
together, the being of man in his time.

No beginning, middle, end—such is the structureless
structure that some modern literary works struggle toward;
and analogously in painting, no clearly demarcated foreground, middleground, and background. To the traditionalist, immersed in the classical Western tradition, all this
will appear negative, purely destructive. But if we do not
keep our gaze narrowly riveted on the tradition of the West
(and in any case this classical canon is only one of the traditions that have arisen in the course of the whole history of
the West), we find that these requirements of logical and
rational form do not hold for other traditions of art in other
cultures. Oriental art, for example, is much more formless,
organic, and sprawling than classical Western art. It has
form, but a different form from that of the West. Why is
this? The question is not a trivial one; it is perhaps as profound as any the West can ask these days, for this difference
in art is not mere happenstance but the inevitable concomi-
tant of a different attitude toward the world.

One of the best indications of this peculiar (to us) sense
of artistic form among Orientals is given by E. M. Forster
in his novel *A Passage to India*. A mixed group, English
and Indians, are at tea, and Professor Godbole, a Hindu,
has been asked to sing, but has let the occasion go by; then,
as all are leaving, the Hindu says, "I may sing now," quite
unexpectedly. (This unexpectedness is significant, for the
song is not to be given a formal setting, but to drop upon

their ears as casually and contingently as life itself.) Forster's description of the song makes our point so beautifully that it is worth quoting in its entirety:

> His thin voice rose, and gave out one sound after another. At times there seemed rhythm, at times there was the illusion of a Western melody. But the ear, baffled repeatedly, soon lost any clue, and wandered in a maze of noises, none harsh or unpleasant, none intelligible. It was the song of an unknown bird. Only the servants understood it. They began to whisper to one another. The man who was gathering water chestnuts came naked out of the tank, his lips parted with delight, disclosing his scarlet tongue. The sounds continued and ceased after a few moments as casually as they had begun—apparently half through a bar, and upon the subdominant.

The song begins, goes on, suddenly stops; but there is not the least trace of an Aristotelian beginning, middle, or end. Compare Godbole's song with the structure of an aria from an Italian opera. In the latter we have a beginning, a development through certain predictable phases toward the inevitable climax of the high note, and then the falling away or denouement, tying up the whole thing in a neat package: here is Aristotelian and rational form in music. But the Oriental song baffles the ear of the Westerner; it appears unintelligible. The reason is that the Westerner demands (or, let us say, used to demand) an intelligibility that the Easterner does not. If the Westerner finds the Oriental music "meaningless," the Oriental might very well reply that this is the meaninglessness of nature itself which goes on endlessly without beginning, middle, or end.

The real reason for the difference between the sense of artistic form in the East and in the West is thus ultimately a difference in philosophic outlook. Since the Greeks, Western man has believed that Being, all Being, is intelligible, that there is a reason for everything (at least, the central tradition that runs from Aristotle through St. Thomas Aquinas into the beginning of the modern period has held this), and that the cosmos is, finally, intelligible. The Oriental, on the other hand, has accepted his existence within a universe that would appear to be meaningless, to the rational Western mind, and has lived with this meaninglessness. Hence the artistic form that seems natural to the Oriental is one that is just as formless or formal, as irrational, as life itself. That the Western artist now finds his own inherited classical form unconvincing and indeed almost intolerable is because of a profound change in his total attitude toward the world —a change that is no less true even when the artist himself has not been able to bring it to conceptual expression. The final intelligibility of the world is no longer accepted. Our existence, as we know it, is no longer transparent and understandable by reason, bound together into a tight, coherent structure. The world that we are shown in the work of the modern painters and writers is opaque and dense. Their vision is not inspired primarily by intellectual premises; it is a spontaneous revelation of the kind of which perhaps only art is capable: it shows us where we stand, whether or not we choose to understand it. If we really open ourselves to the experience of two works of art as widely separated in time as Dante's *Divine Comedy* and Faulkner's *The Sound and the Fury*, the distance that Western man has traveled in the intervening centuries is revealed to us more clearly than through any number of abstract arguments. And the road that has been traveled is irreversible.

(3) The last and most important aspect of what we have called the process of flattening in modern art is *the flattening out of values*. To understand this one can begin at the simplest level in painting, where it means merely that large and small objects are treated as of equal value. Cézanne paints apples with the same passionate concentration as he paints mountains, and each apple is as monumental as a mountain. Indeed, in some of Cézanne's still lifes, if one covers up all of the picture except a certain patch of folded tablecloth, one might very well be looking at the planes and peaks of his Mont St. Victoire. For Cézanne the painting dictates its own values: little and big, high and low, sublime and ordinary outside the painting

are of equal importance if in a given painting they play the same plastic role.

Now all this is quite contrary to the great tradition of Western art, which distinguishes sharply between the sublime and the banal and requires that the highest art treat the most sublime subjects. The mind of the West has always been hierarchical: the cosmos has been understood as a great chain of Being, from highest to lowest, which has at the same time operated as a scale of values, from lowest to highest. Painters were expected to portray the sublime scenes from the Gospel, great battles, or noble personages. The beginning of genre painting in the seventeenth century was the first step toward what we now think of as modern painting, but it was not until the present century that the reversal of Western values was really accomplished. By now, the hierarchical scheme has been abolished altogether. Following Cézanne, the Cubists took as subjects for their most monumental paintings ordinary objects like tables, bottles, glasses, guitars. Now the painter dispenses with objects altogether: the colored shape on his canvas is itself an absolute reality, perhaps more so than the imaginary scene, the great battle, which in a traditional canvas it might serve to depict. Thus we arrive at last at *l'art brut* (raw, crude, or brute art), which seeks to abolish not only the ironclad distinction between the sublime and the banal but that between the beautiful and the ugly as well. Says the painter Dubuffet, one of the more interesting cultivators of this style:

> The idea that there are beautiful objects and ugly objects, people endowed with beauty and others who cannot claim it, has surely no other foundation than convention—old poppycock—and I declare that convention unhealthy. . . . People have seen that I intend to sweep away everything we have been taught to consider—without question—as grace and beauty; but have overlooked my work to substitute another and vaster beauty, touching all objects and beings, not excluding the most despised—and because of that, all the more exhilarating.

. . . I would like people to look at my work as an enterprise for the rehabilitation of scorned values, and, in any case, make no mistake, a work of ardent celebration. . . .

I am convinced that any table can be for each of us a landscape as inexhaustible as the whole Andes range. . . .

I am struck by the high value, for a man, of a simple permanent fact, like the miserable vista on which the window of his room opens daily, that comes, with the passing of time, to have an important role in his life. I often think that the highest destination at which a painting can aim is to take on that function in someone's life.

Such ideas seem scandalous to the Western traditionalist; they undermine the time-honored canon of beauty, countenance the most disorderly elements in existence, and strike against art itself. Yet they are ideas that might be easily understood by an Oriental. For the Oriental, opposites have never been put into separate watertight compartments as with the Westerner: as it is above, so it is below, in the East; the small is equal to the great, for amid the endless expanse of countless universes, each individual universe is as but a grain of sand on the shores of the Ganges, and a grain of sand is the equal of a universe. The lotus blooms in the mud; and generally the Oriental is as willing, in his indifference, to accept the ugly dross of existence as he is its beauty, where the Westerner might very well gag at the taste. We are not concerned here with the question of whether the West is now moving toward forms of thinking and feeling that are closer to what were once those of the East. What is of concern to the philosopher is the fact that here, in art, we find so many signs of a break with the Western tradition, or at least with what had been thought to be *the* Western tradition; the philosopher must occupy himself with this break if he is to recast the meaning of this tradition.

The deflation, or flattening out, of values in Western art does not necessarily indicate an ethical nihilism. Quite the contrary; in opening our eyes to the rejected elements of existence, art may lead us to a more complete and less artificial celebration of the world. In literature, again, the crucial example is Joyce's *Ulysses*. It was not a literary critic but a psychologist, C. G. Jung, who perceived that this book was non-Western in spirit; he sees it as Oriental to such an extent that he recommends it as a much-needed bible to the white-skinned races. For *Ulysses* breaks with the whole tradition of Western sensibility and Western aesthetics in showing each small object of Bloom's day—even the objects in his pocket, like a cake of soap—as capable at certain moments of taking on a transcendental importance—or in being, at any rate, equal in value to those objects to which men usually attribute transcendental importance. Each grain of sand, Joyce seems to be saying (as the Oriental says), reflects the whole universe—and the Irish writer was not in the least a mystic; he simply takes experience as it comes, in the course of the single day he depicts in the novel. Any such break with tradition, where a serious reversal of values is involved, is of course dangerous, for the artist runs the risk of losing the safeguards that the experience of the past has erected for him. A good deal of modern art has clearly succumbed to this danger, and the result is disorder in the art and the artist; but the danger is the price that must be paid for any step forward by the human spirit.

We have seen thus far that modern art, in its formal and structural qualities, is an art of breakdown and bold innovation, the expression of an epoch in which the accepted structures and norms of Western civilization are either in a state of dissolution or at least stand in question. But now, what about the content of this art? What does this content tell us about man? In what ways does it compel the philosopher to recast his traditional concept of man?

Every age projects its own image of man into its art. The whole history of art confirms this proposition, indeed this history is itself but a succession of images of man. A Greek figure is not just a shape in stone but the image of man in the light of which the Greeks lived. If you compare, feature by feature, the bust of a Roman patrician with the head of a medieval saint—as André Malraux has done with a spectacularly sharp eye in his *Voices of Silence*—you cannot account in formal terms for the difference between them: the two heads stare at each other and cancel each other out; they give us two different images of the destiny and possibilities of being a man. The Roman head shows us the face of the *imperium*, of power and empire, the Christian the face of the Incarnation, the humility of the earthly transfigured by the Divine. If we knew nothing at all about Taoism, we could still reconstruct from Chinese Sung painting what the Taoist felt about man and nature. And so it goes. Whenever a civilization has lived in terms of a certain image of man, we can see this image in its art; sometimes the image is present even when it was never articulated in thought, the artist in this way anticipating the philosopher. With primitive or prehumanist art it is another matter; here we are presented with images that are much more primordial and abstract, and we are not able to discern in them the features of man. In those primitive cultures humanism had not yet come into existence. Man was still too close to his totem animal. Yet even in this art if we will, we can see the image—or non-image—of man in the light of which the primitives lived, in the archetypal images from which man's own individuated features have not yet emerged.

And now, what about modern art? What image of man do we find in it?

It is very suggestive that modern artists have discovered primitive art to be valid for them and have found a strange kinship with its forms. To be sure, when the modern artist uses primitive motifs, they mean for him something altogether different from what they meant for the primitive. One cannot undo thirty centuries of civilization. Nevertheless, the extraordinarily vital attraction which primitive art now has for us is of no little significance. The tradition of Western humanism has faltered, become questionable; we are not so sure any more that we know what man is, and we do know in this century what blind forces can disturb or destroy his so-called humanity. Hence we respond to the archetypal images of prehumanist man, more abstract and impersonal than the features of man as we know him.

The one thing that is not clear in modern art is its image of man. We can select a figure from Greek art, from the Renaissance, or the Middle Ages and say with some certainty, "That is the image of man as the Greek, the medieval, or Renaissance man conceived him." I do not think we can find any comparably clear-cut image of man amid the bewildering thicket of modern art. And this is not because we are too close to the period, as yet, to stand back and make such a selection. Rather, the variety of images is too great and too contradictory to coalesce into any single shape or form. May the reason why modern art offers us no clear-cut image of man not be that it already knows— whether or not it has brought this knowledge to conceptual expression—that man is a creature who transcends any image because he has no fixed essence or nature, as a stone or a tree have?

A good deal of modern art has been concerned, in any case, simply with the destruction of the traditional image of man. Man is laid bare; more than that, he is flayed, cut up into bits, and his members strewn everywhere, like those of Osiris, with the reassembling of these scattered parts not even promised but only dumbly waited for. Our novels are increasingly concerned with the figure of the faceless and anonymous hero, who is at once everyman and nobody. Perhaps, again, it is Joyce who began this process of dissection, and he can even evoke an echo of prehumanist art in the incident of Odysseus' encounter with the blind giant Polyphemus, in which the Greek hero calls himself *ou tis*, Noman, the man without an identity. In the novels of Franz Kafka the hero is a cipher, an initial; a cipher, to be sure, with an overwhelming passion to find out his individual place and responsibility—things which are not given to him *a priori* and which he dies without ever finding out. The existence of this cipher who does not discover his own meaning is marginal, in the sense that he is always beyond the boundary of what is secure, stable, meaningful, ordained. Modern literature tends to be a literature of "extreme situations," to use Jaspers' expression. It shows us man at the end of his tether, cut off from the consolations of all that seems so solid and earthly in the daily round of life—that seems so as long as this round is accepted without question.

Naturally enough, this faceless hero is everywhere exposed to Nothingness. When, by chance or fate, we fall into an extreme situation—one, that is, on the far side of what is normal, routine, accepted, traditional, safeguarded —we are threatened by the void. The solidity of the so-called real world evaporates under the pressure of our situation. Our being reveals itself as much more porous, much less substantial than we had thought it—it is like those cryptic human figures in modern sculpture that are full of holes or gaps. Nothingness has, in fact, become one of the chief themes in modern art and literature, whether it is directly named as such or merely drifts through the work as the ambiance in which the human figures live, move, and have their being. We are reminded of the elongated and attenuated figures of the sculptor Giacometti, figures that seem to be invaded by the surrounding void. *"Some live in it and never know it,"* writes Hemingway in the story "A Clean, Well-Lighted Place," which presents in its six or seven pages a vision of Nothing that is perhaps as powerful as any in modern art; and he continues, *"It was all a nothing, and man is a nothing too."* The example of Hemingway is valuable here, for he is not an artist inspired by intellectual themes; quite the contrary, he is a reporter and a poet intent on reporting what it is he really sees in experience, and what he has seen and reports to us in this story is the Nothing that sometimes rises up before the eyes of human beings.* A story by Sartre on the same subject would be much more suspect to us: we would have reason to believe that the Existentialist writer was loading the dice intellectually, reporting on experience out of a previous philosophical commitment. But to reject Hemingway's vision of the

* For a more detailed treatment of the theme of this story see Appendices, pp. 283–286.

Nothing, of Nothingness, might well be to close our eyes to our own experience.

It is worth emphasizing, once again, that the vision of Nothingness with which modern art presents us does express a real encounter, one that is part of the historical destiny of the time. Creative artists do not produce such a vision out of nowhere. Nor in general do audiences or readers fail to respond to it. When a play *Waiting for Godot*, by an Irish disciple of Joyce's, Samuel Beckett—a play in which Nothingness circulates through every line from beginning to end—runs for more than sixteen months to packed houses in the capitals of Europe, we can only conclude that something is at work in the European mind against which its traditions cannot wholly guard it and which it will have to live through to the bitter end. Surely the audience at Beckett's play recognized something of its own experience in what it saw on the stage, some echo, however veiled, of its own emptiness and, in Heidegger's phrase, its "waiting for God." It is not only stuffy and pompous of the Philistine to reject these responses in artist and in audience, but dangerously unintelligent, for he loses thereby the chance of finding out where he himself stands historically.

An epoch, as we have seen, reveals itself in its religion, its social forms, but perhaps most profoundly or, at any rate, lucidly in its art. Through modern art our time reveals itself to itself, or at least to those persons who are willing to look at their own age dispassionately and without the blindness of preconceptions, in the looking glass of its art. In our epoch existential philosophy has appeared as an intellectual expression of the time, and this philosophy exhibits numerous points of contact with modern art. The more closely we examine the two together, the stronger becomes the impression that existential philosophy is the authentic intellectual expression of our time, as modern art is the expression of the time in terms of image and intuition.

Not only do the two treat similar themes, but both start off from the sense of crisis and of a break in the Western tradition. Modern art has discarded the traditional assump-

tions of rational form. The modern artist sees man not as
the rational animal, in the sense handed down to the West
by the Greeks, but as something else. Reality, too, reveals
itself to the artist not as the Great Chain of Being, which
the tradition of Western rationalism had declared intelligible down to its smallest link and in its totality, but as much
more refractory: as opaque, dense, concrete, and in the end
inexplicable. At the limits of reason one comes face to face
with the meaningless; and the artist today shows us the absurd, the inexplicable, the meaningless in our daily life.

This break with the Western tradition imbues both philosophy and art with the sense that everything is questionable, problematic. Our time, said Max Scheler, is the first
in which man has become thoroughly and completely problematic to himself. Hence the themes that obsess both modern art and existential philosophy are the alienation and
strangeness of man in his world; the contradictoriness, feebleness, and contingency of human existence; the central
and overwhelming reality of time for man who has lost his
anchorage in the eternal.

The testimony art brings to these themes is all the more
convincing in that it is spontaneous; it does not spring from
ideas or from any intellectual program. That modern art
which is most successful and powerful moves us because
we see in it the artist subordinate (as must always be the
case in art) to his vision. And since we recognize that man's
being is historical through and through, we must take this
vision of modern art as a sign that the image of man which
has been at the center of our tradition till now must be
re-evaluated and recast.

There is a painful irony in the new image of man that is
emerging, however fragmentarily, from the art of our time.
An observer from another planet might well be struck by
the disparity between the enormous power which our age
has concentrated in its external life and the inner poverty
which our art seeks to expose to view. This is, after all, the
age that has discovered and harnessed atomic energy, that
has made airplanes that fly faster than the sun, and that
will, in a few years (perhaps in a few months), have

atomic-powered planes which can fly through outer space and not need to return to mother earth for weeks. What cannot man do! He has greater power now than Prometheus or Icarus or any of those daring mythical heroes who were later to succumb to the disaster of pride. But if an observer from Mars were to turn his attention from these external appurtenances of power to the shape of man as revealed in our novels, plays, painting, and sculpture, he would find there a creature full of holes and gaps, faceless, riddled with doubts and negations, starkly finite.

However disconcerting this violent contrast between power and impoverishment, there is something a little consoling in it for anyone who is intimidated by excessive material power, as there is in learning that a dictator is a drunkard or marked by some other ordinary failing which makes him seem a trifle more human. If we are to redeem any part of our world from the brute march of power, we may have to begin as modern art does by exalting some of the humble and dirty little corners of existence. On another level, however, this violent contrast is frightening, for it represents a dangerous lagging of man behind his own works; and in this lag lies the terror of the atomic bomb which hangs over us like impending night. Here surely the ordinary man begins to catch a fleeting glimpse of that Nothingness which both artist and philosopher have begun in our time to take seriously. The bomb reveals the dreadful and total contingency of human existence. Existentialism is the philosophy of the atomic age.

In examining our time, we have seen everywhere the signs and omens of a break either with or within the Western tradition; and since Existentialism is concerned with these portents and is indeed one itself, we had better turn back now and cast an eye on this tradition in order to see how deeply the roots of Existentialism extend into it.

THE SOURCES OF EXISTENTIALISM IN THE WESTERN TRADITION

Part Two

HEBRAISM AND HELLENISM

Chapter Four

IN THE celebrated chapter with this same title, in his *Culture and Anarchy*, a book about the contemporary situation in nineteenth-century England that has much to say to us even today, Matthew Arnold writes:

> We show, as a nation, laudable energy and persistence in walking according to the best light we have, but are not quite careful enough, perhaps, to see that our light be not darkness. This is only another version of the old story that energy is our strong point and favorable characteristic, rather than intelligence. But we may give to this idea a more general form still, in which it will have a yet larger range of application. We may regard this energy driving at practice, this paramount sense of the obligation of duty, self-control, and work, this earnestness in going manfully with the best light we have, as one force. And we may regard the intelligence driving at those ideas which are, after all, the basis of right practice, the ardent sense for all the new and changing combinations of them which man's development brings with it, the indomitable impulse to know and adjust them perfectly, as another force. And these two forces we may regard as in some sense rivals—rivals not by the necessity of their own nature, but as exhibited in man and his history—and rivals dividing the empire of the world between them. And to give these forces names from the two races of men who have supplied the most splendid manifestations of them,

we may call them respectively the forces of Hebraism
and Hellenism. Hebraism and Hellenism—between these
two points of influence moves our world. At one time it
feels more powerfully the attraction of one of them, at
another time of the other; and it ought to be, though it
never is, evenly and happily balanced between them.

Hebraism sometimes seems for Arnold to wear too markedly
the stiff bewhiskered face of a British mid-Victorian member of the Dissenting Churches. We have learned a good
deal about the Hebraic mind, since his day, and our picture
of it will be more complicated. Nevertheless, it is well to
begin with this genial and simple passage from Arnold,
which so rightly perceives the distinction between the two
types and sets forth their long historical battle in such clear-
cut terms.

The distinction, as Arnold so lucidly states it, arises from
the difference between doing and knowing. The Hebrew is
concerned with practice, the Greek with knowledge. Right
conduct is the ultimate concern of the Hebrew, right thinking that of the Greek. Duty and strictness of conscience are
the paramount things in life for the Hebrew; for the Greek,
the spontaneous and luminous play of the intelligence. The
Hebrew thus extols the moral virtues as the substance and
meaning of life; the Greek subordinates them to the intellectual virtues, and Arnold rightly observes: "The moral virtues are with Aristotle but the porch and access to the intellectual, and with these last is blessedness." So far all
this is quite simple and clear: the contrast is between practice and theory, between the moral man and the theoretical
or intellectual man. But then Arnold goes on to make another point, which is somehow outside the framework with
which he started:

> To get rid of one's ignorance, to see things as they are,
> and by seeing them as they are to see them in their
> beauty, is the simple and attractive ideal which Hellen-
> ism holds out before human nature; and from the sim-
> plicity and charm of this idea, Hellenism, and human life
> in the hands of Hellenism, is invested with a kind of aerial

ease, clearness, and radiancy; they are full of what we call sweetness and light. Difficulties are kept out of view, and the beauty and rationalness of the ideal have all our thoughts.

While Arnold admires this ideal of sweetness and light, he nevertheless feels that it may not take into consideration one troubling aspect of the human condition, and he goes on to quote a remark that may or may not have been made by Thomas Carlyle:

"Socrates," this saying goes, "is terribly *at ease in Zion*." Hebraism—and here is the source of its wonderful strength—has always been severely preoccupied with an awful sense of the impossibility of being at ease in Zion; of the difficulties which oppose themselves to man's pursuit or attainment of that perfection of which Socrates talks so hopefully, and, as from this point of view one might almost say, so glibly. It is all very well to talk of getting rid of one's ignorance, of seeing things in their reality, seeing them in their beauty; but how is this to be done when there is something which thwarts and spoils all our efforts?

This something is *sin*.

What Arnold perceives here is that deep within Biblical man lurks a certain *uneasiness*, which is not to be found in the conceptions of man given us by the great Greek philosophers. This uneasiness point toward another, and more central, region of human existence than the contrast between doing and knowing, morality and reason. To be sure, Arnold seeks to tie in this uneasiness of Biblical man with his main thesis, which is the distinction between moral practice and intellectual culture, by introducing the idea of sin. But the sinfulness that man experiences in the Bible— as in the Psalms or the Book of Job—cannot be confined to a supposed compartment of the individual's being that has to do with his moral acts. This sinfulness pervades the whole being of man: it *is* indeed man's being, insofar as in his feebleness and finiteness as a creature he stands naked in the presence of God. This idea of man's finiteness takes us beyond the distinctions of practice and theory, morality and knowledge, toward the center from which all such distinctions stem.

It is at this center that we must begin, in our rethinking of Arnold's distinction between Hebraism and Hellenism. We have learned a good deal not only about Hebraic thought but about the Greeks since Arnold's time, and we shall have to qualify his picture of the latter's aerial lightness and ease. The radiant and harmonious Greek Arnold depicted he had inherited from eighteenth-century classicism. We know considerably more now about Greek pessimism and the negation of life that it brought with it. We know more about the Orphic religions, which had their own powerful sense of the sinful and fallen state of man, and which exerted such an influence upon Plato. When Plato says that the body is a tomb and that to philosophize is to learn to die, he is not just tossing off a few idle rhetorical figures. From his Orphic and Pythagorean sources we can see that the whole impulse of philosophy for Plato arises from an ardent search for deliverance from the evils of the world and the curse of time. The Greeks did not produce their tragic plays out of nothing, as Nietzsche was almost the first to observe less than a century ago. Greek tragedy comes out of an acute sense of the suffering and evil of life.

Nevertheless, Arnold is fundamentally right in his distinction between Hebrew and Greek, as is shown by the gifts bestowed on humanity by the two races: the Greeks gave us science and philosophy; the Hebrews gave us the Law. No other people—not the Chinese, not the Hindus—produced *theoretical* science, and its discovery or invention by the Greeks has been what has distinguished Western civilization from the other civilizations of the globe. In the same way, the uniqueness of Western religion is due to its Hebraic source, and the religious history of the West is the long story of the varying fortunes and mutations of the spirit of Hebraism.

1. THE HEBRAIC MAN OF FAITH

The Law, however, is not really at the center of Hebraism. At the center lies that which is the foundation and the basis of the Law, and without which the Law, even in the most Pharisaical tradition, would be but an empty shell. Here we have to think beyond Arnold. To be sure, the Law —the absolutely binding quality of its ritual and commandments—has been what has held the Jewish community together over its centuries of suffering and prevented this people from extermination. But if we go back to the Hebraic sources, to man as he is revealed to us in the Bible, we see that something more primitive and more fundamental lies at the basis of the moral law. We have to learn to reread the Book of Job in order to see this—reread it in a way that takes us beyond Arnold and into our own time, reread it with an historical sense of the primitive or primary mode of existence of the people who gave expression to this work. For earlier man, the outcome of the Book of Job was not such a foregone conclusion as it is for us later readers, for whom centuries of familiarity and forgetfulness have dulled the violence of the confrontation between man and God that is central to the narrative. For earlier man, seeing for the first time beyond the routine commandments of his religion, there was a Promethean excitement in Job's coming face to face with his Creator and demanding justification. The stage comparable to this, with the Greeks, is the emergence of critical and philosophical reflection upon the gods and their ways, the first use of rational consciousness as an instrument to examine a religion that had been up to that time traditional and ritualistic. The Hebrew, however, proceeds not by the way of reason but by the confrontation of the whole man, Job, in the fullness and violence of his passion with the unknowable and overwhelming God. And the final solution for Job lies not in the rational resolution of the problem, any more than it ever does in life, but in a change and conversion of the whole man. The relation between Job and God is a relation between an I and a Thou, to use Martin Buber's terms. Such a relation demands that

each being confront the other in his completeness; it is not
the confrontation of two rational minds each demanding an
explanation that will satisfy reason. The relation between
Job and God is on the level of existence and not of reason.
Rational doubt, in the sense of the term that the later philosophic tradition of the West has made familiar to us, never
enters Job's mind, even in the very paroxysm of his revolt.
His relation to God remains one of faith from start to finish,
though, to be sure, this faith takes on the varying shapes of
revolt, anger, dismay, and confusion. Job says, *"Though he
slay me, yet will I trust in him,"* but he adds what is usually
not brought to our attention as emphatically as the first part
of his saying: *"But I will maintain my own ways before
him."* Job retains his own identity ("his own ways") in confronting the Creator before whom he is as Nothing. Job in
the many shades and turnings of his faith is close to those
primitive peoples who may break, revile, and spit upon the
image of a god who is no longer favorable. Similarly, in
Psalm 89 David rebukes Yahweh for all the tribulations
that He has poured upon His people, and there can be no
doubt that we are here at the stage in history where faith is
so real that it permits man to call God to account. It is a
stage close to the primitive, but also a considerable step beyond it: for the Hebrew had added a new element, faith,
and so internalized what was simply the primitive's anger
against his god. When faith is full, it dares to express its
anger, for faith is the openness of the whole man toward
his God, and therefore must be able to encompass all human modes of being.

Faith is trust—in the sense, at least initially, in which in
everyday life we say we trust so-and-so. As trust it is the
relation between one individual and another. Faith is trust
before it is belief—belief in the articles, creeds, and tenets of
a Church with which later religious history obscures this
primary meaning of the word. As trust, in the sense of the
opening up of one being toward another, faith does not involve any philosophical problem about its position relative
to faith and reason. That problem comes up only later when
faith has become, so to speak, propositional, when it has

expressed itself in statements, creeds, systems. Faith as a concrete mode of being of the human person precedes faith as the intellectual assent to a proposition, just as truth as a concrete mode of human being precedes the truth of any proposition. Moreover, this trust that embraces a man's anger and dismay, his bones and his bowels —the whole man, in short—does not yet permit any separation of soul from body, of reason from man's irrational other half. In Job and the Psalms man is very much a man of flesh and blood, and his being as a creature is described time and again in images that are starkly physical:

> Remember, I beseech thee, that thou hast made me as the clay; and wilt thou bring me into the dust again?
> Hast thou not poured me out as milk, and curdled me like cheese?
> Thou hast clothed me with skin and flesh, and hast fenced me with bones and sinews.

And when Psalm 22 speaks of the sense of abandonment and dereliction, it uses not the high, rarefied language of introspection but the most powerful cry of the physical:

> My God, my God, why hast thou forsaken me? . . .

> Thou art he that took me out of the womb: thou didst make me hope when I was upon my mother's breasts.
> I was cast upon thee from the womb: thou art my God from my mother's belly . . .

> I am poured out like water, and all my bones are out of joint: my heart is like wax; it is melted in the midst of my bowels.
> My strength is dried up like a potsherd; and my tongue cleaveth to my jaws; and thou hast brought me into the dust of death.

Protestantism later sought to revive this face-to-face confrontation of man with his God, but could produce only a pallid replica of the simplicity, vigor, and wholeness of this original Biblical faith. Protestant man had thrown off the husk of his body. He was a creature of spirit and inwardness, but no longer the man of flesh and belly, bones and blood, that we find in the Bible. Protestant man would never have dared confront God and demand an accounting of His ways. That era in history had long since passed by the time we come to the Reformation.

As a man of flesh and blood, Biblical man was very much bound to the earth. "Remember, I beseech thee, that thou hast made me as the clay; and wilt thou bring me into the dust again?" Bound to the dust, he was bound to death: a creature of time, whose being was temporal through and through. The idea of eternity—eternity for man—does not bulk large in the Bible beside the power and frequency of the images of man's mortality. God is the Everlasting, who, though He meets man face to face, is altogether beyond human ken and comparison; while man, who is as Nothing before his Creator, is like all other beings of the dust a creature of a day, whose temporal substance is repeatedly compared to wind and shadow.

> Man that is born of woman is of few days, and full of trouble.
> He cometh forth like a flower, and is cut down: he fleeth also as a shadow, and continueth not.

Hebraism contains no eternal realm of essences, which Greek philosophy was to fabricate, through Plato, as affording the intellectual deliverance from the evil of time. Such a realm of eternal essences is possible only for a *detached* intellect, one who, in Plato's phrase, becomes a "spectator of all time and all existence." This ideal of the philosopher as the highest human type—the theoretical intellect who from the vantage point of eternity can survey all time and existence—is altogether foreign to the Hebraic concept of the man of faith who is passionately committed to his own mortal being. Detachment was for the Hebrew an impermissible state of mind, a vice rather than a virtue; or rather it was something that Biblical man was not yet even able to conceive, since he had not reached the level of rational abstraction of the Greek. His existence was too earth-bound, too laden with the oppressive images of mortality, to permit him to experience the philosopher's detachment. The notion of the immortality of the soul as an intellectual substance (and that that immortality might even be demonstrated rationally) had not dawned upon the mind of Biblical man. If he hoped at all to escape mortality it was on the basis of personal trust that his Creator might raise him once again from the dust.

All of this carries us beyond Arnold's simple contrasting of moral man with intellectual man, though his basic distinction is left intact and in fact deepened. To sum up:

(1) The ideal man of Hebraism is the man of faith; for Hellenism, at least as it came to ultimate philosophic expression in its two greatest philosophers, Plato and Aristotle, the ideal man is the man of reason, the philosopher who as a spectator of all time and existence must rise above these.

(2) The man of faith is the concrete man in his wholeness. Hebraism does not raise its eyes to the universal and abstract; its vision is always of the concrete, particular, individual man. The Greeks, on the other hand, were the first thinkers in history; they discovered the universal, the abstract and timeless essences, forms, and Ideas. The intoxication of this discovery (which marked nothing less than the earliest emergence and differentiation of the rational function) led Plato to hold that man lives only insofar as he lives in the eternal.

(3) There follows for the Greek the ideal of *detachment* as the path of wisdom which only the philosopher can tread. The word "theory" derives from the Greek verb *theatai,* which means to behold, to see, and is the root of the word theater. At a theater we are spectators of an action in which we ourselves are not involved. Analogously, the man of theory, the philosopher or pure scientist, looks upon existence with detachment, as we behold spectacles at the theater; and in this way he exists, to use Kierkegaard's expression, only upon the aesthetic level of existence.

The Hebraic emphasis is on *commitment,* the passionate involvement of man with his own mortal being (at once flesh and spirit), with his offspring, family, tribe, and

God; a man abstracted from such involvements would be, to Hebraic thought, but a pale shade of the actual existing human person.

(4) The eternal is a rather shadowy concept for the Hebrew except as it is embodied in the person of the unknowable and terrible God. For the Greek eternity is something to which man has ready and continuous access through his intellect.

(5) The Greek invented logic. His definition of man as the rational animal is literally as the logical animal, *to zoon logikon;* or even more literally the animal who has language, since logic derives from the verb *legein,* which means to say, speak, discourse. Man is the animal of connected logical discourse.

For the Hebrew the status of the intellect is rather typified by the silly and proud babbling of Job's friends, whose arguments never touch the core of the matter. Intellect and logic are the pride of fools and do not touch the ultimate issues of life, which transpire at a depth that language can never reach, the ultimate depth of faith. Says Job at the end of the Book: "I have heard of thee by the hearing of the ear: but now mine eye seeth thee."

(6) The Greek pursues beauty and goodness as things that are identical or at least always coincident; in fact he gives them a single name, the beautiful-and-good, *to kalokagathia.* The Hebraic sense of sin, to which Matthew Arnold alludes, is too much aware of the galling and refractory aspects of human existence to make this easy identification of the good and the beautiful. The sense of the sinfulness of Biblical man is the sense of his radical finitude in its aspect of imperfection. Hence his good must sometimes wear an ugly face, just as beauty for him may be the shining mask of evil and corruption.

It is unnecessary to extend this list. What is important is to make clear the central intuition that informs each of these two views of man. The reader probably has already divined that the features of Hebraic man are those which existential philosophy has attempted to exhume and bring to the reflective consciousness of our time, a time in which as a matter of historical happening the Hebraic religion (which means Western religion) no longer retains its unconditional validity for the mass of mankind.

This sketch of a comparison perhaps tilts the balance a little too heavily on the side of Hebraism. It is necessary, however, to correct the impression left by Matthew Arnold (and he is here a spokesman for a view that is still prevalent) that the main content of Hebraism is its energy and will toward morality. We have to insist on a noetic content in Hebraism: Biblical man too had his *knowledge*, though it is not the intellectual knowledge of the Greek. It is not the kind of knowledge that man can have through reason alone, or perhaps not through reason at all; he has it rather through body and blood, bones and bowels, through trust and anger and confusion and love and fear; through his passionate adhesion in faith to the Being whom he can never intellectually know. This kind of knowledge a man has only through living, not reasoning, and perhaps in the end he cannot even say what it is he knows; yet it is knowledge all the same, and Hebraism at its source had this knowledge. To be sure, we have stacked the cards somewhat by considering Hellenism more or less as it came to be expressed by the philosophers, and particularly the philosopher Plato; Hellas also produced the tragic poets Aeschylus and Sophocles, who had another kind of knowledge of life. But it was Greece that produced philosophy, logic, science —and also produced Plato, a figure who sums up all the ambiguity of Hellenism as it circles round the momentous issue of reason and the irrational in human life.

2. GREEK REASON

The Anglo-American philosopher Whitehead has remarked that "Twenty-five hundred years of Western philosophy is but a series of footnotes to Plato." Allowing for the disparaging irony of the word "footnotes," we can take this statement as literally accurate. The themes, the questions, and even to a great extent the terms of all subsequent Western philosophy lie in germ in the writings of Plato. All later philosophers betray a filial dependence on Plato—even Aristotle, the great hero of all anti-Platonists. And while existential philosophy is a radical effort to break with this Platonic tradition, yet paradoxically there is an existential aspect to Plato's thought. Such is the richness and ambiguity of Plato as man and philosopher.

Plato began his philosophic career as the result of a conversion. This is surely an existential beginning. He had aspired to be a dramatic poet, the biographer tells us, but after a youthful encounter with Socrates he burned all his manuscripts and dedicated himself to the search for wisdom to which Socrates had given his life. Plato was to be engaged thereafter, for the rest of his life, in a war with the poets that was first and foremost a war with the poet in himself. The steps in Plato's career, after that fateful encounter with Socrates, enact a progress, as we shall see later, that might have the title: *Death of a Poet.* Yet the poet never quite dies in Plato—revile him as he does—and at the end he returns to a great myth of creation, the *Timaeus,* though it is told as an allegory of science and metaphysics. His career is the victory of reason, or the struggle for that victory, over the poetic and mythic functions, and it is all the more remarkable in that it took place in a man who was so richly endowed with the poetic gift.

But this is more than a highly dramatic bit of personal biography: it is an event of the greatest significance in Western history, as it could only be in a man of Plato's greatness. In Plato rational consciousness as such becomes, for the first time in human history, a differentiated psychic function. (Perhaps Socrates achieved this before him, but all we know of Socrates as a philosopher is through Plato's writings.) The momentousness of this emergence of reason can be gauged by setting Greece over against the comparably high civilizations of India and China. These latter had a great flowering of sages at a time close to that of the pre-Socratics in Greece; but neither in India nor in China was reason fully isolated and distinguished—that is, differentiated—from the rest of man's psychic being, from his feeling and intuition. Oriental man remains intuitive, not rational.

Great sages like Buddha and Lao-tse rose above the mythic, but they did not become apostles of reason. The lifting of reason fully out of the primeval waters of the unconscious is a Greek achievement. And from the differentiation Western civilization takes on, subsequently, the character that distinguishes it from the civilizations of the Orient. Science itself, a peculiarly Western product, became possible only through this differentiation of reason and its exaltation as the crowning human power.

This emergence of reason that we can see taking place in the Platonic writings was a momentous historical event that spanned Plato's own lifetime. We can gauge this span by marking out at its beginning two thinkers earlier than Plato, Heraclitus and Parmenides, who were flourishing around 480 B.C., and at its end the achievement of Plato's pupil, Aristotle, who really carried the rational ideal sketched by Plato in the Later Academy to its culmination. In 399 B.C. Socrates was executed for nothing less than the crime of rationalism—an act of reason that destroyed, so the conservative Athenians thought, the gods of the tribe. These dates can be marked as points on a curve, and this curve is one of the most significant ever traced by man in his history. From 480 B.C., the time of Heraclitus and Parmenides, to the death of Aristotle in 322 B.C. is little more than a century and a half. In that century and a half man enters history as the rational animal.

Parmenides and Heraclitus were visionaries and seers. Parmenides wrote in verse, and his poem opens by describing itself as the account of a vision vouchsafed by the goddess, who has taken the poet in her chariot beyond the portals of the day and night. Heraclitus' sayings are dark and oracular, and they are meant to be taken as oracles—visionary disclosures of the real. The Greek word for "I know," *oida*, is the perfect of the verb "to see" and means "I have seen." He who knows is the man who has seen, who has had a vision. For earlier mankind, the sage, the wise man, was the reader of oracles, of dreams and entrails, the fortuneteller, the shaman. And he was the poet who, in giving expression to the "big dreams" of the tribe, voiced its hidden, its deepest and furthest wisdom. At the end of the century and a half in which Plato and Aristotle lived, this ideal sage had been transformed into the man of pure intellect, whose highest embodiment was to be found in the rational philosopher and the theoretical scientist. The vast intuitive visions of nature, as found in the pre-Socratic thinkers, gave way, in Aristotle, to the sobriety of science.

We are so used today to taking our rational consciousness for granted, in the ways of our daily life we are so immersed in its operations, that it is hard at first for us to imagine how momentous was this historical happening among the Greeks. Steeped as our age is in the ideas of evolution, we have not yet become accustomed to the idea that consciousness itself is something that has evolved through long centuries and that even today, with us, is still evolving. Only in this century, through modern psychology, have we learned how precarious a hold consciousness may exert upon life, and we are more acutely aware therefore what a precious deal of history, and of effort, was required for its elaboration, and what creative leaps were necessary at certain times to extend it beyond its habitual territory. We have seen the history of philosophy written as social history, or as economic history, or interpreted from any number of sociological points of view, but we have yet to grasp fully the history of philosophy as part of the psychic evolution of mankind. But of course the concept of evolution cannot here be interpreted in the simple and unilinear fashion of nineteenth-century thought, as in Hegel and Spencer, but rather in its full concreteness and ambiguity, as simultaneously gain and loss, advance and regress.

Nothing better illustrates this last point than the Platonic celebration of reason. The Greeks' discovery represents an immense and necessary step forward by mankind, but also a loss, for the pristine wholeness of man's being is thereby sundered or at least pushed into the background. Consider thus the famous myth of the soul in the *Phaedrus:* the driver of the chariot, reason, holds the reins of white steeds and of black—the white steeds representing the spirited or emotional part of man, which is more docile to the dictates of reason, the black and unruly steeds representing the appetites or desires, which have to be whipped into line by the charioteer. Whips and reins convey only the idea of coercion and restraint; and the charioteer alone wears a human face while the rest of man, the non-rational part, is represented in animal form. Reason, as the divine part of man, is separated, is indeed of another nature, from the animal within him. We are a long distance here from another symbol of light and dark which early mankind, this time the Chinese, handed down to us: the famous diagram of the forces of *yin* and *yang*, in which the light and the dark lie down beside each other within the same circle, the dark area penetrated by a spot of light and the light by a spot of dark, to symbolize that each must borrow from the other, that the light has need of the dark, and conversely, in order for either to be complete. In Plato's myth first appears that cleavage between reason and the irrational that it has been the long burden of the West to carry, until the dualism makes itself felt in most violent form within modern culture.

The same superhuman, or inhuman, exaltation of reason can be seen in another of the Platonic myths, the celebrated allegory of the cave in the *Republic*. The myth begins with a very grim picture of the human condition as it actually is: Men sit in the darkness of a cave, in chains, their backs to the light and able to see only the shadows of objects cast on the wall they face. One of the prisoners becomes free, turns around to see the objects of which he had previously seen only the shadows, and the light itself that casts the shadows; he may even progress to the mouth of the cave and see the sun beyond.

This is a myth of man's progress from darkness to light, ignorance to knowledge, from dereliction to salvation. As a young man, we are told, Plato had studied the doctrines of Cratylus, a follower of Heraclitus who had taught that all things were in flux and that there was no escape anywhere from death and change; the young Plato, tormented by this vision, desired at all costs a refuge in the eternal from the insecurities and ravages of time. Hence the enormous attraction for him of the science of mathematics, which opens up a realm of eternal truths. Here at least, in pure thought, man can find an escape from time. Hence too the tremendous emotional force for him of the theory of eternal forms or Ideas, since these latter were an everlasting realm to which man has access. We have to see Plato's rationalism, not as a cool scientific project such as a later century of the European Enlightenment might set for itself, but as a kind of passionately religious doctrine—a theory that promised man salvation from the things he had feared most from the earliest days, from death and time. The extraordinary emphasis Plato put upon reason is itself a religious impulse.

Light and darkness are universal human symbols for the contrasting states of redemption and dereliction. You will find them in all cultures—in Hindu, Buddhist, Taoist, and Christian thought. The sage or saint is always the enlightened man, he who walks in the light. Plato's myth, taken simply as a story, could be adopted by any of these religions. The use that Plato makes of it, however, is altogether his own, and strikingly different from the use any religion has made of these symbols. For when he has finished the story, Plato goes on to explain it as an allegory: the progress from the cave into the light, in the myth, will correspond to the actual stages to be followed in the education of the guardians of the state, and the chief content of this education, its sole content from the age of twenty to thirty-five, is to be mathematics and dialectic. At this point we may imagine a great Eastern sage such as Buddha or Lao-tse looking somewhat askance: the enlightenment they sought, which was the redemption of the individual, would not have come through any such severely intellectual and logical training. And one's own observation of professional mathematicians hardly supports the view that they are the most whole and intact psychological specimens mankind has to offer. In Plato's extraordinary emphasis upon mathematics we see the vestiges of Pythagoreanism, in which mathematics has been given a sacred, a religious status.

Behind Plato's emphasis upon mathematics lies his theory

of Ideas: the "really real" objects in the universe, *ta ontos onta*, are the universals or Ideas. Particular things are half real and half unreal—real only insofar as they participate in the eternal universals. The universal is fully real because it is eternal; the fleeting and changing particular has only a shadowy kind of reality because it passes and is then as if it had never been. Humanity, the universal, is more real than any individual man. This is the crucial emphasis of Platonism as it was passed on to all subsequent philosophy and that against which contemporary existential philosophy is in rebellion. Kierkegaard and Nietzsche in the nineteenth century were the first to reverse this Platonic scale of values and to establish the individual, the single one, precisely in the way in which he is an exception to the universal norm, as taking precedence over the universal.

Everything else in Plato follows from his identification of true Being, of "real reality," with the Ideas. Since art, for example, deals with the objects of the senses, therefore with particulars, it deals only with shadows and is itself a form of untruth. Philosophy and theoretical science have a higher value than art because in them alone truth is realized, as it is not in the arts. The earlier meaning of truth, which embraced also the utterances of the poets, has here been shifted to make it a purely intellectual concept. Psychologically speaking, the significance of Plato's theory of Ideas is to transfer the weight of emphasis from sensory reality to a supersensible reality. Perhaps nothing short of this would have served historically, at that time: For man to enter history as the rational animal, it was necessary for him to be convinced that the objects of his reasoning, the Ideas, were more real than his own individual person or the particular objects that made up his world. The great step forward into rationalism required its own mythology—such perhaps is always the ambiguity of human evolution.

Plato's thought, as we have seen, values (which means, finds "really real") the eternal over the temporal, the universal over the particular, reason over the non-rational other half of man. In all these valuations it is profoundly anti-existential—a philosophy of essence rather than of existence. Yet it remains existential in its conception of the activity of philosophizing as fundamentally a means of personal salvation. Plato had no conception of metaphysics as such, as a purely theoretical branch of philosophy devoted to the study of Being as Being. He was an Athenian to the end, which means that his interest in political life, the *polis*, was the one to which all other human interests were subordinate. Athens did not produce metaphysicians; these came rather from other parts of the Greek world, from Ionia, Milesia, Sicily, southern Italy; and the founder of metaphysics as a strict and separate discipline was Aristotle, a native of Stagira in Macedonia. But for Plato, the Athenian, all metaphysical speculation was simply instrumental in the passionate human search for the ideal state and the ideal way to live—in short, for a means to the redemption of man. The figure of Socrates as a living human presence dominates all the earlier dialogues because, for the young Plato, Socrates the man was the very incarnation of philosophy as a concrete way of life, a personal calling and search. It is in this sense too that Kierkegaard, more than two thousand years later, was to revive the figure of Socrates—the thinker who lived his thought and was not merely a professor in an academy—as his precursor in existential thinking. All of this adds to the richness and ambiguity of the Platonic writings. But the figure of Socrates himself undergoes some radical transformations as we follow the growth and systematization of Plato's rationalism. In the earlier, so-called "Socratic," dialogues the personality of Socrates is rendered in vivid and dramatic strokes; gradually, however, he becomes merely a name, a mouthpiece for Plato's increasingly systematic views, and the dialogues tend toward monologues, mere formal essays. In the *Phaedrus* Socrates is still a friend to poets: all the greatest gifts to man, he tells us, come out of a form of inspired madness, and the poetic man, haunted by the muses, is ranked near to the philosopher in the hierarchy of human values. In *The Sophist,* however, a late dialogue, the poets are lumped together in disrepute with the Sophists as traffickers in nonbeing, dealers in untruth. The figure of Socrates himself by then has shrunk from a flesh-and-blood person to a shadowy abstract reasoner. In the later dialogues he even takes a back seat: the principal figure in *The Sophist* is the Eleatic Stranger; in *The Laws* it is the Athenian Stranger; and in the *Parmenides* the venerable figure of Parmenides lectures Socrates on the intricacies of dialectic. Part of this may be due simply to fading memory: the Socrates who died in 399 B.C. had stamped himself so strongly on the young man's mind that for the next thirty or forty years he virtually dominated Plato's life; but with the passage of time even this vivid figure had to grow fainter and, in unconscious compensation, Plato had to assert himself at the end against Socrates. Those unknown figures—the Eleatic Stranger and the Athenian Stranger—are simply the shadow of Plato himself, those portions of his personality which had not been able to speak through the mouth of Socrates but had at last forced themselves to be recognized. Because of his meeting with Socrates, Plato had ceased to be a poet, and finally, at the end of the trail, in his least poetic dialogue, *The Laws,* he advises the death penalty for those whose thought opposes the religious orthodoxy of the state —the very crime for which Socrates had been put to death by the Athenian orthodoxy and in revolt against which Plato himself had taken up his own career as a philosopher! Unconsciously, at the end, he took his revenge upon the figure that had dominated his life.

When we come to the end, with Aristotle, of the great historical cycle that began with the pre-Socratics, philosophy had become a purely theoretical and objective discipline. The main branches of philosophy, as we know it today as an academic subject, had been laid out. Wisdom is identified as Metaphysics, or "First Philosophy," a detached and theoretical discipline: the ghost of the existential Socrates had at last been put to rest. (The progress of this great historical curve is all the more remarkable if we consider Aristotle's own individual development, as it has been established by Werner Jaeger: as a young man and still a Platonist, Aristotle himself conceived of philosophy as the

personal and passionate search for redemption from the
wheel of birth and death.) The foundations of the sciences,
as the West has known them, had been laid, and this was
only possible because reason had detached itself from the
mythic, religious, poetic impulses with which it had hitherto been mixed so that it had no distinguishable identity
of its own.

The West has thought in the shadow of the Greeks;
even where later Western thinkers have rebelled against
Greek wisdom, they have thought their rebellion through
in the terms which the Greeks laid down for them. We must
therefore understand Greek rationalism in all its depth and
breadth if we are to understand some of the later revolts
against it, and particularly the modern effort of existential
philosophy at last to think beyond it. The rationalism of the
Greeks was not the mere passing salute to reason that a
present-day orator might toss off before an academic audience. The Greeks were thoroughgoing, stringent, and bold
in their thinking—and never more so than when they placed
reason at the top of the human hierarchy. Which is greater,
the artist or the thinker? Is Mozart, the creator of music,
inferior to the physicist Helmholtz, the theorist who explained the nature of sound? Which is the higher life—that
of Shakespeare, the greatest poet of the English language,
or of Newton, the greatest English scientist? We today
would hesitate to answer such questions; and in our timid-
ity we might even reject them as meaningless. Not so the
Greeks. A young Greek who felt a disposition toward both
poetry and theory, and wanted to choose one for a career,
would want to know which was the better life, and Plato
and Aristotle would have made no bones about their reply:
the theoretical life is higher than the life of the artist or
that of the practical man of politics—or of the saint, for that
matter, though they did not yet know of this kind of
existence. In his *Nicomachean Ethics* Aristotle gives us a
remarkably flexible and well-rounded picture of human
nature and the many different kinds of goals, or goods, at
which it may aim; but the ethical question still seems un-
answered for him until he has declared which of all pos-

sible goods is the best, and in the tenth and final book of this work he expresses his own preference (stated, of course, as an objective truth) for the life of pure reason, the life of the philosopher or theoretical scientist, as the highest life. Here his own words must be observed carefully:

> It would seem, too, that this [Reason] is the true self of every man, since it is the supreme and better part. It will be strange, then, if he should choose not his own life, but some other's. . . . What is naturally proper to every creature is the highest and pleasantest for him. And so, to man, this will be the life of Reason, since Reason is, in the highest sense, a man's self. (*Eth. Nic.* X, 7.)

Reason, Aristotle tells us, is the highest part of our personality: that which the human person truly is. One's reason, then, is one's real self, the center of one's personal identity. This is rationalism stated in its starkest and strongest terms —*that one's rational self is one's real self*—and as such held sway over the views of Western philosophers up until very modern times. Even the Christianity of the Middle Ages, when it assimilated Aristotle, did not displace this Aristotelian principle: it simply made an uneasy alliance between faith as the supernatural center of the personality and reason as its natural center; the natural man remained an Aristotelian man, a being whose real self was his rational self.

Aristotle did not have, as Plato did, a realm of eternal essences, which is alone "really real," to guarantee the primacy of reason. Nevertheless, he too found a metaphysical ground for this primacy, in the intelligibility of all Being as it rests on a First Cause. To know, says Aristotle, is to know the cause, and human reason can ascend to knowledge of the First Cause of all things, the Unmoved Mover of the Universe, God. So long as the human intellect has held out to it the prospect of surveying the whole cosmos from its ultimate height to its lowest depth, to the end that it may see the ultimate and sufficient reason why this cosmos exists and why it exists in the manner it does— so long as such a goal is promised to the intellect, then all

the spectacles afforded by art, all the worldly triumphs of
the practical life, will dwindle by comparison. The value of
art or of the practical life must necessarily be ranked lower
than that of a theoretical vision so complete and all-
encompassing. The connection between theoretical reason
as the highest human function and the possible completeness of its vision of the cosmos is an intrinsic one: the latter
secures the supreme value of the former. For where the
ultimate reason of things may be known, who would ab-
stain from the effort to reach it, or be distracted by other
goals which partake of the finitude and incompleteness of
our poor feeble human existence? "Happy is he who can
know the causes of things," said the Roman poet; and the
happiest man would be he who could know the ultimate
causes of things.

What happens, however, to this view that the highest
man is the theoretical man if we conceive of human existence as finite through and through—and if human reason,
and the knowledge it can produce, is seen to be finite like
the rest of man's being? Then the possibility that the system
of human knowledge may be closed and completed, that all
of Being may be ultimately embraced in one vision, disappears; and man is left patiently treading the endless road
of knowledge that never reaches conclusion. If science were
to continue its researches uninterruptedly for a thousand
years, it would not disclose to us the ultimate ground of
things. Being finite, we should never arrive at the highest
object of knowledge, God, which this rationalist tradition
has celebrated as the goal that outshines all others. This
conception of human finitude places in question the su-
premacy that reason has traditionally been given over all
other human functions in the history of Western philosophy. Theoretical knowledge may indeed be pursued as a
personal passion, or its findings may have practical application; but its value above that of all other human enterprises
(such as art or religion) cannot be enhanced by any claim
that it will reach the Absolute. Suppose, for example, that
there were a road and we were told we ought to walk it;
in response to our question "Why?", we might be told that

we ought to do so because the walking itself would be pleasant or useful (good for our health); but if we were told that there was a priceless treasure at the end of the road, then the imperative to walk would carry overwhelming weight with us. It is this treasure at the end of the road that has disappeared from the modern horizon, for the simple reason that the end of the road has itself disappeared.

Hence, we in our day have to come back to those old, apparently naïve questions of the Greeks from a different angle, as Nietzsche was the first to do: Which is higher, science or art? Who is the highest—the theoretical or the practical man? or the saint? or the artist? The man of faith or the man of reason? If man can no longer hold before his mind's eye the prospect of the Great Chain of Being, a cosmos rationally ordered and accessible from top to bottom to reason, what goal can philosophers set themselves that can measure up to the greatness of that old Greek ideal of the *bios theoretikos,* the theoretical life, which has fashioned the destiny of Western man for millennia?

CHRISTIAN SOURCES

Chapter Five

1. FAITH AND REASON

THOUGH strongly colored by Greek and Neo-Platonic influences, Christianity belongs to the Hebraist rather than to the Hellenist side of man's nature because Christianity bases itself above all on faith and sets the man of faith above the man of reason. Again and again, at the beginning of Christianity, St. Paul tells us that the faith he preaches is foolishness to the Greeks, for they demand "wisdom"—which of course to the Greek meant rational philosophy and not religious faith. But the historical fact that Christianity arose in a world which already knew about reason through the Greeks distinguishes Christian faith from the Hebraic faith of the Old Testament. Ancient Biblical man knew the uncertainties and waverings of faith as a matter of personal experience, but he did not yet know the full conflict of faith with reason because reason itself did not come into historical existence until later, with the Greeks. Christian faith is therefore more intense than that of the Old Testament, and at the same time paradoxical: it is not only faith beyond reason but, if need be, *against* reason. This problem of the relation between faith and reason, stated by St. Paul, is not only the root problem for centuries of Christian philosophers to come, it is the root itself of later Christian civilization.

The problem is still with us, in our modern civilization, though naturally it presents itself to us in a very different guise than it did to St. Paul. For what is faith? Philosophers through the centuries have attempted to analyze or describe it, but all their talk cannot reproduce mentally the fact itself. Faith is faith, vital and indescribable. He who has it knows what it is; and perhaps also he who sincerely and painfully knows he is without it has some inkling of what it is, in its absence from a heart that feels itself dry and shriveled. Faith can no more be described to a thoroughly rational mind than the idea of colors can be conveyed to a blind man. Fortunately, we are able to recognize it when we see it in others, as in St. Paul, a case where faith had taken over the whole personality. Thus vital and indescribable, faith partakes of the mystery of life itself. The opposition between faith and reason is that between the vital and the rational—and stated in these terms, the opposition is a crucial problem today. The question is one of where the center of the human personality is to be located: St. Paul locates this center in faith, Aristotle in reason; and these two conceptions, worlds apart, show how at its very fountainhead the Christian understanding of man diverges utterly from that of Greek philosophy, however much later thinkers may have tried to straddle this gulf.

From the point of view of reason, any faith, including the faith in reason itself, is paradoxical, since faith and reason are fundamentally different functions of the human psyche. But the paradoxical quality of Christian faith is further heightened by its specific content: that the Son of God became man, died, and rose from the dead. On this matter St. Paul knows that his adversaries are not merely the Greek philosophers but the faithful Hebrews too. To the Greeks, he tells us, Christianity is foolishness, to the Jews a scandal; if the Greeks demand wisdom, the Jews on the other hand demand a sign—i.e., a definite miraculous event to show that this Jesus of Nazareth is really the promised Messiah. Not the Incarnation—that the Infinite God became finite man, which to Kierkegaard, later, is the absolute paradox and scandal of Christianity—but the resurrection of Jesus is the overriding article of the faith that takes possession of Paul's mind. (It is extremely doubtful, in fact, that there is any clear-cut doctrine of the Incarnation in St. Paul.) The central fact for his faith is that Jesus did actually rise from the dead, and so that death itself is conquered—which is what in the end man most ardently longs for. The problem of death lies at the center of the religious consciousness—Unamuno was really following St. Paul when he argued this—and at the center of much more of the philosophic consciousness than this consciousness itself realizes. Plato believed in the eternal Ideas because he was afraid to die. (This is not personal derogation, for the man who is not afraid to die is not really alive.) And because the soul shared in the eternal Ideas, it too could be eternal, and so the man Plato himself might survive death. But Paul's instincts are shrewder: he knows that neither Platonic nor any other kind of reason can convince us of immortality; nothing short of a miracle will do—and the most astounding one at that, a stumbling block to the skeptical among Greeks and Jews alike. Nowadays we would say that a miracle like the resurrection merely contradicts the natural order, whereas the Incarnation contradicts even logic, but we speak thus looking backward from the vantage point of Kierkegaard. It was not so in the earliest Christianity, where faith, more naïve and primitive, came closer to the heart of the matter.

And it was not so more than a century after Paul, with the Church Father *Tertullian* (150–225), who is often cited as an existential precursor of Kierkegaard. Like Kierkegaard, Tertullian was a brilliant intellectual and a powerful writer, who pitted all his power of mind and his rhetoric against the intellect itself. And like Kierkegaard he too insists on the absolutely paradoxical quality of the Christian faith; but notice in the oft-quoted lines of his *De Carne Christi* where he places the weight of emphasis, as the central paradox:

The Son of God was crucified; I am unashamed of it because men must needs be ashamed of it. And the Son of God died; it is by all means to be believed, because it is absurd. And He was buried and rose again; the fact is certain because it is impossible.

Here the parallel with Kierkegaard ends, as all such historical parallels between men of vastly different epochs must: There is no Kierkegaard before Kierkegaard, no Nietzsche before Nietzsche, and in general nobody before himself simply because in history nothing individual and great happens before it does—before the conditions of its being are present. Tertullian was a Christian writer at the beginning of Christianity, when the faith was aggressive, expanding, conquering; Kierkegaard toward its end, when it was in retreat and half buried under the wave of an advancing secular civilization.

The violence of the conflict between faith and reason, which finds expression in anti-rationalism, in a Tertullian, is mitigated by the time we come to a figure like St. Augustine (354–430), who is also often cited as an existential precursor and is indeed a more consequential one than Tertullian. The existentialism of St. Augustine lies in his power as a religious psychologist, as expressed most notably and dramatically in his *Confessions*. Augustine had an almost voluptuous sensitivity to the Self in its inner inquietude, its trembling and frailty, its longing to reach beyond itself in love; and in the *Confessions* he gives us a revelation of subjective experience such as even the greatest Hellenic literature does not, and could not, because this interiorization of experience came through Christianity and was unknown to the earlier Greeks. Where Plato and Aristotle had asked the question, What is man?, St. Augustine (in the *Confessions*) asks, Who am I?—and this shift is decisive. The first question presupposed a world of objects, a fixed natural and zoological order, in which man was included; and when man's precise place in that order had been found, the specifically differentiating characteristic of reason was added. Augustine's question, on the other hand, stems from an altogether different, more obscure and vital center within the questioner himself: from an acutely personal sense of dereliction and loss, rather than from the detachment with which reason surveys the world of objects in order to locate its bearer, man, zoologically within it. Augustine's question therefore implies that man cannot be defined by being located in that natural order, for man, as the being who asks himself, Who am I?, has already broken through the barriers of the animal world. Augustine thus opens the door to an altogether different view of man than had prevailed in Greek thought.

He opens the door, but he does not really go inside. For the other side of St. Augustine is Augustine the Neo-Platonist. As a formal theologian, he was concerned with the justification of God's ways to man and particularly a justification of God's cosmos; and when he was required thus to think cosmically, rather than personally, he found the metaphysics of Plato's *Timaeus* and of the Neo-Platonist Plotinus at hand and suited to his purpose. The duality that gave rise on the one hand to Augustine the existential lyricist of religious experience and on the other to Augustine the formal theologian (thinking with the concepts of Greek metaphysics) is one that lay concealed beneath all the centuries of medieval philosophy that followed; but it did not erupt into painful consciousness until the modern period, when the containing structure of the church, which had held the conflicting elements together in a kind of suspension, could no longer serve this purpose.

The opposition or duality in Augustine can be illustrated on one crucial point: the problem of evil. On page after page of the *Confessions* he reveals to us with marvelous power the presence of the evil and the negative in our existence; but as a formal theologian, in his *Enchiridion* (a manual of theology), he has to make the negative disappear from that existence or be sublimated into some larger harmony. All evil, he tells us, is a lack of being, hence a form of non-being; and since the negative is not real, as positive being is, we are somehow to be consoled. St. Augustine was here engaged in an effort at theodicy, a justification of the goodness of God's cosmos; after Augustine, theodicy was the central project of all Christian metaphysicians, down through Leibniz and Hegel. Leibniz's cosmic optimism came to its comic end in the Dr. Pangloss of Voltaire's *Candide,* Hegel's in the existential revolt of Kierkegaard. Hegel is the end of the line because once the spirit of existential revolt has entered the modern world we are forced to take the side of Ivan Karamazov, who says that he "has to decline the ticket"—the ticket of admission to a cosmos where so much evil has to exist as the necessary precondition of good. Similarly, we are forced today to take the side of Augustine's *Confessions* against his *Enchiridion* because we recognize theodicy for what it is, the tragicomedy of rationalism *in extremis.* Theodicy is an attempt to deal with God as a metaphysical object, to reason demonstratively about Him and His cosmos, to the end that the perfection of both emerges as a rational certainty. Behind this lies the human need to seek security in a world where man feels homeless. But reason cannot give that security; if it could, faith would be neither necessary nor so difficult. In the age-old struggle between the rational and the vital, the modern revolt against theodicy (or, equally, the modern recognition of its impossibility) is on the side of the vital, since it alone holds firm to those inexpugnable elements of our existence that Augustine described in his *Confessions,* but then as metaphysician attempted to think away.

St. Augustine saw faith and reason—the vital and the rational—as coming together in eventual harmony; and in this too he set the pattern of Christian thought for the thousand years of the Middle Ages that were to follow. The formula after Augustine became "Faith seeking understanding": that is, faith taken as a datum, a given fact within the individual's existence, then seeking to elaborate itself rationally as far as it can. In a Neo-Platonic cosmos it was easy for faith to seek its own understanding, for that cosmos itself, though the philosophers themselves did not know it, rested on a faith: given a universe through which God already radiated as an infinite sun, one could find analogies and simulacra everywhere to the dogmas of faith. If one could not prove the dogma of the Trinity, one could at least show likenesses to the Trinity everywhere in nature and man. This made the dogma more plausible, even if in its intimate nature it remained a mystery to reason. That such a dogma absolutely contradicts reason was something the medieval philosophers never perceived or acknowledged. Faith, contrary to Tertullian, had become faith *beyond* reason, but never against, or in spite of it. On the whole, throughout the Middle Ages the position of reason—and this in itself may seem a paradox—remained unassailable.

The consolidation of the Church, institutionally and dogmatically, helped in this. As the Church enunciated its faith in article after article of dogma, the medieval philosopher was left free to be as rational as he wished, since the non-rational part of him was contained and expressed in the structure of the Church and could thus take care of itself. Secular historians have often represented the medieval Church as placing a galling restraint upon the free intelligence of medieval thinkers. This is undoubtedly true from the point of view of the modern secular mind (to which, by the way, there was no counterpart in that earlier period); but it is not at all the way in which the medieval thinkers themselves felt about the dogmas of their faith. These dogmas were experienced as the vital psychic fluid in which reason itself moved and operated and were thus its secret wellspring and support. It remained for later Protestant philosophers, like Kant, to experience the fateful, but necessary, split between reason and dogma, in such a way that Kant can point out that the traditional proofs of the existence of God really rest on an unconscious faith. What the medieval thinker often took to be reason was in fact faith; and the error occurred not because of a deficiency in logical acumen on the part of those thinkers, but because their reason itself was rooted in their historical *existence*—the existence, in short, of an Age of Faith.

From time to time, of course, there were rumblings of discord within the medieval harmony. The tension between the vital and the rational in man involves such a delicate balance that it can split apart into open warfare even where man is totally contained in a universal Church. The instincts of man are so earth-bound that they shrewdly sense it whenever the approach of logic threatens them. And so we find in the eleventh century, the age of naïve and beautiful Romanesque art, when the logical works of Aristotle were just beginning to circulate in the West, a violent controversy ensuing between "theologians" and "dialecticians." The theologians were the spokesmen for faith, the dialecticians for logic. It was once again the old conflict between faith and reason, but this time sharpened by the sense of a naïve and rude age that the very coming of reason was itself a threat. The most remarkable figure in the controversy was *Peter Damiani* (1007–1072), the most forceful spokesman for the party of the theologians, who attacked the exaltation of grammar and logic (what nowadays we would call semantics) as the temptation of the Devil. The Devil in fact, Damiani says, was the first grammarian, tempting Adam in the Garden of Eden with the promise "Ye shall be as gods," and thus teaching him to decline the word "God" in the plural. Logic is quite useless, according to this theologian, in helping us to know God because God in His nature is so incomprehensible and omnipotent that He transcends the basic law of logic, the principle of contradiction; God can even abolish the past, make what has happened not to have happened. Logic is a man-made tool, and God cannot be measured according to its requirements. We are not far here from the later protest of Pascal: "Not the God of the philosophers, but the God of Abraham, Isaac, and Jacob."

The enlightenment went on, nevertheless, despite such rumblings; and Greek reason, in the form of the works of Aristotle, became known more and more in the West. It took prodigious labors on the part of the philosophers of the twelfth and thirteenth centuries to effect the final medieval concordat between faith and reason. The moment of synthesis, when it came in the thirteenth and early fourteenth centuries, produced a civilization perhaps as beautiful as any man has ever forged, but like all mortal beauty a creature of time and insecurity. The fact that the philosophers had to labor so prodigiously in bridging the gap should show us how delicate is the balance between the vital and the rational, and that no harmony between them can be acquired ready-made. The medieval harmony was achieved at a price: In the thought of *St. Thomas Aquinas* (1225?–1274?), the crowning work of the synthesis, man is—to use Bernard Groethuysen's image—really a centaur, a being divided between the natural and theological orders. In the natural order Thomistic man is Aristotelian—a creature whose center is reason and whose substantial form is the rational soul; and St. Thomas, the Christian, never bats an eye in commenting upon the passage in Aristotle's *Ethics* which states flatly that reason is our true and real self, the center of our personal identity, but merely expounds it in straightforward agreement. This might be excused as simply the pedagogic exposition of a teacher identifying himself with his text; but in the *Summa Theologica* he repeats that the speculative, or theoretical, intellect is the highest function of man, that to which all the others are subordinate. This rational animal in the natural order is subordinated, to be sure, to the supernatural; but again through an intellectual vision—the final one, of the essence of God—which informs and purifies the will. This is a synthesis indeed, but how far we have traveled from the experience of Biblical man or of the early Christian, whose faith was felt as something that pierced the bowels and the belly of a man's spirit!

And despite the synthesis, despite the fact that philosophers in this epoch had come to live with the assumption that faith and reason agree, the ancient problem of the relation between the vital and the rational still did not disappear; it simply went underground and popped its head up elsewhere: this time in the controversy between Voluntarism and Intellectualism. After St. Thomas, *Duns Scotus* (1265?–1308) and his followers advocated a doctrine that went contrary to the Thomists—that of the primacy of the will over the intellect. In an age of unbounded rationalism (among the philosophers, that is: the actual concrete life of the time was far from that), such a doctrine was the faint but remembered echo of primitive Christianity's cry as voiced by St. Paul when he said that he came not to bring wisdom to the philosophers but a saving will to all mankind. Scotus, a Franciscan and therefore an Augustinian, was also remembering the existential voice of St. Augustine's *Confessions*.

St. Thomas, the Intellectualist, had argued that the intellect in man is prior to the will because the intellect determines the will, since we can desire only what we know. Scotus, the Voluntarist, replied that the will determines what ideas the intellect turns to, and thus in the end determines what the intellect comes to know. Put this way, the problem looks as insoluble as which came first the chicken or the egg. And indeed this matter of the primacy of intellect or will is one of the oldest and most vexing questions in philosophy—it is the issue behind Socrates' perpetual query whether virtue is really knowledge and therefore all the perversities of the will merely forms of ignorance. The question has perhaps to be put differently: not in terms of whether will is to be given primacy over the intellect, or the intellect over the will—these functions being after all but abstract fragments of the total man—but rather in terms of the primacy of the thinker over his thoughts, of the concrete and total man himself who is doing the thinking. At least Voluntarism seems to be aware that it is the heart which pumps blood to the brain, and so its own heart is rather in the right place; however excessive or extreme the various voluntarisms have been in the history of philosophy, the fact remains that Voluntarism has always been, in intention at least, an effort to go beyond the thought to the concrete existence of the thinker who is thinking that thought.

2. EXISTENCE VS. ESSENCE

Contemporary Thomists would not accept this comparison between Duns Scotus and St. Thomas because they are just now in the process of discovering St. Thomas as the true and authentic existentialist. When Existentialism first appeared on the scene in France, M. Jacques Maritain was scathing and peevish in his denunciation of it, but then later announced that all it contained had been said already in the thirteenth century by St. Thomas. Imitation is the sincerest form of flattery!

In fact, the issues between Aquinas and Scotus are complicated by another profound and technical problem: *the relation between essence and existence.* And to shed some light on this problem we shall have to anticipate a little what will be given more extended treatment later.

The essence of a thing is *what* the thing is; existence refers rather to the sheer fact *that* the thing is. Thus when I say "I am a man," the "I am" denotes the fact that I exist, while the predicate "man" denotes *what kind* of existent I am, namely a man.

Modern Existentialism, particularly in the writings of Sartre, has made much of the thesis: existence precedes essence. In the case of man, its meaning is not difficult to grasp. Man exists and makes himself to be what he is; his individual essence or nature comes to be out of his existence; and in this sense it is proper to say that existence precedes essence. Man does not have a fixed essence that is handed to him ready-made; rather, he makes his own nature out of his freedom and the historical conditions in which he is placed. As Ortega y Gasset puts it, man has no nature, only a history. This is one of the chief respects in which man differs from things, which do have fixed natures or essences, which are once and for all what they are. However differently the various Existentialists may put this thesis, they are all agreed on it as a cardinal point in their analysis of man. Sartre proclaims the point as applying, be it noted, only to the case of man; it is only with man that it seems to him to have any significance. Whether or not existence precedes essence in things generally—in the stone, the tree, or a table—or whether the reverse is true is a question that would hardly seem to matter very much, since a thing at any moment is always precisely what it is, and it would not make much sense to raise the question when existence and essence exactly coincide.

In the history of philosophy, however, the question has been raised not only for man but for all beings. The problem breaks down into two separate but related questions: (1)

Does existence have primacy over essence, or the reverse? and (2) In actual existing things is there a real distinction between the two? Or are they merely different points of view that the mind takes toward the same existing thing?

The reader may wonder whether questions that sound as abstract and remote as these have any real flesh-and-blood import at all. But its technicality alone need not make a question irrelevant to life, if the technicality results from carrying a question that is indeed one of life and death, as the phrase goes, to the farthest reaches of thought. These two questions touch upon the most fundamental matters of philosophy, and indeed the whole history of Western philosophy revolves around the answers that have been given to them. How one answers them determines one's view of one's own life and the life of nature. A glance back at Plato, the father of Western philosophy, will show us the human consequences of the answers to these questions.

Essences Plato called Ideas. These Ideas, as we saw in the previous chapter, were for him "really real," more real than the particular things that derived their own individual being from participation in the Ideas. The circle, that is, about which the geometrician reasons is the essence common to every individual circle in nature, and without which the individual circles could not exist; it is more real than the individual circle that he may draw on the blackboard for illustration. Now, the circle that the mathematician reasons about is one he never draws upon the blackboard; it cannot be drawn because it never comes into existence; it is outside time and therefore eternal. So too it never comes to be in actual physical space; and it is non-spatial in the same sense in which it is non-temporal. All the Ideas, for Plato, thus constitute a realm of absolute realities beyond time, change, and existence, and existence is merely a shadowy replica of essence. When an Idea comes into existence, it is through a fall (a kind of original sin) from some higher realm of Being. Time itself—that invisible and tormenting medium of our own individual existence—becomes merely a shadowy image of eternity.

It requires very little imagination to see how, holding

such a philosophic position, one's attitudes toward life become colored all the way down the line by the Platonic bias. All of Plato's writings, the whole of his philosophy, are in fact a working out of the consequences of this fundamental conviction of the priority of essence over existence for every field of human experience: for government, ethics, aesthetics; even extending down to the condemnation of the life of the body. Whatever we may think of it, throughout the centuries Platonism has exercised a powerful influence upon the imaginations and lives of men, and in view of the miraculous fertility of that influence we cannot say that the question of existence versus essence is an idle one, or that it is remote from the concerns of life.

Plato's is the classic and indeed archetypal expression of a philosophy which we may now call *essentialism*, which holds that essence is prior in reality to existence. *Existentialism*, by contrast, is the philosophy that holds existence to be prior to essence. The history of Western philosophy has been one long conflict, sometimes explicit but more often hidden and veiled, between essentialism and existentialism. And it would seem also to be the case that, to the degree to which this history takes its beginnings from Plato, essentialism has always come out on top. This may not be due altogether to the compelling influence of Plato; it may also be due to the very nature of philosophy itself, to the hidden tendency of human reason. We shall have more to say on this question later.

With the foregoing distinctions perhaps a little clearer, let us return now to the point in history where we left matters between St. Thomas Aquinas and Duns Scotus.

On the question of existence in relation to essence it would seem that St. Thomas is the existentialist. He held that existence is prior to essence in the sense that what primarily constitutes the being of anything is its act of existing (*actus essendi*). Moreover, he said, in all created things— all things except God that ultimately derive their existence from God—there is a real difference between the thing's existence and its essence. I am not my essence, since if I were —if essence and existence were identical in me—it would be of my essence to exist, and I would never die. For all contingent beings, beings that are born and that die, existence therefore can never coincide with essence. There is within the being of contingent things a hiatus or cleft, as it were, between existence and essence.

Duns Scotus, on the other hand, maintained the primacy of essence over existence. In the matter of the order of the attributes of God, at any rate, he set God's essence first as the basic attribute, and His existence after it. To be sure, it might be argued by the Scotist that since God's being is absolutely one and undivided, in contrast to the complexity and self-dividedness that we find among the things of nature, it does not make much difference whether we assign to essence or existence the status of primary attribute because the two words as applied to God designate the very same thing—God Himself. The order of the divine predicates would thus seem to be merely a matter of verbal arrangement. But this arrangement does show the philosophic cast of mind of the arranger; and even though the attributes in this case denote the same reality in the thing, he who puts essence first, and on grounds of strictest philosophic principle, does so because he considers it more basic than existence. In this respect the Scotist philosophy was certainly more essentialistic than that of St. Thomas.

With regard to the second of our questions—whether existence and essence in actually existing things are really distinct—Duns Scotus also held a position different from the Thomist one: There is, Scotus says, no real distinction between the essence and existence of a thing, as St. Thomas had maintained; the two are but different ways in which the mind lays hold of the existing thing.

This question of the identity of essence and existence is one of the most tangled in the history of Scholastic philosophy, and it is still hotly debated between two schools of Catholic philosophers, the Jesuits and the Dominicans. After Scotus, in the sixteenth century, the great Spanish theologian Francis Suarez—really the last voice of medieval Scholasticism—upheld the Scotist position on the question. Suarez became the great philosophical teacher for the Jes-

uits, and indeed the interpreter *par excellence* for them of
what St. Thomas was supposed to have meant. Hence
the continuing, and even contemporary, debate between
Suarezians and Thomists (Dominicans), a controversy that
is relevant in that the issue still being debated throws an
unexpected and clarifying light on the whole of modern
thought.

Much of this light comes from a remarkable, even great,
book, *Being and Some Philosophers,* by the distinguished
scholar of medieval philosophy, Etienne Gilson. Whether or
not we agree with him that all existential roads lead to
Rome—or, more exactly, to the Paris of the thirteenth century where St. Thomas taught his doctrine of the priority
of existence—Gilson has presented a marvelous analysis of
the way in which the Scotist influence worked upon the
great philosophers of the seventeenth century, Descartes,
Spinoza, and Leibniz, and through them has permeated
the thinking of the last three centuries. Descartes, Spinoza,
and Leibniz were all philosophers with a pronounced
mathematical bent, and therefore it was likely that they
should find congenial a philosophy that exalted essence
over existence The mathematician is enthralled by the
timeless self-identity of essences, and hence always gravi-
tates spontaneously to one form of Platonism or another.
Moreover, the seventeenth century and those following it
were concerned with the extraordinary expansion of mathematics and mathematical physics, and these two disciplines
won prestige beyond that of every other intellectual enterprise because of the extraordinary conquests over nature
they made possible: hence this bias toward essence with
which the contemporary era in philosophy began continued
supreme and in fact almost unchallenged until Kierkegaard
appeared in the nineteenth century. The roots of a thing
always go deeper into the soil than our vision of the plant
above the surface would lead us to imagine; and in this
case it comes as something of a surprise to know that one
fateful direction of modern thought had its roots in the
disputes of theologians in the thirteenth and fourteenth
centuries.

Modern Catholic philosophers, to whom we alluded earlier, have made a great deal of St. Thomas as representing the original and true form of what a Christian existentialism should be, an assumption enabling some Thomists to assume a rather papal and condescending attitude toward modern Existentialism as toward a degenerate scion. The existentialism of St. Thomas, however, is extremely debatable; and one faithful son of the Church, Miguel Unamuno —whose testimony should carry as much weight initially as any medieval scholar's, since he was at once a scholar and poet—has rejected the mentality of St. Thomas as expressed in the *Summae* as being purely legalistic. The *Summae* plead a case, says Unamuno, they buttress the Church as an institution, in the way that the old codifications of Roman law buttressed an empire; and in this respect we must remember how much of the spirit of the old Roman Empire the medieval Church had inherited. A good deal of the Thomistic existentialism current nowadays looks indeed like a case of special pleading after the fact. A book like Gilson's, for example, shows so strongly the influence of Kierkegaard (albeit at work on a mind that is granitically Thomist) that it is safe to say the book could not have been written if Kierkegaard had not lived. Without Kierkegaard, indeed, Gilson would not have found in St. Thomas what he does manage to dig out, and the fact is that a good many other Thomists found quite different things before the influence of Kierkegaard made itself felt. And, to go one step further, what Gilson finds is not enough. The historicity of truth is inescapable, however perennial the problems of philosophy may be, and we should be suspicious in advance of any claim that the answer to modern problems is to be found in the thirteenth century. Granting St. Thomas' thesis of the primacy of existence and of the real distinction between existence and essence, we are still very far from an answer to those questions which have led modern thinkers like Heidegger and Sartre to a reopening of the whole subject of Being.

The fact is that the Thomistic distinction between essence and existence leads us into very grave embarrassment when we try to understand our own human existence as men. In his treatise *On Being and Essence* (*De Ente et Essentia*) St. Thomas cites as an example of essence the traditional definition, "Man is a rational animal." This essence is the common characteristic of a whole species. A question then arises, and it is the famous question of universals: How does this essence, which is one as a species, exist as a plurality of individual members of the species? This essence is particularized in each individual: my rational-animality is mine, as distinctly my own and different from that of my friend Peter as my flesh and blood are mine and not his. In fact according to St. Thomas it is my individual matter, my flesh and blood, that individuates the universal essence. "Signate matter," Aquinas calls it, and he describes it as matter that exists in determinate dimensions—that is, it is just this particular matter of mine that fills this space which I am now occupying and that excludes any other solid body from filling the same space. Now it is precisely here that the difficulty arises that begets that classical view we referred to earlier of man as a centaur, irremediably split between two parts of his being; here he is divided between the essence and the individuating matter that locates his body uniquely in space and time. The characteristics or qualities that inhere in this individual matter St. Thomas calls "accidents," since they are not a necessary part of the essence. But what, we may ask, in the case of any individual human being is the accident and what is the essence? Is it at all clear that in that singular and internal biography of our own selves from birth to death there is a compartment into which certain happenings and characteristics are dumped as being accidental, while in another compartment are other characteristics and events considered as essential? Or, more precisely, are the qualities of here and now—the temporal and spatial qualities that are accorded to me in virtue of that matter which individuates the essence—accidental to my being as a human person?

If I turn a candid gaze "to the things themselves," as Husserl would say, toward my own individual existence as it has been my actual care and concern through life, quite apart now from any metaphysical presuppositions whatever, can I say that the fact that I exist here and now, rather than there and then, is an accident of my being? I was born and have lived an American in the twentieth century. From the point of view of an essence of man that exists individually in me but is nevertheless really distinct from my existence, such facts are indeed accidents; but they have formed the burdens and tasks of *my* life, and there is not a part of its warp and woof into which they have not entered. Or, let us take the example of which Sartre has at once properly and improperly made a great deal: the fact of human sexuality. Is the individual's sexuality part of the essence of his existence or only an accident? I cannot, in introspection, imagine myself harboring any essence, like a nugget at the center of a nest of Chinese boxes, that is not touched by the fact that my life has been lived from birth as a member of one sex and not of the other. The argument applies to all the factual conditions of man's being—man's *facticity*, as Sartre calls it: if we *exist* our facticity, then we *are* it, and it makes up the total essence of what we are. These factual conditions, particularly of the historical epoch in which we live, color every portion of our being. Existence and essence, as we take them at any rate in the actual life of the human person, interpenetrate.

The Scotist thesis of the identity of essence and existence would seem then to do more justice to the actual facts of our experience. But, on the other hand, the Thomistic arguments work very well against this position, which ends up by making existence itself a kind of "accident" that occurs to essence. Moreover, with this view it becomes difficult to explain the radical contingency of the human being, since if the essence and existence of the actually existing person are identical, why should his existence not therefore be necessary so that he lives forever?

But if neither of these medieval positions works, if there is neither an identity of essence and existence nor a real distinction between them, what then?

The fact is that neither position can work because the very notions with which they deal are too abstract and

schematic. The medieval conceptions of essence and existence do not do justice to the full concreteness of modern
experience, particularly to our experience of man himself.
They need a complete overhauling. That is why Heidegger
announced that it was necessary for these questions about
Being to be renewed, and he has been the first philosopher
to attempt a radical rethinking of the tradition itself. A
tradition is kept alive only by such renewal, not by mechanical and idle parroting of the formulae it has be-
queathed to the present. But renewal really means renewal,
and is therefore a very radical adventure. We should not
be surprised therefore that though modern Existentialism,
to the degree that it moves in the mainstream of Western
thought, inevitably harks back to traditional problems, it
nevertheless comes up with conclusions that are bound to
shock some of the traditionalists. Time, alas, is of our essence; and our mere recognition of this fact—a recognition
that was altogether beyond the anhistorical medieval man—
is so radical that it creates a gulf between us and the medieval past. The solutions of that past can never be totally
ours, marvelous as we have come to realize its philosophy
as having been.

3 · THE CASE OF PASCAL

However numerous these antecedents and precursors,
what we know today as Existentialism could not have come
to be before the conditions of its being were there. Philosophers breed ideas; and if anything keeps them anchored to
existence, it is not philosophy itself but something that
comes from outside it—either religion, or the personal
drama, anguish, or rebellion of the philosopher's own life.
So in the past it was the dynamite of Hebraism or Christianity that blew to bits the classical temple of Greek rationalism. Before even the possibility of modern Existentialism
could be created it was necessary to create its world, and
this could have come about only through science, which
suddenly projected man out of the Middle Ages. So when

we come to *Pascal* (1623–1662), himself a great scientist, we are no longer dealing, as in the case of St. Augustine, with a precursor of Existentialism. Pascal *is* an existentialist.

Nothing could be more confusing than the indifferent lumping together of Pascal and St. Augustine as great psychologists of religion. To be sure, they were both concerned with the inner life of the religious man, his anguish and restlessness. But the world St. Augustine inhabited was the Neo-Platonic cosmos, a luminous crystal palace with the superessential Good fixed on its highest point, radiating outward like a beacon and diminishing in brilliance as it shone down through the rest of the perfect structure. Pascal's was the desolate and desiccated world of modern science, where at night the sage hears not the music of the shining heavenly bodies but only the soundless emptiness of space. "The silence of these infinite spaces frightens me," Pascal said, voicing the reaction of the human heart to the universe that seventeenth-century science had fabricated for man. In that world of frightful and empty space man was homeless. Accordingly, he evolved a different image of himself from that of the man who inhabited—and believed himself at home in—a Greek or Neo-Platonic cosmos. In the world of Pascal, faith itself became a much more desperate gamble and a much more daring leap.

Consequently, the struggle between faith and reason gave rise to a more profound psychological discord within man's being. Despite the arguments of theologians during the Middle Ages about matters of faith and reason, those ages never experienced this division of man within himself. In the *Divine Comedy*, Dante is led by Virgil, the symbol of human reason, through the depths of Hell and up the slopes of Purgatory; but when it comes to the journey through Heaven, the sphere of the elect who have made it there only by God's grace, Virgil disappears and Beatrice, symbol of Divine Revelation, takes over as guide. Reason, in short, guides us to faith, and faith takes over where reason leaves off—such is the happy and harmonious lot of man in the ordered, crystalline cosmos of Dante. But the universe of Pascal does not present us with the numerous similitudes and analogies to the Divine Being on which the medieval philosophers had hung their faith, as on so many pegs. In Pascal's universe one has to search much more desperately to find any signposts that would lead the mind in the direction of faith. And where Pascal finds such a signpost, significantly enough, is in the radically miserable condition of man himself. How is it that this creature who shows everywhere, in comparison with other animals and with nature itself, such evident marks of grandeur and power is at the same time so feeble and miserable? We can only conclude, Pascal says, that man is rather like a ruined or disinherited nobleman cast out from the kingdom which ought to have been his. Thus he takes as his fundamental premise the image of man as a disinherited being.

Consequently, the psychology of a Pascal will be different from that of a St. Augustine. Pascal's observations of the human condition are among the most "negative" that have ever been made. Readers of Sartre who have protested that his psychology is too morbid or sordid, and possibly therefore only an expression of the contemporary Paris school of despair, would do well to look into Pascal: they will find his view of our ordinary human lot every bit as mordant and clinical as Sartre's. "The natural misfortune of our mortal and feeble condition," Pascal says, "is so wretched that when we consider it closely, nothing can console us." Men escape from considering it closely by means of the two sovereign anodynes of "habit" and "diversion." Man chases a bouncing ball or rides to hounds after a fleeing animal; or the ball and fleeing game are pursued through the labyrinth of social intrigue and amusement; anything, so long as he manages to escape from himself. Or, solidly ensconced in habit the good citizen, surrounded by wife and family, secure in his job, need not cast his eye on the quality of his days as they pass, and see how each day entombs some hope or dream forgotten and how the next morning wakes him to a round that becomes ever narrower and more congealed. Both habit and diversion, so long as they work, conceal from man "his nothingness, his forlorn-

ness, his inadequacy, his impotence and his emptiness."
Religion is the only possible cure for this desperate malady
that is nothing other than our ordinary mortal existence itself.

Where classical philosophers discuss the nature of man
—as Aristotle does in his *Ethics* or St. Thomas in his treatise
on man in the second part of the *Summa Theologica*—such
talk seems to us nowadays to smack of the textbook: the
creature the thinkers are discussing may be man, but he
does not resemble us in the least. In what Pascal says about
the human condition, however, we recognize ourselves all
too painfully. As a psychologist, he is a contemporary.

Perhaps Pascal was a better psychologist than were the
philosophers because he himself was no philosopher. He
has left us in one brief remark his final judgment of the
value of philosophy itself: it is, he tells us, "not worth an
hour's trouble." And considering the quality of Pascal's
mind and his deepest interests as a man, this is an entirely
reasonable judgment. To put it somewhat paradoxically, he
was too intelligent to be a professional philosopher. To have
put himself through the slow and laborious course of training in any academic philosophy would have been to hobble
dreadfully his marvelous intelligence, and in any case it was
unnecessary for him to do so in order to know what he ultimately needed to know as a man. In this respect he resembles Kierkegaard and Nietzsche, philosophers who went
beyond philosophy and so were able to see how it looked
from the outside, from the point of view of religion and
art, in their cases, from that of science, in his. Kierkegaard
and Nietzsche did possess a technical grounding in philosophy, however, while Pascal's education was scientific and
humanistic. He had read some of the classical philosophers,
like the Stoics, but apparently only to find out what they
had to say about the condition of man and not to follow
their metaphysics, for which he had very little taste. His
passionate interest as a youth was in science, and he was
one of the most precocious scientific geniuses that ever
lived, making fundamental discoveries in mathematics before he was twenty-one.

After the death of his father, Pascal, still a young man, came into a fairly comfortable inheritance and was able to cut something of a figure in the world. We know, at any rate, that he kept for a while a coach-and-six, which was enough to establish him as a gentleman and man of the world. In order to understand the mind of Pascal we have to imagine him entering that social world of Paris in the reign of Louis XIV, when the observation and study of man was the consuming passion of worldly and acute minds like Saint-Simon and La Rochefoucauld, and recognizing that here was a different kind of datum from that he had dealt with in his mathematical and physical researches. And not only was the material different, but it required an altogether different kind of intelligence for its comprehension. Pascal, unlike Spinoza, was too intelligent not to recognize that doing geometry was altogether different from doing the study of man.

Out of this realization came his famous distinction between the mathematical and the intuitive mind—*l'esprit de géométrie* and *l'esprit de finesse*. It would not be too much of an exaggeration to say that the whole of Bergson's philosophy is virtually contained in the few pages that Pascal dedicates to this fundamental distinction. French culture has in these matters a marvelous sense of conservation. The most inbred of cultures, it is nevertheless among the richest because it preserves and elaborates what it has in its own kitchen. (This is also the spirit of French cooking, which does not throw away anything but uses it to create a stock— the fundamental element in cooking, Escoffier tells us—or else to throw into a *pot au feu* that can be kept simmering indefinitely.) Because it kept sight of Pascal's distinction, French culture never quite surrendered itself to the clear and distinct ideas of Descartes. Now, the mathematical mind, as Pascal describes it, is defined precisely by its pre-occupation with clear and distinct ideas, from which it is able to extract by deduction an infinite number of logical consequences. But the material with which the intuitive mind is dealing is so concrete and complex that it cannot be reduced to clear and distinct ideas that can be set forth in a few simple axioms. In a human situation the waters are usually muddy and the air a little foggy; and whatever the intuitive person—whether he be a politician, courtier, or lover—can perceive in that situation is not by virtue of well-defined logical ideas. Quite the contrary: such ideas are more likely than not to impede his vision. What Pascal had really seen, then, in order to have arrived at this distinction was this: that man himself is a creature of contradictions and ambivalences such as pure logic can never grasp. This was something the philosophers had not yet grasped.

By delimiting a sphere of intuition over against that of logic, Pascal had of course set limits to human reason. Perhaps nowhere did he use his own *esprit de finesse* more shrewdly than in his estimate of the value of reason, and perhaps no writer has ever balanced more judiciously the claims and counterclaims of reason: As a mathematical genius he had known all the power and glory of reason, but he also saw its corresponding feebleness and limitations. Three centuries before Heidegger showed, through a learned and laborious exegesis, that Kant's doctrine of the limitations of human reason really rests on the finitude of our human existence, Pascal clearly saw that the feebleness of our reason is part and parcel of the feebleness of our human condition generally. Above all, reason does not get at the heart of religious experience. As Pascal had very little use for formal philosophy, so he had even less for formal or rational theology, whose supreme task is the fabrication of rational proofs for the existence of God. Such proofs, Pascal held, are beside the point: one day they seem valid to us, the next day not, and if we postpone our salvation until the proofs are satisfactory we shall stand forever wavering from one foot to the other. There are today, Pascal said, extremely intelligent minds who find the proofs for the existence of God entirely convincing, and equally intelligent minds that find them misconceived or inconclusive; and each side suspects the other of bad faith. But the fact is that the proofs convince those who want to be convinced, fail to convince those who do not want to be convinced, and so are not really proofs at all. In any case, God as the *object* of a rigorous demonstration, even supposing such a demonstration were forthcoming, would have nothing to do with the living needs of religion. He would become as neutral an entity as the abstract circle or triangle about which geometricians reason. It is here that Pascal raises his famous outcry: "Not the God of the philosophers, but the God of Abraham, Isaac, and Jacob."

He himself had had a religious experience, connected with what he thought to be a miraculous recovery from an illness, and so overpowering had been the visitation that he wrote down a note about the experience and sewed it into his clothing, as if it were a secret that he had to keep as close as possible to himself and never forget. Whatever we may think of the validity of such experiences, for Pascal himself this lightning from heaven needed no proofs: it was of the order of life itself, not of rational theology. His life thereafter turned round that single and shattering experience, and he dedicated that life to religion; particularly to an attempt at a great explanation and defense of the Christian religion, which he never completed and of which we have only those glorious ruins, the *Pensées*. Another equally drastic experience, this time rather negative than positive, was equally decisive for his thinking. While he was driving by the Seine one day, his carriage suddenly swerved, the door was flung open, and Pascal almost catapulted down the embankment to his death. The arbitrariness and suddenness of this near accident became for him another lightning flash of revelation. Thereafter he saw Nothingness as a possibility that lurked, so to speak, beneath our feet, a gulf and an abyss into which we might tumble at any moment. No other writer has expressed more powerfully than Pascal the radical contingency that lies at the heart of human existence—a contingency that may at any moment hurl us all unsuspecting into non-being. Death does not arrive punctually by appointment. The idea of Nothingness or Nothing had up to this time played no role at all in Western philosophy. At the very beginning of Greek philosophy, Parmenides had warned against following the path of non-being, for non-being, he said, cannot even be thought. During the ages of Scholastic philosophy the Nothing, *nihil*, had been a purely conceptual entity, an empty abstraction that lay at the farthest reaches of thought. But for Pascal it was no longer an abstraction but an experience. At a certain moment of his existence, Nothingness had suddenly and drastically revealed itself to him. Thereafter, Pascal searched everywhere for evidences of the contingent in human existence—in the length of Cleopatra's nose, which altered the destinies of Mark Antony and the Roman Empire, in the grain of sand in Cromwell's kidney that put an end to his military dictatorship. And long before Heidegger and Sartre introduced their jawbreaking names for all the categories that define human contingency, Pascal had seen that to be born is itself for the individual the prime contingency, since it means to be born at *this* time, *this* place, of *these* parents and *this* country—all of these brutally given facts on which his life has to seek to found itself.

Nothingness, for Pascal, opens as it were both downward and upward. He lived in the age of the microscope and the telescope, when the tight, tidy, finite cosmos of Aristotle and the medieval thinkers was being expanded in both directions, toward the infinitesimally minute and the infinitely great. We go downward, cleaving matter and space, and finding the unbelievable and minute organizations of life at lower and lower levels; and always there are things beyond these that exceed our comprehension because of their minuteness. Or we go outward into space and find the universe dwarfing us by its vastness. Man thus occupies a middle position in the universe, as Pascal saw, between the infinitesimal and the infinite: he is an All in relation to Nothingness, a Nothingness in relation to the All. This middle position of man is the final and dominant fact of the human condition with which Pascal leaves us, and it suggests perfectly what we can expect of the range and powers of man's reason. It is also a perfect image of the finitude of human existence, invaded as it were on both sides by the Nothing. Man *is* his finitude. And if we add a consideration of the infinite duration of time to this predominately spatial and material image, we get Pascal's ultimate judgment on the nature of human existence:

> When I consider the short duration of my life, swallowed up in the eternity before and after, the little space which I fill, and even can see, engulfed in the infinite immensity of space of which I am ignorant, and which knows me not, I am frightened, and am astonished being here rather than there, why now rather than then.

Reading this, we are no longer in the world of a Tertullian or a St. Augustine, in the violent fervor of an expanding and conquering Christianity; nor in the Romanesque world of a Peter Damiani or St. Bernard when the most naïve and beautiful works of Christian art were being created; nor in the world in which Duns Scotus debated the positions taken by St. Thomas and in which Christian faith was so strong that it could make a miraculous marriage with the philosophy of Aristotle. No; it is our world, the modern world, that Pascal depicts, and reading him we enter that world as our home just because we are as homeless there as he was.

Pascal died in 1662. There followed a century of such blinding light, the century of the Enlightenment, that his example seemed not to be needed and so was forgotten. The light of the Enlightenment became thus its own darkness. The accomplishments of this extraordinary era cannot be undervalued. In that century the conquests in mathematics and physics were extended; the universe of Newton became a consolidated conquest and, due to the marvelous fertility and ingenuity of mathematical analysis, seemed to afford answers to all the problems of nature. The great victories won by reason in mathematics and physics suggested inevitably its extension into all other fields of human experience in order to dispel the shadows of ancient superstition: into law, custom, government, and history. The idea of Progress was announced not only as fact, but as a law of history. The perfectibility of human nature was to be realized through the universal application of reason. The philosopher Condillac outlined a scheme of universal history, whose guiding thread was the progress of man from darkness to light—a progress that had gone steadily forward in the past and would continue so indefinitely. Philosophers became critics, attacking the medieval barbarisms of the society around them. The century found its symbol and summation in that curious episode at the height of the French Revolution when the goddess of Reason, in the person of a well-known actress, was enthroned in the Cathedral of Notre Dame. Our Lady of Reason in the temple of the Queen of Heaven—an ironical switch that might have suggested to anyone faintly familiar with the personality and history of goddesses that extremely stormy weather lay ahead, and not only for France but for European civilization as a whole.

But there were also some unhappy souls in the universe of Newton and of the goddess of Reason, and to these we must now lend an ear. The first voices to be heard are, as we might expect, those of the poets. Poets are witnesses to Being before the philosophers are able to bring it into thought. And what these particular poets were struggling to reveal, in this case, were the very conditions of Being that are ours historically today. They were sounding, in poetic terms, the premonitory chords of our own era.

THE FLIGHT FROM LAPUTA

Chapter Six

ANYONE who has read Swift's *Gulliver's Travels* probably will not have forgotten the episode of the voyage to Laputa, which is among the most bizarre of that great and fantastic book. Laputa is an island that floats in the air. It is driven by the power of an immense magnet and navigated by means of magnetic lines of force, which to our latter-day minds suggests something like a radar apparatus. Swift's technology was not so advanced that he could imagine machinery that would enable the inhabitants of the Zeppelinlike island to cut themselves off altogether from the earth: the lines of force used to navigate by are still those of the earth, and so to that degree the Laputans are earthbound. Nevertheless, they are the nearest things to creatures of the air that Gulliver encounters anywhere on his long and varied journey, and their character belongs as much as possible to the aerial element.

What this aery quality in their nature consists of, we are not long in finding out. When the shipwrecked Gulliver is rescued and brought up to this island, he finds the inhabitants the oddest-looking creatures he has ever seen. Their eyes do not focus on the person or object before them; instead one eye is turned upward as if in perpetual contemplation of the stars, and the other turned inward in empty and vacuous introversion. Their garments are decorated with emblems of the sun, moon, stars, and of various musical instruments. Mathematics and mathematical astronomy are the subjects to which we would expect these

aery creatures to devote themselves, since those are the
most abstract studies, the most detached from ordinary ter-
restrial claims. But why music, the most directly emotional
of the arts? Emotion, of course, is not the aspect of music
that Swift had in mind; he meant the Laputans' music to
have the significance it had in the Pythagorean or Platonic
tradition, when it was thought of as a purely mathematical
study, a branch of applied arithmetic. Laputa might thus
be called the kingdom of the pure Platonists, and Swift's
imagination gave this people a local habitation to match
the spirit of its Platonism: an island that floats in the blue.
That vigorous coarseness of Swift's temperament, which expressed itself even in the name he chose for this place, *la
puta,* suggests and may even have been inspired by Luther's equally vigorous and coarse exclamation, "The whore
reason!"

Because they control the air over the land below, the Laputans hold subject the ordinary earthly people in their
vicinity. The subjects, however, seem to be a good deal
happier than their rulers. The Laputans in fact, despite
their power, are a dreary and sad lot. These cerebral people
are incapable of the ordinary human interchange involved
in conversation. When they go into society they have to be
accompanied by a servant boy carrying a stick at the end
of which is a bladder filled with pebbles or dried peas;
these rattle as the boy strikes the mouth or the ears of his
master, as the case may be, to signal him when he is to talk
and when to listen while conversing with another Laputan.
The absent-minded intellectual might otherwise drift off
into speculation and forget altogether about the person in
front of him. At dinner in Laputa, Gulliver finds the food
is served cut in all manner of geometrical shapes. When a
tailor comes to fit Gulliver with a suit of clothes, he takes
the measurements by means of sextant, quadrant, and
other scientific gadgets; then brings back a very ill-fitting
garment. Geometry evidently does not provide a very accurate means of measuring the organic human form; an ordinary tape measure, made flexible in order to follow the
contours of the body, would do better. On a visit to their

academy of sciences Gulliver finds the Laputans engaged in all manner of fantastic and harebrained schemes of research. Actually, these researches might not seem so fantastic to us today; they do have analogies in contemporary scientific invention. Clearly, we are further advanced in the ways of Laputa than Swift's imagination led him to be.

We need not go into all the details by which Swift visited his scorn upon these abstract minds. In fact, nothing very much happens during Gulliver's sojourn among the Laputans that is not overshadowed in one's memory simply by the weird image of the people themselves. However, one tiny incident serves to set the whole episode in its proper human perspective. The Laputan wives are not very happy with their Platonist husbands; and shortly before Gulliver's arrival in the kingdom there had been a great scandal at court because the wife of the prime minister had run away, despite all efforts to restrain her, to the mainland below to take up with an old footman who got drunk regularly and beat her. Women as creatures of nature will prefer passion to pure reason, even if the passion is accompanied by drunkenness and blows. A beating is at least a recognition of one's own individual existence.

In this part of *Gulliver's Travels* Swift does not seem in the least to be trying to play the prophet. His temperament was too downright, positive, and passionately concrete to bother very much about assuming the mantle of prophecy. Sufficient unto the day is the evil thereof—and he had enough to do to put up with the imbecility of English politics and to bear with the tedium of life in Ireland, where he had been sent, as he himself puts it, to die like a rat in a hole. Nevertheless, this episode from *Gulliver* (a book that appeared in 1726) can be taken as a forecast of the cultural history of western Europe, or at least of one sizable slice of that history, over the next hundred and fifty years. The prophet's power is in proportion to his character, and the testimony of Swift gains all the more force in coming from the kind of man he was. Were there any of the high and exotic color of romanticism about Swift, we might set down his prophetic diatribe as the eccentric product of a romantic temperament unlucky enough to be born before its time. But Swift is a great writer of prose because he wrote prose and not something else: his is perhaps the best example in English literature of simple, straightforward, even plain prose; and the temperament of the man matched the temper of his writing. Nowhere did he espouse any ir-rational attitude toward life; he repeatedly extolled the virtues of reason, but it was always down-to-earth and practical reason that he had in mind. He had little taste—and little capacity, for that matter—for the more abstract exercises of reason: the Laputa episode of *Gulliver's Travels* might almost be taken as Swift's final vengeance upon the examiners at Trinity College who failed him because he did not do well enough in logic. Coming from such a prosy and non-romantic temperament, the image of Laputa is proba-bly the most powerfully prophetic we could find. The men and movements of which it does stand as a prediction will find themselves at times in the desperate quandary of the prime minister's wife, ready to throw themselves into the arms of a drunken footman if that is the only way out of the sterile kingdom of reason. In the search for the Diony-sian, after all, one cannot always be expected to be bound by good taste.

Who, then, are these men and movements that Swift predicts?

1. THE ROMANTICS

The whole movement of Romanticism, which not long after the appearance of Swift's work thrust up its first shoots in England, is at bottom an attempt to escape from Laputa. However we choose to characterize Romanticism—as a pro-test of the individual against the universal laws of classi-cism, or as the protest of feeling against reason, or again as the protest on behalf of nature against the encroach-ments of an industrial society—what is clear is that it is, in every case, a drive toward that fullness and naturalness of Being that the modern world threatens to let sink into oblivion. The Romantic movement was not confined to one country, but passed like a great spasm of energy and enthusiasm over the whole of Europe—England, France, Germany, Italy—finding somewhat different national expressions in each country but always preserving the same inner characteristics. Among its English representatives, the figures of three poets—Blake, Wordsworth, and Coleridge—deserve our passing attention.

Blake is recognized easily enough as the poet *against* the industrial revolution. The imagery of wheels, forges, furnaces, smoke, and Satanic mills is strewn throughout his poems. But he was a poet of considerably more intellectual substance than an early, rather patronizing essay by T. S. Eliot has led most of our current literati to think. Blake was not merely a critic of industrial society as such, but of that particular attitude of mind from which industrialism springs:

> The atoms of Democritus
> And Newton's particles of light
> Are sands upon the Red sea shore
> Where Israel's tents do shine so bright.

Mills and furnaces are evil, to Blake, because they are the external manifestations of the abstract and mechanical mind which means the death of man. Robert Graves has argued that in his prophetic books Blake was seeking to resurrect an ancient bardic tradition dating back to the days of pre-Christian Britain. This may very well be the case, but I think we should not neglect to observe that Blake calls these books "prophetic," that prophecy has to do with the future, and that Blake, as a genuine seer, was concerned with the vision of what man might become. One of these works, *The Marriage of Heaven and Hell*, is of particular significance here because in a good many ways it anticipates Nietzsche, as it also anticipates a good deal of the psychologist Jung in our century. "Drive your plow over the bones of the dead" is not the aphorism of a man who is seeking merely to hearken back to the "green & pleasant land" of ancient Britain. If man marries his hell to his heaven, his evil to his good, Blake holds, he will become a creature such as the earth has not yet seen. Nietzsche put the same insight paradoxically: "Mankind must become better and more evil."

This point is worth emphasizing here at the outset, in connection with Blake, because Romanticism did in many of its manifestations take on the trappings of a revival of or a return to the past, to the Gothic ages or Homeric Greece, or to any past age of enchantment that seemed to stand outside the tawdriness of the present; in some quarters the movement has almost come to be defined in those terms. But basically, although they were sometimes unconscious of it, the Romantics were moved by a vision of the future, of human possibilities, rather than of the past; of what man might become rather than of what he actually was or had been. Hence the vitality among them of the tradition which takes the poet to be a genuine seer.

Wordsworth is so respectable a figure—we can see him almost as a gaitered and benign English clergyman—that he helps us to avoid the error of locating the inner meaning of Romanticism in a search for exoticism, a gaudy parade of colored lights and high romance. With the exception of the German poet Hölderlin, Wordsworth was probably the most philosophic poet of Romanticism; and it is to be regretted that no English philosopher has made the kind of commentary on his poems that Heidegger has made on those of Hölderlin. Whitehead, who owes much of his own philosophy to Wordsworth's feeling for nature, has thrown out a few brilliant asides on his work, and that is all we have. Wordsworth was not a philosophical poet because he knew something about Platonism and a little about German Transcendentalism that he had picked up from Coleridge, and expressed these bits of philosophy gnomically in some of his best-known poems. Nor is he at his final philosophical depth when he criticizes, and quite acutely, the intellect as something that severs us from the immediate feeling for nature:

> Our meddling intellect
> Misshapes the beauteous forms of things:
> We murder to dissect.

Wordsworth is not at his most philosophic when he is being

pithy or gnomic, or otherwise drawing an explicit moral. A deeper philosophy resides in some of his poems in which he was able, almost miraculously, to locate man in nature, to reveal his being as a being-in. Thus one of the great poems, "Resolution and Independence," begins with the magnificent lines:

> There was a roaring in the winds all night,
> The rain came heavily and fell in floods.

The poet wanders over the moors, encounters an old man who is gathering leeches at a pond, hears his story, and then concludes, moved by the old man's example, with some stoical comments on the necessity of facing life with courage. But what sticks in the mind is the marvelous way in which the leech gatherer is located in nature, along with stone and tree and moor. Whitehead called this quality the togetherness-of-things, and he claimed to have come by this philosophical insight through studying the poets of nature like Wordsworth. But Whitehead's expression is not yet adequate: it is not that man is a thing essentially together with other things in the natural landscape: rather, before he is a thing, he is-in; his being is a being-in before it is the being of a thing.

Wordsworth himself never expressed this meaning conceptually; perhaps he had not arrived at the point of grasping it conceptually, perhaps this meaning of Being cannot very well be grasped conceptually. But it is there, revealed in his poetry; and it is indeed what gives positive meaning to all those other poems in which he is simply moralizing, protesting that urban man—by which he means modern man—by cutting himself off from nature has cut himself off from the roots of his own Being.

Though he was immensely more learned philosophically than Wordsworth, nevertheless in this particular respect Coleridge's work is of less philosophic significance. In his most successful and famous poems—such as *The Ancient Mariner, Kubla Khan, Christabel*—he exhibits chiefly the "romance" aspect of Romanticism, the freedom of the imagination to find its materials outside the stringent categories of neoclassicism. But in one poem, and a very great one, *Dejection: An Ode*, Coleridge produced something so modern that we can call it existential even though it was written before the Existentialists. The ode is a lament on his failing powers as a poet, powers that have dried up because Coleridge is no longer able to find joy in nature. These powers are identical with the power to be in communion with nature. What makes Coleridge's statement of the matter so impressive is that he himself participates in the feeling; Wordsworth's protests against the severance of man from nature were laments for his fellow men who were being thus cut off, not for himself—his own powers of communion with nature seemed to have survived intact. But Coleridge, who was himself one of the wretched—cut off, forlorn, miserable, derelict—was the first to explore this thoroughly modern mood from the inside. What happens to man when he is thus severed from nature? Here Coleridge encounters, in thoroughly existential fashion, anxiety itself. He cannot pin down this anxiety, cannot attach it to any definite object, event, or person; it is the revelation of void or nonbeing.

> A grief without a pang, void, dark, and drear,
>   A stifled, drowsy, unimpassioned grief,
>   Which finds no natural outlet, no relief,
>   In word, or sigh, or tear—

All the German idealism with which poor Coleridge's head was crammed had nothing to say to him about this experience; it did not even provide the terms necessary for its philosophic comprehension. Kierkegaard had not yet introduced the analysis of dread into philosophy. Coleridge the poet, however, saw and knew before Coleridge the philosopher.

Coleridge's melancholy condition in this respect is precisely that of Faust at the beginning of Goethe's drama. Both are in or near the condition of breakdown, trapped in a paralysis of feeling in which everything has turned to dust and ashes, including the meddling intellect that has

tyrannized over both. Coleridge has lost life to German
metaphysics:

> by abstruse research to steal
> From my own nature all the natural man;

Faust to a reckless attempt to master all of human learning,
which Goethe dismisses in the final statement of intellectual
disenchantment: *"Gray is all theory, green is life's glowing
tree."* Coleridge's poem is so intensely personal that we cannot take this parallel with Goethe to be a case of literary
imitation: it was due rather to a kind of experience that
had become momentous for the men of that period, as it
still is today. Midway in his life—and it was a long life—
Goethe insisted on detaching himself from the movement
of Romanticism. So far as that gesture applied to the sentimentality of an early work like *Werther* it was certainly
valid; but the theme of *Faust* had laid hold of Goethe in
his very earliest days, when he was at his most romantic,
and it was a theme that continued to occupy him throughout his life. Since his greatest work deals with the central
problem of Romanticism, it cannot be left out of any account of the movement, and indeed Goethe's final handling
of the problem, in the poem, was the culmination of all
his youthful experience of Romanticism.

We have particularly to call attention to *Faust*, in this
connection, because it deals with the very problem with
which Nietzsche was later to wrestle, both in his own life
and in his philosophy: How is man to be born out of contemporary despair into a more complete and vigorous being
than history has yet known? Goethe never uses Nietzsche's
word Superman, but there can be no doubt that what we
encounter in the Second Part of *Faust* (completed just before the poet's death) is Goethe's own conception of a
superior mortal, in fact a Superman, for in his old age Faust
has almost transcended his humanity. At the beginning of
the play, with the well of life gone dry inside him, Faust
decides to commit suicide and is just raising the poison gob-
let to his lips when he is stopped by hearing from the street
an Easter hymn to Christ's resurrection. At the moment of

crisis it is the remembrance of Christianity that intervenes: Faust-Goethe is still tied to the collective being of mankind for whom the symbol of resurrection is inevitably Christ. Since he is not to commit suicide, how then is Faust to be reborn? Mephistopheles appears; Faust makes his pact with the Devil and from a withered old scholar is transformed into a radiant and handsome youth. It is the same solution to the problem of human energy that Blake preached: the marriage of hell and heaven, the pact with one's own devil; or, in Nietzsche's terms, the marriage of one's good and evil in order to arrive at the point that is beyond good and evil because it is the source of them both —the Self in its craving to live and grow.

The original Faust was an old medieval scholar who turned to magic and the black arts; and in Marlowe's version, *Doctor Faustus*, Faust is the demoniacal magician who seeks power over popes and emperors. Goethe internalized Faust's quest, indeed turned him into a man of his own time, yet the original overtones of magic and alchemy still surround this character. Goethe himself had read a good deal of alchemy at one time, and part of the original fascination of the historical Faust, for him, was the dark halo of magic around him, the sign of a craving to transcend ordinary humanity. Now, magic and alchemy are perfectly appropriate symbols for our aspirations toward freedom. The problem of free will does not present itself to us in life in the cool and sterilized abstractions of the philosophers. To free oneself, to break the chains of a situation, whether inner or outer, that imprisons one is to experience something like the magical power that commands things to do its bidding. The figure of the magician is, as it were, the primitive image of human freedom. Scholars tell us that the ideograms in some of the older Chinese writings that are usually translated "men of virtue" might be more accurately rendered as "men of magic"; and indeed the sage, the virtuous man, he who could command himself and therefore others, must have struck earlier mankind as something of a magician. In any case, magic and alchemy recur throughout the whole course of the Romantic movement,

always as the deep archetypal symbols of aspiration toward
a higher and fuller level of Being. Even Goethe in his old
age, by then the cool and classic Olympian, introduces into
the Second Part of *Faust* an alchemical scene in which
a little man, *homunculus*—Is he perhaps future man?—is
brewed in a retort.

It is in later French Romanticism, as it passes over into
Symbolism, that this spiritual craving of poets for magic and
alchemy becomes more noticeable. Baudelaire was the most
remarkable figure in this phase of the movement, the initia-
tor or precursor of almost everything that we know as "modern poetry." He was the first poet of the city, as others before him had been poets of the countryside. As such, he
sounds a new and more extreme note of human alienation.
Where Wordsworth had been a rural man, observing and
condemning the city but always writing about it from outside, Baudelaire is inside the city, the swarming anthill of
alien and faceless men, in whose streets he is utterly a
stranger. Romantic melancholy, as we have seen in the case
of Coleridge, is nothing less than man's discovery of his
own estrangement from Being; in Baudelaire this becomes
Spleen, and takes on the dimensions of revolt. It is not only
a social revolt against the materialism of bourgeois society,
but a metaphysical revolt against the kind of world created
by the positivism and scientism of the present age. The poet
does not find reality in such a world, he must search for it
in some other hidden sphere of Being. Hence, Baudelaire's
doctrine of "*correspondances*," according to which the poet
must seek out the arcane and obscure images in nature,
somewhat like one of the ancient astrologers or diviners.
Poetry is no longer an art merely of making verses, but a
magical means of arriving at some truer and more real
sphere of Being. Poetry becomes a substitute for a religion.

For this last attitude, of course, Baudelaire and his followers have been very much taken to task by some French
Catholic critics. Such critics are certainly right in their judgment that poetry would not have developed these extraordinary aspirations if man had remained within his historic
container, Christian faith. But it will not do to lecture these

poets smugly, as if they were delinquent children who have run away from home. The fact is that there was no home for them to stay in. They themselves did not create the human condition into which they were thrown by the nineteenth century; they merely experienced it as their fatality, while others, less sensitive, were not aware of what had happened in the world. We are not dealing here with a mere aesthetic perversion, but with a genuine human revolt—a point that becomes indisputable in the case of the poet Rimbaud, whose revolt was in fact so genuine that the poet literally paid for it with his life. It is a mistake to consider the Romantic poets as excessive and self-indulgent aesthetes; for them the value of the aesthetic attitude was always metaphysical and concerned with the total human condition.

It seems a very long step from the serenity of Wordsworth to the violence of Rimbaud, who heralded "the era of assassins." Yet the filiation is direct; only a few conditions had to change or grow more acute to produce, instead of the earlier, the later Romantic. The rest of mankind might be cut off from contact with nature, but Wordsworth, as we have seen, remained secure in the belief that he at least possessed the mana and was in touch. He did indeed have that mana, and though the possession of it may have been fleeting, Wordsworth's self-conceit was such that he never perceived himself at any time as being without it. Hence he never shared the despair of his fellow Romantics. But the poet has only to lose the mana, or the security of his belief in himself as never being without it, and he finds himself sharing the forlorn and derelict fate of the rest of mankind. His despair has only to become desperation, and to ally itself with a violent will to power, a will to reconquer by the most extreme measures if necessary, the lost province of Being from which modern man has been extruded—and we have Rimbaud. Rimbaud remained true to his vision: he ended by giving up poetry and leaving Europe—a civilization he thought doomed—to go off and run guns in Abyssinia. The demands he had made of poetry, as a revelation of an unknown truth, were too severe; in the end he spoke of it with disgust as "one of my follies." In any case, it became irrelevant to his final project, the forging of the Self. For the man who seeks to transcend humanity, poetry is not enough: it will only lead back to the squabbles of sectarian literati or the exegeses of dry-as-dust professors, and the poet will be caught up again in the web of a banal and mechanical civilization. Rimbaud burst like a rocket in the sky of French poetry, and then by the very force of his trajectory was carried beyond it. But in the course of this brilliant flight he brought all the hidden problems of Romanticism to the fore.

For one thing, Rimbaud's unconditional break with Western civilization—the civilization of the white man—was the sign of a break *within* this civilization. Rimbaud was thus among the first of the creative artists to announce primitivism as one of the goals of his art and of his life. From Gauguin to D. H. Lawrence primitivism has been such a varied and rich source in modern art that academicians or rationalists would be ill advised to dismiss it out of hand as a mere symptom of "decadence." One might ask, in any case, whether it is not the civilization itself that has become decadent rather than those creative individuals within it who struggle to rediscover the wellsprings of human vitality. With Rimbaud primitivism was far from being a sentimental décor for the spirit, an illicit longing after the South Seas and maidens in sarongs; rather it was a passionate and genuine struggle to get back to the primitive—which is to say, primary—sources of Being and vision. We need not approve of the particular means Rimbaud used for this in order to acknowledge the validity and necessity of his task. Rimbaud surrendered himself in the end to the demon of the will to action, thus proving himself a true child of Western civilization. He does not seem to have found any other course possible. While following it, however, he revealed the tremendous potential of energy and action that Romanticism harbored explosively within itself. Romantic melancholy was no mere matter of languor or the vapors; nor was it an outbreak of personal neurosis, impotence, or sickness among a few individuals; rather it was a revelation to modern man of the human condition into which he had fallen, a condition that is nothing less than the estrangement from Being itself. Once having lost contact with the natural world, however, man catches a dizzy and intoxicating glimpse of human possibilities, of what man might become, in comparison with which the old myths of the magician and the sorcerer seem pallid indeed. Rimbaud was the poet of these possibilities as Nietzsche was to be their thinker.

2. THE RUSSIANS: DOSTOEVSKI AND TOLSTOY

From Paris to Moscow or St. Petersburg is a long journey; and it looks like even a longer step from later French Romanticism and Symbolism to the realistic fiction of the great Russian writers. It is indeed a complete change of literary climate. What one prizes above all in the Russian writers is their direct grasp of life, their radical scorn of the artifices and artificialities of literary form and symbol, which became so consuming a preoccupation among French poets. In his *What is Art?* Tolstoy has some pages passionately denouncing Baudelaire and his followers as decadent and artificial writers. Yet for all this difference in their attitude toward the nature of literature itself, we shall find in the Russian writers the same insights about modern man. So far as Existentialism is concerned, we are here on even richer soil.

Conditions in nineteenth-century Russia thrust the writer into a position where he was forced to confront the ultimate problems of human life. Hence, no matter how realistic may be its literary tone, Russian fiction is thoroughly metaphysical and philosophical at bottom. The contrast between East and West was as sharp then as now, though it yielded much richer fruits for nineteenth-century writers. Russia was absorbing Western culture at breakneck speed, and the strain of this absorption produced throughout her whole society a situation of extraordinary tension and ambivalence. The very backwardness of the country, which gave rise to a

smoldering but profound sense of inferiority in cultured
Russians, could at the same time be the cause of an overweening feeling of superiority toward western Europe and
all its refinements. The West stood for the Enlightenment,
true, but Russia—with her vast spaces, mud, illiterate peasantry, and archaic Church—at least was in contact still with
old Mother Earth; and the Russian Slavophile, convinced
of his nation's messianic destiny, could spurn, as he does
today, the decadence of the West. The word "intelligentsia"
is of Russian origin; its coinage bears witness to the fact
that intellectuals, whatever their original social or economic
class, felt themselves a distinct cultural group in Russia because by their very nature they were alienated from the
rest of the society. Outside of the small glow of light cast
by the cultured circles in Moscow and Petersburg, Russia
was an immense wasteland populated by primitive peasantry and ineffectual gentry. The intelligentsia were so conscious of themselves as a class because the head, in their
country, was so far removed from the body social. The ad-
vent of Communism in 1917 belongs in the general scheme
of Russian development, which began in the eighteenth
century with the violent imposition of Western ways by
Peter the Great. Social and political reforms exerted from
above, the forcing of new ways down upon the old, cannot
fail to produce acute dislocation and tension. The Russian
writers of the nineteenth century had an opportunity (as
they no longer have) to convert this human upheaval, if
not into a form of social critique, at least into a spiritual
revelation.

Because they were placed outside of Western culture—
driven on the one hand to devour it greedily, as the indispensable tool of their own literary profession, on the other
hand impelled to stand apart from it in order to assert their
own identity—the Russian writers were in a unique and
privileged position, from which they could see this culture
in a way that Western eyes could not. The sharp contradiction between their own existence as intellectuals and that
of the rest of the vast, shapeless, backward social body of
Russia enabled them to see this as a contradiction central to

the whole culture of the Enlightenment. Intellectuals as a class suffer to the degree that they are cut off from the rest of mankind. But intellectuals are the embodiment of reason, and reason itself if cut off from the concrete life of ordinary mankind is bound to decay. When the head is too far away from the body, the head withers—or goes crazy. The whole of the European Enlightenment, in the eyes of these writers, faced this threat. It would be a mistake to consider this feeling of Tolstoy and Dostoevski as a mere manifestation of Russian nationalism, or as the Russian sense of inferiority converting itself into one of superiority; rather, the Russian condition placed these men in a position to see a threat that was really there.

A society that is going through a process of dislocation and upheaval, or of revolution, is bound to cause suffering to individuals, but this suffering itself can bring one closer to one's own existence. Habit and routine are great veils over our existence. As long as they are securely in place, we need not consider what life means; its meaning seems sufficiently incarnate in the triumph of the daily habit. When the social fabric is rent, however, man is suddenly thrust outside, away from the habits and norms he once accepted automatically. There, on the outside, his questioning begins. Thrust out into the cold air of the Western Enlightenment, with its ideals of reason, progress, and liberalism, the Russian found his old religion a burning question. God, freedom, and immortality became topics not for the professional philosopher but for Everyman. We are told how Russian youths used to sit up all night arguing these matters. Such naïveté and passion were on their way out in the West, where the same arguments had taken place a century earlier. Precisely because Russia was a backward country in this respect—because it had no developed tradition of professional or professorial philosophy—there was no insulating screen between the questions and the personal passion such questions ought to arouse. The absence of a philosophical tradition, however, does not mean necessarily the absence of a philosophical revelation: the Russians did not have philosophers, but they did have Dostoevski and

Tolstoy; and the substitute was perhaps not a total loss. When in the next century a professional philosopher, Heidegger, began to re-examine the meaning of death, he took as his starting point a story by Tolstoy, *The Death of Ivan Ilyich;* and entire volumes have been written on the subject of Dostoevski's existential insights by thinkers like Berdyaev and Shestov.

The first novel Dostoevski wrote after his return from imprisonment in Siberia was *Memoirs from the House of the Dead*. Since the book came after the decisive events of his life—his near execution by a firing squad and his penal servitude in Siberia—it can be taken as the beginning of the real Dostoevski. The narrative that comprises the second part of the book, which is the novel proper, is fairly negligible; but the first part, the description of prison life in Siberia, is of crucial importance in understanding Dostoevski's deepest insights into human nature. An experience like his in this Siberian prison lay outside the whole humanistic tradition of European culture and could only be expected to yield knowledge of man that that tradition had not yet come upon. No classicist or rationalist, armed with the Aristotelian definition of man as the rational animal, could have been exposed to such a welter of humanity and still have retained his ancient convictions. What Dostoevski saw in the criminals he lived with is what he came finally to see at the center of man's nature: contradiction, ambivalence, irrationality. There was a childishness and innocence about these criminals, along with a brutality and cruelty, altogether not unlike the murderous innocence of a child. The men he knew could not be categorized as a criminal type and thus isolated from the rest of the species, man; these criminals were not "types," but thoroughly individual beings: violent, energetic, intensely living shoots from the parent stalk. In them Dostoevski was face to face with the demoniacal in human nature: perhaps man is not the rational but the demoniacal animal. A rationalist who loses sight of the demoniacal cannot understand human beings; he cannot even read our current tabloids.

In *The House of the Dead* the philosophic theme remains unstated; it is implicit simply in the human material with which the novelist is dealing. In *Crime and Punishment*, however, Dostoevski embarked upon the kind of thematic novel that is so distinctly his. The hero, Raskolnikov, is the alienated intellectual—alienated at once from the collective body of mankind and from his own being. Hungry and solitary, he spins out of the bowels of his own reason a Nietzschean theory (before Nietzsche) of the Superman who through his own superior daring and strength rises above all ordinary moral codes. Then to put his theory to the test he kills an old pawnbroker. But the criminal is unequal to his crime: Raskolnikov's theory has not reckoned with his own self, and the guilt over his crime brings on a breakdown. Precisely the feelings that had been repressed in this intellectual—the ordinary human horror at the taking of life—erupt and take their revenge. What drove Raskolnikov to the crime had nothing to do with the justifications he fabricated to himself: He reasoned, "I am poor, this old pawnbroker is a louse; by killing and robbing her, I can relieve my mother of the awful strain of paying for my studies"; but in fact, as he admits finally to the girl Sonia, he killed in order to prove to himself that he was not a louse like the ordinary run of mankind. The will to power—the demoniacal will to power—was thus discovered by Dostoevski before Nietzsche made it his theme. But, unlike Nietzsche, Dostoevski did not lose sight of the thoroughly dialectical, or ambivalent, nature of this drive: The will to power is weakness as well as strength, and the more it is cut off and isolated from the rest of the human personality, the more desperate, in its weakness, it can become. Thus Raskolnikov kills out of insecurity and weakness, not out of an excess of strength: he kills because he is desperately afraid that he is nobody. And indeed he is, for his mind has so lost touch with the rest of him that he is not, properly speaking, a self.

These destructive and even criminal possibilities of reason were the philosophic themes on which Dostoevski played his most persistent variations. In *The Brothers*

Karamazov the appealing Ivan Karamazov is led, through a stubborn pride of intellect, into a revolt against God; his final breakdown, due to a medically vague "brain fever," is dramatically appropriate—nemesis striking down its victim through the offending organ. In *The Possessed* a group of political intellectuals are shown as being possessed by devils, ready to scheme, lie, even kill for the abstract ideals of Progress, reason, socialism. The political events of the last two decades have made *The Possessed* seem far less fantastic than some of our own intellectuals thought it during the Marxist period of the thirties. Nevertheless, some liberal minds still feel Dostoevski goes too far; that despite his amazing accuracy as a prophet of the political course of Russia as it was to be acted out some fifty or sixty years later, too much of his message is tied to an archaic and messianic Christianity.

To be sure, Dostoevski as a thinker is not always a safe guide: the thought in his case too evidently partakes of the being of the thinker, and therefore often has a frenzied and hysterical quality. But Dostoevski as a psychologist—or rather, as the artist who reveals a certain psychological stratum in man—sets before us data on the human condition that it would be folly for us to ignore. "He might have been a liberator of mankind," Freud remarked of him, dryly, "instead he chose to be its jailer." The implication is that Dostoevski would be more acceptable to a certain type of modern mind had he been a Freudian; but in that case he would also have been much less of a psychologist. The work of Dostoevski in which his attack upon the Enlightenment seems to carry most conviction for present-day readers is the novelette *Notes from Underground*. The impact made by its dark fulminations against human nature is due, curiously enough, to the fact that our ears have been somewhat attuned to such things by modern psychoanalysis; and to the fact that in this work Dostoevski's psychological explorations are less visibly connected with his Christian faith. We seem to have reached a point where we are willing to believe the worst about human nature so long as that worst is not attached to any hope of religious redemption.

Notes from Underground appeared in 1864. The first part of this work is one of the most amazing monologues in all literature: The Underground Man, a petty clerk in the Russian bureaucracy, voices his spite, indignation, resentment, and his rebellious longing for freedom. Time and again in his tirade he refers to "the great crystal palace" as the symbol of the Enlightenment, with its dream of a thoroughly rational ordering of human life. This Crystal Palace had been given material form, as the building that housed the International Exposition in London in 1851. It was fitting that this Exposition, in which the bourgeois century congratulated itself on its material progress, should have been held in England, the country that had led in the industrial revolution and in the development of liberal and parliamentary government. Dostoevski's Underground Man was the Russian answer to all those pious dreams enshrined in the Crystal Palace. The Underground Man, who is everyman or at least one underlying stratum in everyman, rejects everything for which that Palace and the liberal nineteenth century stood. In a rational utopia, he cries, man might die of boredom, or out of the violent need to escape this boredom start sticking pins in his neighbor—for no reason at all, just to assert his freedom. If science could comprehend all phenomena so that eventually in a thoroughly rational society human beings became as predictable as cogs in a machine, then man, driven by this need to know and assert his freedom, would rise up and smash the machine. What the reformers of the Enlightenment, dreaming of a perfect organization of society, had overlooked, Dostoevski saw all too plainly with the novelist's eye: Namely, that as modern society becomes more organized and hence more bureaucratized it piles up at its joints petty figures like that of the Underground Man, who beneath their nondescript surface are monsters of frustration and resentment. Like Nietzsche after him, Dostoevski was the great explorer of *resentment* as a powerful and sometimes unaccountable motive in man.

Dostoevski is too complex and volcanic a figure to be swallowed at one gulp. There was something of the criminal in him as well as the saint. The critic Strakhov in his bio-

graphical notice may have weighed certain evidence too
heavily against the novelist, but there seems nevertheless to
have been a repulsive and unsavory side to Dostoevski's
character. Perhaps it was just these human contradictions,
in all their virulence, however, that made Dostoevski so in-
comparable a witness to the existential truth about man. In
any case, his grasp of nihilism as the basic fact in modern
life was itself never nihilistic. We know this from one passage in *The Idiot*, in which Dostoevski reveals what had
been and was always to be the pivot about which his life
turned. A story is told by Prince Myshkin—the fool of Christ,
another of Dostoevski's own masks—as coming from another
man, unidentified; but we of course know it to have been
Dostoevski's own experience. Here is the story in Myshkin's
words:

> This man had once been led out with the others to the
> scaffold and a sentence of death was read over him. . . .
> Twenty minutes later a reprieve was read to them, and
> they were condemned to another punishment instead.
> Yet the interval between those two sentences, twenty
> minutes or at least a quarter of an hour, he passed in the
> fullest conviction that he would die in a few minutes.
> . . . The priest went to each in turn with a cross. He
> had only five minutes more to live. He told me that those
> five minutes seemed to him an infinite time, a vast
> wealth. . . . But he said that nothing was so dreadful at
> that time as the continual thought, "What if I were not
> to die! What if I could go back to life—what eternity!
> And it would all be mine! I would turn every minute
> into an age; I would lose nothing, I would count every
> minute as it passed, I would not waste one!" He said
> that this idea turned to such a fury at last that he longed
> to be shot quickly.

In this story, which describes Dostoevski's own reprieve
after he had been condemned to be executed by a firing
squad, is the ultimate affirmation: in the face of death life
has an absolute value. The meaning of death is precisely
its revelation of this value. Such is the existential view of it,

elaborated later by Tolstoy in his story *The Death of Ivan Ilyich* and by Heidegger in the context of a whole system of philosophy.

To go from Dostoevski to Tolstoy is a little like emerging from the lurid air of some subterranean forge into the clear daylight. It has been said that every man is born either a Platonist or an Aristotelian; it might be said with equal justice that he is born either a Tolstoyan or Dostoevskian. If Dostoevski is the novelist of the abnormal and the morbid, of the convulsions of the human spirit at its heights and in its depths, Tolstoy is by contrast the supreme portrayer of the normal and the organic. Tolstoy himself felt very keenly this temperamental antipathy to the other man, and for many years he dismissed Dostoevski as a "morbid mediocrity." That view changed, however, and toward the end of his life *The Brothers Karamazov* became Tolstoy's bedside book, the one he read and reread endlessly. This reconciliation between the two writers is appropriate, for despite the tremendous differences in the literary and human atmospheres they create, both bring the same revelation to the philosophic mind.

As a simple and convenient key to Tolstoy's existentialism, we may begin with one brief passage from his *Anna Karenina*. Karenin, the husband, has suddenly and unexpectedly become jealous of his wife Anna. This jealousy strikes him as offensive to his wife and to his own moral breeding, for he has been taught that "one" ought to trust one's wife. Karenin is a thoroughly rational type, a dry and officious intellectual, whose whole life has been constructed on such rational precepts as to what "one" (the impersonal and collective one) must be and do. But there, all the same, is the incalculable and living fact of his jealousy staring him in the face:

> He felt that he was standing face to face with something illogical and irrational, and did not know what was to be done. Alexey Alexandrovitch was standing face to face with life, with the possibility of his wife's loving some

one other than himself, and this seemed to him very irrational and incomprehensible because it was life itself. All his life Alexey Alexandrovitch had lived and worked in official spheres, having to do with the reflection of life. And every time he had stumbled against life itself he had shrunk away from it. Now he experienced a feeling akin to that of a man who, while calmly crossing a bridge over a precipice, should suddenly discover that the bridge is broken, and that there is a chasm below. That chasm was life itself, the bridge that artificial life in which Alexey Alexandrovitch had lived. For the first time the question presented itself to him of the possibility of his wife's loving some one else, and he was horrified at it.

The great goal for Tolstoy, both as novelist and man, was just this "standing face to face with life." Truth itself—the truth for man—is just this standing face to face with life. Such truth cannot come from the intellect, for the intellect may in fact veil it, placing us like Karenin in that impersonal zone where we know only "the reflection of life" through concepts, precepts, all the abstract formulae of social routine; rather, truth is of the whole man. Tolstoy tells us repeatedly, in his later tracts, that the truth he is after is not what he knows merely by the intellect but what he knows with his whole being. More impressively, however, he has actually embodied this view of truth in the structure of his greatest novels.

These novels unfold so simply and naturally that they do not seem to us to be plotted in the usual sense of literary contrivance and manipulation, but to be parts of the great organic process of life itself. Nevertheless, there is always a Tolstoyan subplot moving parallel to this effortless and organic sweep of life: people are born, love, marry, suffer, move toward death, but in the midst of this unfolding panorama there is one character, the emissary of Tolstoy and the bearer of the spirit, whose story amid all these other natural involvements is that of the search for truth—for his own truth and the truth of life itself. Thus we have Levin in *Anna Karenina* and Pierre in *War and Peace*. The things that happen to them in the course of the novels—encounters, love, marriage, suffering—are only so many stages on the way the spirit takes in search of its truth. In the end Tolstoy shows them each as finding this truth. And what is it? It is not, as we have seen, an intellectual truth. Levin and Pierre are both at odds with the intellectuals of the city, who far from having found the answer they seek are indeed, in the artificiality of their life and its estrangement from nature, more remote from the truth than are the simple peasantry. (Here Tolstoy, despite his realism, speaks in the deepest tradition of Romanticism, as a good Wordsworthian, but with a vigor and boldness beyond anything in Wordsworth.) The truth Pierre and Levin come to possess is not intellectual, moreover, because there are no propositions—and no system of propositions—they can assert that would adequately express what it is they have learned out of all their tribulations. Theirs is not an intellectual, but an existential truth. It consists in nothing more nor less than that they now stand more directly "face to face with life itself." They are open to what is; and if we were to cast about for a philosophic expression for this, the nearest we could come would be Heidegger's description of truth as the openness toward Being.

To grasp the Tolstoyan meaning of truth is to grasp the unity of all his writings—novels, tracts, autobiography—a unity so strong as to make his work virtually unique. Perhaps this was so because Tolstoy himself was so much more than a writer. But anyone who would stand face to face with life itself must also stand face to face with death, for death is an inescapable part of life. It is here that Tolstoy's passionate quest for truth met the acid test of courage; and he was equal to it. His preoccupation with death is not morbid brooding, mere fecklessness, or cowardice, but the measure of his intense passion for life. It is this that makes his story, *The Death of Ivan Ilyich,* perhaps the most powerful description in any literature of what it means to face death. Ivan Ilyich is a thoroughly ordinary and average bourgeois—in fact, Everyman; he has acquired success in the average way, found love and marriage and a family in the average way—as, likewise, the lack of love in the average way: altogether, a likable and pleasant fellow. He falls from a ladder, but the accident seems slight and he thinks nothing of the pain in his side. The pain stays, however, and grows; he begins to go from doctor to doctor, but no diagnosis seems to serve. Then the horrifying thought dawns upon him that he may be going to die. The reality of death lies not in the physical structure, the organs that medical science examines; it is a reality *within* Ivan Ilyich's own existence:

> To Ivan Ilyich only one question was important: was his case serious or not? But the doctor ignored that inappropriate question. From his point of view it was not under consideration, the real question was to decide between a floating kidney, chronic catarrh, or appendicitis. It was not a question of Ivan Ilyich's life or death, but one between a floating kidney and appendicitis.

Nor does death's reality consist in its being a mere external social fact, an event that happens to everybody:

> The syllogism he had learned from Kiezewetter's Logic: "Caius is a man, men are mortal, therefore Caius is mortal," always seemed to him correct as applied to Caius, but certainly not as applied to himself. That Caius—man in the abstract—was mortal, was perfectly correct, but he was not Caius, not an abstract man, but a creature quite, quite separate from all others.

The reality of death is precisely that it sunders Ivan Ilyich from all other human beings, returns him to the absolute solitude of his own individual self, and destroys the fabric of society and family in which he had lost himself. But awful and inexorable as the presence of death is, it gives to the dying man the one revelation of truth in his life, even though the content of this revelation is chiefly the pointlessness of the way he has lived.

Tolstoy could not have written this story had not he himself stood face to face at one time with death. Maxim Gorky knew Tolstoy well for a time, and in his *Reminiscences of*

Tolstoy has given us a remarkable picture of the old man, indomitably earth-bound, sunning himself like a lizard, and capable old as he was of such outbursts of sexual profanity as to make Gorky, himself a pretty robust type, blush in embarrassment. But this same old man could say to Gorky one day: *"If a man has learned to think, no matter what he may think about, he is always thinking of his own death. All philosophers were like that. And what truth can there be, if there is death?"* All philosophers, unfortunately, have not been like that; and Tolstoy himself would have snorted with anger and derision at the remark of Spinoza, so typical in this of the philosophic tradition: "The free man never thinks of death, but only of life"—as if one could think of life without thinking of death. In his *My Confession,* the story of his own spiritual crisis in middle life and one of the greatest of existential documents, Tolstoy tells how he himself met the dread presence which finally overwhelms poor Ivan Ilyich. A happy man; with family, wealth, and fame; in the full possession of all his physical and mental powers: nevertheless he suddenly became aware of the possibility of death, yawning like a chasm beneath his feet. The revelation was all the more dreadful in view of his boundless energy and mastery of life; that such a chasm should appear at all seemed to him absurd and irrational. He recounts how he attempted to take stock of himself, to think, to search through science and philosophy for some answer to this absurd and grinning presence. But reason holds no answer to this problem of death: the solution is always the same, as in an equation in which zero equals zero. The wisdom of the sages—Socrates, Buddha, Ecclesiastes, Schopenhauer—tells us only that in the face of death life is meaningless and an evil; meanwhile, millions of ordinary people who know nothing of the thought of these sages go on living, begetting children, perpetuating the race. The meaning of life, if there is one, says Tolstoy, must be found in these ordinary souls and not in the great intellects of the race. Whatever ultimate meaning there is is vital and not rational. The peasantry are wiser in their ignorance than the savants of St. Petersburg in their learning.

My Confession is not the argument of a professional philosopher, but it is a powerful act of thinking (to which no summary can do justice) nonetheless, and a great work of art to boot. In it, as in his greatest novels, we encounter that peculiarly Tolstoyan power to cut through all artifices and complications in order to come directly to the heart of his matter. Is not this a power not only of art but of thought? And perhaps as valid as a means to truth as the ingenious dialectic of any philosopher?

All the foregoing refugees from Laputa, though they differ widely in temperament and literary art, come together in a remarkable way in their criticism of modern life and the peculiar threat it raises to the being of man. They make an impressive group of witnesses, and their testimony can be dismissed out of court as the aberration of poets only by those Platonic (or Laputan) intellectuals who have already excluded poetry from their ideal Republic. The historians of ideas have acquired a magical belief in labels not unlike the old magical belief in spells; they seem to think that they need only apply the proper rubrics— "Romanticism," "Irrationalism," "Symbolism," "the Russian soul," or what not—to conjure away the realities with which these writers dealt, much as the medieval bishop thought he could exterminate the vermin simply by excommunicating them. The work of all these writers pointed to something that was happening to Western man that could not be arrested; something of such power and momentum that it had eventually to erupt into philosophy itself. This eruption took place in the existential philosophers, to whom we now come. The malaise of poets over the last hundred and fifty years, far from being the itch of merely personal neurosis, discloses rather the human climate in which philosophers too, whether they knew it or not, drew their breath.

THE EXISTENTIALISTS

Part Three

KIERKEGAARD

Chapter Seven

"It was *intelligence*," Kierkegaard says, writing of himself and his task in his *Journals*—"*it was intelligence and nothing else that had to be opposed. Presumably that is why I, who had the job, was armed with an immense intelligence.*" This is the candid statement of genius about itself, without boast and without false modesty. Kierkegaard does not disparage intelligence; quite the contrary, he speaks of it with respect and even reverence. But nonetheless, at a certain moment in history this intelligence had to be opposed, and opposed with all the resources and powers of a man of brilliant intelligence. No better summation can be made of what Kierkegaard had to do and what he accomplished.

Of the immensity of his intelligence there can be no doubt. The fecundity of his mind astounds us each time we return to his writings. A century after he wrote, we are still in the process of garnering, sifting, and trying to systematize the insights he strewed so profusely through his pages. He wrote at breakneck speed, his mind in a kind of feverish blaze, bursting with ideas of which sometimes only a darting gleam or glint could be got down on the page. Hence the discontinuities and shifts in so much of his writing, the tacks and turns, asides and parables, in which the slower mind of the reader may sometimes get lost. The power of Kierkegaard's almost febrile intelligence was such that it was capable of devouring the life of its possessor by turning almost every experience into reflection. But, unlike so many

great minds, Kierkegaard was aware of this in himself, and
so forewarned against the subtle and omnivorous depreda-
tions of his intellect. His intellectual power, he knew, was
also his cross. Without faith, which the intelligence can
never supply, he would have died inside his mind, a sickly
and paralyzed Hamlet.

As the nineteenth century recedes, the foothills that close
up had seemed to tower fall into proper perspective and
the true heights rise more starkly. More and more, for us
today, Kierkegaard begins to be visible above his century,
a solitary peak but central to the whole chain. And this
belated fame, in a century that has departed as far from
him almost as it has from the Middle Ages, is a paradox,
as was the man himself. Certain great German forerunners
of Kierkegaard had also attempted a critique of the intelligence; and earlier opponents of rationalism, men like
Hamann and the later Schelling, had spoken out forcefully
for the instinctive, the intuitive, the mythical against a
time that seemed no longer able even to understand such
things. By comparison with the German Romanticists Kierkegaard traced a much narrower orbit in his writings; but
the narrower the orbit, the closer we are to the center, hence
the less energy lost on matters peripheral. Justice Holmes
once remarked that the hallmark of genius, in a great
lawyer or jurist, was his ability to cut through technicalities
and go for the jugular. Kierkegaard's one theme and his
one passion was Christianity, but Christianity embraced
neither speculatively nor romantically; his concern, rather,
was with what it means concretely for the individual to be
a Christian. The central fact for the nineteenth century, as
Kierkegaard (and after him Nietzsche, from a diametrically
opposite point of view) saw it, was that this civilization
that had once been Christian was so no longer. It had been
a civilization that revolved around the figure of Christ, and
was now, in Nietzsche's image, like a planet detaching itself from its sun; and of this the civilization was not yet
aware. In contrast with this great historical datum, this
fork in the road for the whole of mankind and not just for
its savants, most of the questions debated by philosophers

—the nature of sense-data, perception, judgment, canons of induction and deduction, and the rest—look like what they are, mandarin pastimes. The thinker whose thought is central, however, is always attuned to some urgent question of his time of which the time itself is not aware. In Holmes's brutal and telling phrase, Kierkegaard (like Nietzsche after him) goes for the jugular. That is one explanation of his power over us today.

1. THE MAN HIMSELF

Kierkegaard, of course, never put to himself the question of his own relevance to his time in this speculative and detached way. He did not take up the problem of Christianity because history, civilization, and Western man were at issue. That would have been something for the professional speculators, the learned *Privatdocenten* and professors of philosophy, to deal with. The problem for Kierkegaard was throughout a personal one: he had chosen to be a Christian, and he had constantly to renew that choice, with all the energy and passion of his being. All that he thought and wrote shows this personal cast. He called his book *Fear and Trembling* "a dialectical lyric," and the phrase would in fact be a good description of nearly all his writing. His thought was the lyric of Kierkegaard the man: frankly and avowedly an act of self-expression. For all its lyricism, however, it has its own subtlety, exactness, and dialectical acumen. Indeed, the thought of the "subjective thinker," as Kierkegaard called himself, always has its own rigor, distinct from that of the objective theorist. Kierkegaard does not merely tell us that being precedes thought, or that all thought is an expression of some concrete being; he shows us this truth in the flesh, as it were, by showing us a thought that is without disguise an act of being, i.e., of his own personal and passionate existence. He never aimed at being a philosopher and all his philosophy was indeed incidental to his main purpose, to show what it means to be a Christian; just as this was in turn incidental to his own personal task in life—that of becoming one.

The reader who wishes to understand Kierkegaard ought to begin with his purely devotional works, such as *Training in Christianity* or *Works of Love*, which he signed with his own name and not with pseudonyms; in these the true center both of his life and of his work resides. The ultimate source of Kierkegaard's power over us today lies neither in his own intelligence nor in his battle against the imperialism of intelligence—to use the formula with which we began— but in the religious and human passion of the man himself, from which the intelligence takes fire and acquires all its meaning. This still can arouse us today to the problem of our own subjectivity. We open a book, as Pascal says, expecting to encounter an author, and we meet a man. Even to those for whom Christianity is a mournful echo of a dead past, Kierkegaard still can make, in Karl Jaspers' phrase, an appeal to their own existence. Being a Christian, after all, is one way of being a man—for Kierkegaard personally it was the only way—and to have this way illumined, to be summoned to its tasks, is also to be called on to be a man, however divergent our own choice of a way may be.

Kierkegaard the man, however, is not an ingratiating figure in everyone's eyes. During his own lifetime he met with an unfriendly press and he is not exactly without one even now. He was a bizarre and eccentric figure, to be sure, and his physical appearance was no help to him in his native city of Copenhagen, where the street urchins used to run after him yelling "Either/or! Either/or!" He had fine eyes, but there the attractive features ended; a spindly figure, a humped back, and a tousled head of hair made him look altogether rather like a scarecrow. He accepted his ill-favored body, however, with what seems to have been wry good humor; it was his first instruction in comic irony, so important a weapon later in his intellectual arsenal, for here was irony close to home in the disproportion between this frail and ungainly body and the infinite claims of the spirit which it housed. He always was able thereafter to see comedy and pathos together as one human side of religion.

If his fellow townsmen held his odd physical appearance

against him, subsequent critics have dealt almost as harshly with the personality behind this unprepossessing exterior. "Kierkegaard the cripple!" is a phrase invoked not merely against the man's body but against his spirit too. Recent psychoanalytic critics have clumsily wielded their scalpels upon him in an effort to cut the man down to size—in order, apparently, to cut down his thought. Much too much mystification has been made of one decisive event, of a human and emotional nature, in a life that was otherwise one of dedicated uneventfulness: his becoming engaged to, and subsequently breaking off with, Regina Olsen. If Kierkegaard had not been an existential thinker, his broken engagement would now be only a subject for gossip; but man and thinker being one, in his case, the incident does in fact shed a great light on his thought and is worth going into if only to clear up some of the mystification.

Why Kierkegaard should have broken this engagement should not be such a mystery when he himself put forward pretty adequate reasons for doing so. To make it a mystery that can only be explained by some unspoken and unspeakable blight within his character is simply to cast doubt on there being such a thing as a religious personality for which the ordinary life of marriage and family is impossible, simply because it has other tasks. The religious type may seem an abnormal one, to our secular and naturalistic minds; but there it is, it exists, and in sufficient plenty throughout history. Only a very parochial and dogmatic mind can fail to accord to this type at the least its own psychological right to be. Kierkegaard's case, to be sure, was complicated because he himself longed passionately for marriage, home, family—the blisses and the tedium of the commonplace; his writings are packed with eulogies of these. His most touching picture of the man of faith is of an ordinary bourgeois paterfamilias sunk deep in the life of domesticity. Naturally, then, he never ceased to regret the loss of Regina; for him it was a sacrifice as drastic as Abraham's sacrifice of Isaac, his firstborn; and Kierkegaard had personal as well as religious motives in exploring, in *Fear and Trembling*, that old Biblical story. In a moment of melancholy in his *Journals,* he even goes so far as to say: "If I had faith, I would have stayed with Regina"—a remark of immediate and momentary grief that has given some suspicious critics grounds for crowing over the lack of genuineness of Kierkegaard's faith. But what his remark really means is that the loss of Regina was a painful loss, and therefore that the choice not to have her was a decisive choice, which in fact split the man in two and had to be met ultimately as a choice of himself. Here the philosophical and personal meanings of this episode meet and become one.

Had he given up the girl and sunk into an aimless and irreligious life, we would be justified in finding his renunciation only an act of impotent neurosis. At the moment of renunciation, indeed, there flashed before Kierkegaard's mind another pair of alternatives: a life of unbridled sensuality or an absolutely religious one. We who are able to look back on his life spread out before us as a whole are not likely to believe that this first alternative was really possible for Kierkegaard. He had the vocation from the start—to be sure, it was a mixed, tormented, and ambiguous vocation, but a triumphant one too. He chose what he had to become. This does not in the least mean that it was not a free choice; on the contrary, it had to be renewed freely day by day, throughout the rest of his life, if it were to be given meaning. Kierkegaard was, that is, what he had to be; but he had to be it by making the free choice every day to renew that choice. "I cannot do otherwise," said Martin Luther at the moment of performing what was the highest act of freedom of his life. If a man who wants to get married but cannot converts his renunciation into a dedication and an eventual triumph, we cannot then judge the value and the *meaning* of his life—including as it now does that act of renunciation—by the categories of neurosis.

Having lived through the breaking of his engagement, Kierkegaard could not ever become a Hegelian. The drastic Either/Or of choice had cut through his life as decisively as a sword, and no philosopher's balm could remove the pain of loss. The man who has chosen irrevocably, whose choice has once and for all sundered him from a certain *possibility* for himself and his life, is thereby thrown back on the *reality* of that self in all its mortality and finitude. He is no longer a spectator of himself as a mere possibility; he is that self in its reality. The anguish of loss may be redeemed, but can never be mediated. Reality for the man who has been called upon to make such a choice is just the reality of his own mortal, finite, bleeding self, and this reality can never be absorbed in a whole in which that finite suffering becomes unreal. The Absolute of Hegel embraces all reality and swallows up every contradiction and every finite evil. It is, as it were, the philosophic counterpart of that great Crystal Palace from which every shadow or dark spot of our ordinary human reality has been cast out. When Lear cries out in that appalling line, "Never, never, never, never, never!", he is naming just that reality of the negative which we as finite mortals cannot escape. But in the philosophy of Hegel the negative is not ultimately real, for the Absolute Reality is pure and positive being. Kierkegaard, of course, being thoroughly human, hoped that his loss would be made good, that Regina might be restored to him; but he knew this could only be through a miracle of faith. The cosmic rationalism of Hegel would have told him his loss was not a real loss but only the appearance of loss, but this would have been an abominable insult to his suffering.

Kierkegaard already knew all this, but the experience of the broken engagement clinched it for him. The episode of the engagement thus becomes a human drama in which the ultimate meaning is religious and philosophical. For the thinker, as for the artist, what counts in life is not the number of rare and exciting adventures he encounters, but the inner depth in that life, by which something great may be made out of even the paltriest and most banal of occurrences.

Kierkegaard has been criticized as being overmelancholy, excessively introverted, even morbid—a Hamlet more brooding than the original Dane. Melancholy he certainly was, and the *Journals* abound in sighs, tears, and self-laceration. But what is a journal for if not to unburden one-self? One is expected, out of good breeding, to refrain from weeping and sighing in public, but is one also expected to keep on one's social mask while writing in a diary? The remarkable thing about Kierkegaard was that the cloud of sighs and tears he shed never got in the way of his seeing what he was after: no man ever hewed more strictly to the line of his own truth. His melancholy, moreover, was lightened by humor and irony, and a wonderful sense of the beauties of homely life. Kierkegaard was indeed one of the most intensely introverted of men, and even of writers. But introversion and extraversion, as Jung suggests, are not at all of our choosing; and the rosiest extravert is just as effectively imprisoned in his own centrifugal self as the introvert is in his centripetal one. Kierkegaard was able to make a very great deal out of his tendency to morbid introspection. He was aware of his own self-imprisonment and was able to see its conditions more clearly than any religious writer before him.

Kierkegaard succeeded, in Nietzsche's words, in becoming the individual he was; analysis of him will not advance our understanding if it attempts, in a kind of critical daydream, to transform him into some altogether different individual. Rather than try to explain Kierkegaard away, it might be better to allow him now to explain himself.

2. SOCRATES AND HEGEL; EXISTENCE AND REASON

His own explanation of his point of departure as a thinker is given in a characteristically vivid and Kierke-gaardian passage in the *Concluding Unscientific Postscript.* While he sat one Sunday afternoon in the Fredriksberg Garden in Copenhagen smoking a cigar as was his habit, and turning over a great many things in his mind, he suddenly reflected that he had as yet made no career for himself whereas everywhere around him he saw the men of his age becoming celebrated, establishing themselves as renowned benefactors of mankind. They were benefactors be-

cause all their efforts were directed at making life easier
for the rest of mankind, whether materially by constructing
railroads, steamboats, or telegraph lines, or intellectually by
publishing easy compendiums to universal knowledge, or—
most audacious of all—spiritually by showing how thought
itself could make spiritual existence systematically easier
and easier. Kierkegaard's cigar burned down, he lighted another, the train of reflection held him. It occurred to him
then that since everyone was engaged everywhere in making things easy, perhaps someone might be needed to make
things hard again; that life might become so easy that
people would want the difficult back again; and that this
might be a career and destiny for him.

The irony is delicious and thoroughly Socratic, and ap-
propriately so, since the task it marked out for Kierkegaard
was parallel to that of Socrates. As the ancient Socrates
played the gadfly for his fellow Athenians stinging them
into awareness of their own ignorance, so Kierkegaard
would find his task, he told himself, in raising difficulties for
the easy conscience of an age that was smug in the conviction of its own material progress and intellectual enlightenment. He would be a modern and Christian gadfly
as Socrates had been an ancient and pagan one.

Now, it was no accident that the name of Socrates came
to Kierkegaard's mind in his meditation on his life's task.
The ancient Greek sage held a special place in his affec-
tions, due not only to the power of the Socratic personality
but also to basic philosophic principle. In his estimate of
Socrates, as on most other points, Kierkegaard is the dia-
metrical opposite of Nietzsche: the two agree only in the
importance they attach to the gadfly of Athens. Kierkegaard was interested not at all in the Socrates who figures
in some of Plato's writings as the mouthpiece of Platonism;
his attachment rather was to the man Socrates, the concrete man of flesh and blood, who said that he had no
system or doctrine to teach, that in fact he had no knowledge of his own, but could only play the midwife to other
men in bringing to birth the knowledge they had within
themselves. In comparison with a modern philosopher like

Hegel, who claims to have knowledge of the whole of reality or at least can find a place for everything within his System, old Socrates would seem to cut a very poor figure indeed. However, if philosophy is, as the etymology of the word signifies, the love of wisdom, then Socrates was a genuine philosopher—a lover of wisdom—even though he did not claim to know *about* this love. We do not ordinarily say a man is a lover even if he knows all *about* love, unless he does in fact love. And indeed the more he loves, the less confidence he is likely to have in any theory *about* love. For Socrates philosophy was a way of life, and he *existed* in that way. Since he did not profess to have any theory of philosophy, he did not accept pay as a professor. He could teach only by example, and what Kierkegaard learned from the example of Socrates became fundamental for his own thinking: namely, that existence and a theory about existence are not one and the same, any more than a printed menu is as effective a form of nourishment as an actual meal. More than that: the possession of a theory about existence may intoxicate the possessor to such a degree that he forgets the need of existence altogether. The lover may become more fascinated by his theory about love than by the person of the beloved, and so cease to love. There is, in short, a fundamental discrepancy between existence and theory; and this discrepancy Kierkegaard proceeded to explore in a way more radical than had hitherto been done in Western thought.

In the course of this exploration he had to engage in a sweeping polemic against Hegelian philosophy. We miss altogether the point of this polemic, however, if we think of it as merely a local skirmish against an odd and now outdated system of thought. Kierkegaard fought against the Hegelian climate of his time, but the ultimate issues were neither local nor temporary because in these issues Hegel was simply the spokesman for the whole tradition of Western philosophy. Hegel was not an odd lunatic, as some people nowadays think, but a very great philosopher; Kierkegaard was a greater man, however, and for that reason, if for no other, was able to catch Hegel out. What strikes us today as extreme, audacious, or even crazy in what Hegel says often seems so only because he was speaking aloud what had been the hidden presuppositions of Western philosophy since its very beginning with the Greeks. When Hegel says, "The Real is rational, and the rational is real," we might at first think that only a German idealist with his head in the clouds, forgetful of our earthly existence, could so far forget all the discords, gaps, and imperfections in our ordinary experience. But the belief in a completely rational cosmos lies behind the Western philosophic tradition; at the very dawn of this tradition Parmenides stated it in his famous verse, "It is the same thing that can be thought and that can be." What cannot be thought, Parmenides held, cannot be real. If existence cannot be thought, but only lived, then reason has no other recourse than to leave existence out of its picture of reality. As the French scientist and philosopher Emile Meyerson says, reason has only one means of accounting for what does not come from itself, and that is to reduce it to nothingness. Which is exactly what Parmenides did, and what philosophers after him continued to do. The process is still going on today, in somewhat more subtle fashion, under the names of science and Positivism, and without invoking the blessing of Hegel at all.

Hegel's peculiar offense lay not in following the tradition by leaving existence out of his system, but rather in the way in which he tried to bring it in, having begun by excluding it. At law, I suppose, this would come under the heading of a compound felony. All his philosophical predecessors, or nearly all of them, had committed the theft, but poor Hegel was caught in the act of trying to restore the misappropriated article. The means he chose were most unfortunate: he tried to bring back existence through logic. Reason, become omnipotent, would generate existence out of itself! Even here, Hegel was not really flying in the face of tradition, as it might seem; he was only giving a more audacious expression to the overinflation of reason and its powers that had been the peculiar professional deformation of almost all earlier philosophers. This conjuring up of existence, like a rabbit out of a hat, Hegel accomplished by means of his famous dialectic, the instrument Marx later turned with such devastating results upon social and economic history. We begin, says Hegel, with the concept of Being, a pure empty concept without existence; this begets its opposite, Nothing, and out of the pair comes the mediating and reconciling concept that is the synthesis of both. This process goes on until at the proper stage of the dialectic we reach the level of Reality, which is to say, Existence. The details of the derivation we need not go into here; what concerns us is the general structure of Hegel's argument, through which thought begets existence. It does not require much imagination to see the human implications of this sample of Hegelian dialectic.

There was nothing recondite about the kind of existence for which Kierkegaard, in refuting Hegel, fought such a brilliant and passionate battle. It was indeed our ordinary human existence—concrete, personal, and finite—which he saw reason on the point of ingesting into itself. Reason's offense was a religious one, to Kierkegaard, because Christianity for him was through and through a personalistic religion, depending on an historical incarnation and an historical revelation, and could not be understood purely under the aspect of eternity. Hegel, on the other hand, still called himself a Christian but believed that philosophy encompassed religion and made the religious truth a mere symbolic approximation to itself. If Hegel had recognized, and admitted, that he had actually passed out of Christianity, the matter would stand differently, and one could let the whole Hegelian System pass unchallenged as a magnificent *jeu d'esprit*, an exuberant display of dialectical virtuosity. But Hegelianism threatens Christians more than does any professedly anti-Christian philosophy, because the System can only lead to confusion and misunderstanding as to what Christianity really is, and therefore to self-deception among those who continue to believe they are Christians when in fact they are not. Better to be a non-Christian and know it than to be a non-Christian and not know it—so any honest disciple of Socrates would be compelled to point out.

If Kierkegaard had merely argued, against Hegel, that existence cannot be derived from reason, he would have gone no farther than some other schools of modern philosophy whose thought does not move beyond the sphere of logic. But Kierkegaard did in fact go much farther than this; and to see where he stood on the relation of reason to existence, we have to see him in a broader philosophical context, one that lies outside his particular relation to Hegel.

Kant, before Hegel, had made a statement on the subject of existence and reason that has become decisive for modern philosophy. Kant declared, in effect, that existence can never be conceived by reason—though the conclusions he drew from this fact were very different from Kierkegaard's. "Being," says Kant, "is evidently not a real predicate, or concept of something that can be added to the concept of a thing." That is, if I think of a thing, and then think of that thing as existing, my second concept does not add any determinate characteristic to the first. Kant gives the example of the concept of a hundred dollars: if I think of a hundred real dollars and a hundred possible dollars, my concept is still of one hundred dollars, not a cent more nor less. To be sure, in the order of existence and not of concepts, there is a world of difference between the real and the merely possible: a hundred real dollars will make me a hundred dollars richer, while a hundred possible dollars leave my financial position exactly where it was. But that is in life and not in thought. So far as thinking is concerned, there is no definite note or characteristic by which, in a concept, I can represent existence as such.

Now when Kant made this point, he was speaking, or intended to speak, from the more positivistic and scientific side of his philosophy. From the point of view of theoretical knowledge existence is negligible, because knowledge wants to know *about* a thing, and the fact that it exists does not tell me anything *about* it. Ultimately, what I want to know about the thing is what characterizes it in the way

of definite *observable* qualities; and existence, far from
being an observable quality, is in fact too general, remote,
and tenuous a property to be represented at all to the mind.
Hence, all modern Positivism takes its cue from Kant's doctrine and discards all thinking about existence (metaphysics, as this school calls it) as pointless because existence
cannot be represented in a concept, and hence thinking
about it will never lead to any definite results in observation. The crossroad in modern philosophy is precisely here,
and Kierkegaard takes a road leading in the opposite direction from that taken by Positivism. If existence cannot be
represented in a concept, he says, it is not because it is too
general, remote, and tenuous a thing to be conceived of
but rather because it is too dense, concrete, and rich. *I am;*
and this fact that I exist is so compelling and enveloping
a reality that it cannot be reproduced thinly in any of my
mental concepts, though it is clearly the life-and-death fact
without which all my concepts would be void.

Kant can justly be called the father of modern philosophy, for out of him stem nearly all the still current and
contending schools of philosophy: Positivism, Pragmatism,
and Existentialism. The difference between Positivism and
Existentialism, to confine ourselves to these two, can be seen
simply as the different response to Kant's point that existence cannot be a concept.

And this difference makes all the difference. Philosophers
before Kierkegaard had speculated about the proposition
"I exist," but it was he who observed the crucial fact they
had forgotten: namely, that my own existence is not at all
a matter of speculation to me, but a reality in which I am
personally and passionately involved. I do not find this
existence reflected in the mirror of the mind, I encounter it
in life; it is my life, a current flowing invisibly around all
my mental mirrors. But if existence is not mirrored as a
concept in the mind, where then do we really come to
grips with it? For Kierkegaard this decisive encounter with
the Self lies in the Either/Or of choice. When he gave up
Regina, thus forever giving up the solaces of ordinary life
for which he longed, Kierkegaard was encountering his

own existence as a reality more potent and drastic than any concept. And so any man who chooses or is forced to choose decisively—for a lifetime, and therefore for eternity since only one life is given us—experiences his own existence as something beyond the mirror of thought. He encounters the Self that he is, not in the *detachment* of thought, but in the *involvement* and pathos of choice.

3. AESTHETIC, ETHICAL, RELIGIOUS

To make his position clear, Kierkegaard elaborated three levels of existence—the aesthetic, ethical, and religious—and his clarification of these levels represents one of his most significant contributions to philosophy.

The child is the perfect and complete aesthete, in terms of this distinction, for the child lives solely in the pleasure or pain of the moment. Some people do grow up retaining something of this childlike immediacy of response, this capacity for existing in the moment. They are sometimes beautiful to watch, these immediate ones, says Kierkegaard, as they glow in the moment responding to some simple and beautiful object with all the grace of their nature and their blood. They are also thrown as quickly and immediately into despair if the flower that delights them fades. The aesthete, in the stricter sense, is someone who chooses to live solely for such privileged and pleasurable moments. Kierkegaard explores the aesthetic attitude with great subtlety and sympathy; but, he says, in the end it must collapse into despair. Ancient Epicureanism shows this, for it is haunted by the images of despair that it has sought to banish from its thinking. The most beautiful Epicurean poems of the Greeks and the Romans are always haunted by sadness: there is a grinning skull behind the flowers. Lucretius, the greatest poet of Epicureanism, has the passion of madness, and the tradition is that he did toward the end of his life go mad. Life yields so many weeds along with its flowers that the man who has staked his whole life on its pleasurable moments has to become desperate in his search for them, as Don Juan becomes desperate in his search for new loves. The aesthete is driven into a panicky flight from the prospect of boredom, and this flight—which is in fact a flight from himself—becomes his form of desperation and therefore of despair.

Kierkegaard's treatment of the aesthetic is given a new and radical twist when he extends the attitude to include also that of the intellectual "aesthete," the contemplative who tries to stand outside life and behold it as a spectacle. The word "aesthetic" comes from the Greek verb meaning to sense or perceive; it has the same root as the word "theory" and the word "theater." At a theater we view spectacles in which we ourselves are not involved. The spectacle may be either interesting or boring, and the "interesting" and the "boring" are the dominant categories under which the aesthete views all experience. The intellectual who looks at things with detachment, the philosopher who claims to be the spectator of all time and existence—both are fundamentally aesthetes in their attitude. Here Kierkegaard attacks what had been held to be the highest value in the tradition of Western philosophy, the thinker's speculative detachment from life; in so doing he laid down what was to be a cardinal point in all the subsequent existential philosophies. Plato, Spinoza, and the others were aesthetes without knowing it.

The aesthetic attitude can be only a partial, never a complete, attitude toward life. Kierkegaard does not discard it, but preserves it within the more integrated and total attitude that must supplant it as we become more seriously involved with ourselves and our life. Thus the three "stages on life's way," as Kierkegaard calls them, are not to be taken as different floors of a building; if I rise from the aesthetic to the ethical it does not mean that I have left the lower floor entirely behind me. Rather, both attitudes are stages on the way from the periphery to the center of the self, and the periphery is still preserved even when we have learned to dwell a little closer to our center. The fact is that the aesthete, at the very moment of choosing the aesthetic way of life, contradicts himself and enters upon the ethical. He chooses himself and his life, resolutely and consciously in the face of the death that will come as certain; and his choice, by its very consciousness and resoluteness, is a piece of finite pathos in the face of the vast nothingness stretching before and after his life. The aesthete may not wish to dwell on this somber background to his choice, but that background is surely there even if we, to use Tolstoy's phrase, are not able to stand face to face with it. It is thus by an act of courage that we begin to *exist* ethically. We bind ourselves to ourselves for a lifetime.

Does Kierkegaard add anything, by this, to the traditional discussions of ethics by philosophers? I think he does; and it may take philosophy a long time to absorb the full import of what he has to say about the ethical as a level of our human existence. In the traditional kind of ethics philosophers are concerned with analyzing the concepts of good, bad, right, and wrong, and with deciding to which things or kinds of things these predicates may be attached. This is a purely formal kind of analysis; indeed, in modern times philosophers have shifted their inquiry to an analysis of the language of ethics. Such linguistic analysis does not in the least require that the man who makes it himself exist ethically. It is thus perfectly possible—and in fact often happens—that a philosopher who has worked out a complete theory of values in the abstract may yet remain in a childish or donnish existence that has never felt the bite of the ethical upon it. One's values may thus be all down on paper, but one's actual life goes on as if the ethical did not exist. A formal theory of ethics would be perfectly empty if it were not for the fundamental act of ethical existence by which we let values come into our life. The fundamental choice, says Kierkegaard, is not the choice between rival values of good and bad, but the choice by which we summon good and bad into existence for ourselves. Without such a choice, an abstract system of ethics is just so much paper currency with nothing to back it up.

Kierkegaard speaks often of the ethico-religious, as if the two levels of existence were one; and for a mind so abrupt and powerful as his there is no doubt that it was a single leap from the aesthetic into the religious. For a really passionate temperament that has renounced the life of pleasure, the consolations of the ethical are a warmed-over substitute at best. Why burden ourselves with conscience and responsibility when we are going to die, and that will be the end of it? Kierkegaard would have approved of the feeling behind Nietzsche's saying, "God is dead, everything is permitted," and he himself was fascinated by the bold amoral figure of the Seducer or Don Juan who, though secretly in despair, is at least living passionately. He never wearies of telling us that what is at stake in Christianity is our own eternal happiness and not the maintenance of a morality that may be socially desirable or is at least socially approved.

The real line of difference between the ethical and the religious Kierkegaard draws in his *Fear and Trembling*, and it has to do with the uniqueness of the individual, the singleness of the single one, and with the calling of the religious man, who has to break with the ordinary moral code that his fellow citizens approve. He uses the example of Abraham's sacrifice of his son Isaac, but he has in mind throughout himself and his sacrifice of Regina. An ethical rule, he says, expresses itself as a universal: all men under such-and-such circumstances ought to do such and such. But the religious personality may be called upon to do something that goes against the universal norm. All men ought to cherish and preserve the lives of their sons; but Abraham is called by God to sacrifice Isaac his son. This calling is anguish, for Abraham is suspended between the fear of disobeying God and the doubt that this call may be from Him—he feels it may instead be the demoniacal voice of pride asking for a sacrifice that need not be made. So Kierkegaard could never be sure, when he broke his engagement to take up the cross of his religious life, that he was choosing rightly and not succumbing to some demoniacal egotism. How does this break with the ethical differ, if at all, from that advocated by Dostoevski's Raskolnikov and by Nietzsche, who said the superior individual, the Superman, is justified in breaking any moral rule he wishes in order to advance his own power? The difference is that

Kierkegaard does not deny the validity of the ethical: the individual who is called upon to break with the ethical must first have subordinated himself to the ethical universal; and the break, when he is called upon to make it, is made in fear and trembling and not in the callous arrogance of power. The validity of this break with the ethical is guaranteed, if it ever is, by only one principle, which is central to Kierkegaard's existential philosophy as well as to his Christian faith—the principle, namely, that the individual is higher than the universal. (This means also that the individual is always of higher value than the collective.) The universal rule of ethics, precisely because it is universal, cannot comprehend totally me, the individual, in my concreteness. Where then as an abstract rule it commands something that goes against my deepest self (but it has to be my deepest self, and herein the fear and trembling of the choice reside), then I feel compelled out of conscience —a religious conscience superior to the ethical—to transcend that rule. I am compelled to make an exception because I myself *am* an exception; that is, a concrete being whose existence can never be completely subsumed under any universal or even system of universals.

Now, Abraham and Kierkegaard were both in exceptional situations; most of us are not called upon to make such drastic sacrifices. But even the most ordinary people are required from time to time to make decisions crucial for their own lives, and in such crises they know something of the "suspension of the ethical" of which Kierkegaard writes. For the choice in such human situations is almost never between a good and an evil, where both are plainly marked as such and the choice therefore made in all the certitude of reason; rather it is between rival goods, where one is bound to do some evil either way, and where the ultimate outcome and even—or most of all—our own motives are unclear to us. The terror of confronting oneself in such a situation is so great that most people panic and try to take cover under any universal rule that will apply, if only it will save them from the task of choosing themselves. Unfortunately, in a good many cases there is no such universal rule or recipe available, and the individual can do nothing but muddle through on his own and decide for himself. Life seems to have intended it this way, for no moral blueprint has ever been drawn up that covers all the situations for us beforehand so that we can be absolutely certain under which rule the situation comes. Such is the concreteness of existence that a situation may come under several rules at once, forcing us to choose *outside* any rule, and from *inside* ourselves. The most exhaustive ethical blueprint ever drawn up is the system of moral theology of the Catholic Church; and yet the Church has to supplement this by casuistry and the confessional.

Most people, of course, do not want to recognize that in certain crises they are being brought face to face with the religious center of their existence. Such crises are simply painful and must be got through as quickly and easily as one can. Why, in any case, should the discovery of the religious come to us at the moment in which we feel most sundered and alone, as Abraham did on Mount Moriah or as Kierkegaard did face to face with his own deprivation? Kierkegaard's answer to this is pretty traditional: "The fear of the Lord," says the Bible, "is the beginning of wisdom"; and for modern man, before that fear and as a threshold to it, are the fear and trembling in which we begin to be a Self.

That Kierkegaard, as a psychologist of religious experience—as such he is without peer—dwells so much upon emotions like fear and trembling, anxiety or dread, and despair is often taken as an indication of the excessive morbidity of his temperament. Kierkegaard does show a certain predilection for these moods, admittedly, or let us say at least that in dealing with them he is at his most potent, both dramatically and dialectically. What is important, however, is that there is no morbidity, no tinge either of exaggeration or sensationalism, in his treatment of these moods. Such moods are a part of life—a larger part than we moderns like to believe—and Kierkegaard chooses to face up to them. If the abstractness of modern society can be said to lead to a repression of all the emotions, certainly the most deeply repressed are those we call "negative." The "positive" emotions such as love or joy lend themselves to all kinds of sentimental caricatures in popular art, which are probably more damaging to the spirit than outright repression of such feelings would be. But what love does not know the ache of fear, what joy is not tinged with regret? Modern man is farther from the truth of his own emotions than the primitive. When we banish the shudder of fear, the rising of the hair of the flesh in dread, or the shiver of awe, we shall have lost the emotion of the holy altogether.

The most powerful of Kierkegaard's distinctly psychological treatises is probably *The Sickness Unto Death*, a study of the various modalities of despair. Despair is the sickness unto death, the sickness in which we long to die but cannot die; thus, it is the extreme emotion in which we seek to escape from ourselves, and it is precisely this latter aspect of despair that makes it such a powerful revelation of what it means to exist as a human individual. We are all in despair, consciously or unconsciously, according to Kierkegaard, and every means we have of coping with this despair, short of religion, is either unsuccessful or demoniacal. Kierkegaard advances two general principles that are in advance of nearly all current psychologies: (1) Despair is never ultimately over the external object but always over ourselves. A girl loses her sweetheart, and falls into despair; it is not over the lost sweetheart that she despairs, but over herself-without-the-sweetheart: that is, she can no longer escape from herself into the thought or person of the beloved. And so on, for all cases of loss, whether it be money, power, or social rank. The unbearable loss is not really in itself unbearable; what we cannot bear is that in being stripped of an external object we stand denuded and see the intolerable abyss of the self yawn at our feet. (2) The condition we call a sickness in certain people is, at its center, a form of sinfulness. We are in the habit nowadays of labeling morally deficient people as sick, mentally sick, or neurotic. This is true if we look at the neurotic from outside: his neurosis is indeed a sickness, for it prevents him from functioning as he should, either totally or in some particular area of life. But the closer we get to any neurotic the more we are assailed by the sheer human perverseness, the willfulness, of his attitude. If he is a friend, we can up to a point deal with him as an *object* who does not function well, but only up to a point; beyond that if a personal relation exists between us we have to deal with him as a *subject,* and as such we must find him morally perverse or willfully disagreeable; and we have to make these moral judgments to his face if the friendship is to retain its human content, and not disappear into a purely clinical relation. At the center of the sickness of the psyche is a sickness of the spirit. Contemporary psychoanalysis will have eventually to reckon with this Kierkegaardian point of view; among some schools there is already an uneasy edging in its direction.

Kierkegaard's insight is superior here because he is a "subjective thinker." He thus plants himself within the subjectivity of the person, and his concern is with the "inwardness" of the human being. But to see what this "inwardness" means we have now to consider the problem of truth itself.

4. SUBJECTIVE AND OBJECTIVE TRUTH

If the religious level of existence is understood as a stage upon life's way, then quite clearly the truth that religion is concerned with is not at all the same as the objective truth of a creed or belief. Religion is not a system of intellectual propositions to which the believer assents because he knows it to be true, as a system of geometry is true; existentially, for the individual himself, religion means in the end simply *to be religious.* In order to make clear what it means to be religious, Kierkegaard had to reopen the whole question of the meaning of truth. His was the first radical reappraisal of the subject since the thirteenth century when St. Thomas Aquinas' monumental *De Veritate* had settled the meaning of truth for the next five centuries of philosophy; and like that earlier treatment, Kierkegaard's stand on the question may well have marked a turning point in European philosophy.

Objective truth is easily recognized, and indeed today it has come to be almost the only sense of the term in our usage. If I know that twice two is four, this knowledge is in the highest degree impersonal; once I know it, I know it, and I need not struggle continuously to make it my own: it is a reliable piece of lumber in the mental attic, one on which I can put my hand any time I have need for it. But the truth of religion is not at all like that: it is a truth that must penetrate my own personal existence, or it is nothing; and I must struggle to renew it in my life every day. What is in question here, says Kierkegaard, is one's own personal *appropriation* of the truth—"appropriation" coming from the Latin root *proprius,* meaning "one's own." A learned theologian may be in possession of all the so-called truths of rational theology, able to prove and disprove propositions and generally hold his own dialectically with the best; and yet in his heart God may have died or never lived. On the other hand, an illiterate peasant who knows nothing of formal theology, who may not even be able to state accurately the tenets of his creed, nevertheless may succeed in *being* religious. He is in the truth, as we say, and people who know him can recognize this fact from his presence, his bearing, his way of life. In the Oriental religious and philosophical tradition, where truth has never been defined as belonging basically to the intellect, the Master is able to discern whether or not a disciple has attained enlightenment from how he behaves, what kind of a person he has come to *be,* not from hearing him reason about the Sutras. This kind of truth is not a truth of the intellect but of the whole man. Strictly speaking, subjective truth is not a truth that I *have,* but a truth that I *am.*

In the thirteenth century St. Thomas banished Augustinianism or at least relegated it to a subsidiary place: truth in the strictest sense, he said, is in the intellect, and specifically in the intellect as it forms propositions that correspond with reality. Starting with this understanding of truth, the centuries that followed were able to develop and consolidate all that we now know as science. But what happens if the question is now reopened, and if philosophers go back for their answers to an older, prephilosophic understanding of the meaning of truth? If we were to understand truth anew (and in this ancient sense), would not our fundamental attitudes be so changed that our whole civilization would become different? These are precisely the questions that, as we shall see, lie at the center of Heidegger's philosophy. With Heidegger, philosophers have only just begun to *think* about what lies implicit in the Kierkegaardian distinction between subjective and objective truth.

5. THE ATTACK UPON CHRISTENDOM

When we advance from the aesthetic to the religious level of existence, Kierkegaard says, we become really serious; we are not serious persons until we have become religious. This seriousness has nothing to do with the solemnity of the bourgeois or the official—that stuffed-shirtedness that Sartre has sneered at in the *"salauds";* it is the simple and forthright seriousness of someone who has at last arrived at his center, and who is therefore at last totally engaged in the project of his life, with all that it entails. This person exists under the eye of eternity, and therefore what he does in the moment is absolutely real. It is quite fitting therefore that the last act in Kierkegaard's life should have been a thoroughly existential one: an attack upon the Christianity of his native Denmark, and by extension upon the public and acknowledged Christianity of the whole modern world. This polemic has been published in English as *The Attack upon Christendom,* but a good part of it Kierkegaard published as a series of pamphlets under the title *The Instant.* The title he gave these last writings, where thinking had in fact become an existential deed, as powerful as a blow of the fist, is significant, for it tells us that here the thinker stands and wills to stand thoroughly and absolutely rooted in his situation. Home is not only the place from which we start, but that to which we must inevitably return. When he had completed the last of the pamphlets, Kierkegaard collapsed; he had literally burned himself out, and two months later he was dead. He had done his work.

Before he published those pamphlets, however, Kierkegaard had set forth in an earlier essay, *The Present Age*, some criticisms of his time that were to prove brilliantly prophetic; the essay has been the source of nearly all the Existentialist criticisms of modern society—including those by Jaspers, Ortega, Berdyaev, and Marcel. So well has Kierkegaard's prophecy held up in fact that even contemporary efforts at journalistic sociology, like Riesman's *The Lonely Crowd* or Whyte's *The Organization Man*, are still repeating and documenting his insights. The chief movement of modernity, Kierkegaard holds, is a drift toward mass society, which means the death of the individual as life becomes ever more collectivized and externalized. The social thinking of the present age is determined, he says, by what might be called the Law of Large Numbers: it does not matter what quality each individual has, so long as we have enough individuals to add up to a large number —that is, to a crowd or mass. And where the mass is, there is truth—so the modern world believes. Behind this social observation, of course, lay Kierkegaard's ultimate conviction that Christianity is something that concerns the individual alone; and this conviction, as the basis for his criticism of modern times, was not fully developed until his later polemic against contemporary Christendom. *The Present Age*, brilliant as it is, is merely a tuning up for the full orchestral blast of *The Attack upon Christendom*.

In the modern world it makes no sense and is in fact a gigantic swindle to speak of Christian nations, Christian states, or even Christian peoples: this is the sum and substance of Kierkegaard's attack. But his expression is so direct and powerful, he rings so many momentous changes upon this single theme, that *The Attack upon Christendom* takes its place among the greatest polemics ever written. The style itself is at the farthest remove from the fanciful complexity of his earliest aesthetic writings; here the expression is direct, vigorous, even coarse. Kierkegaard had become serious, and with a vengeance. There can be no doubt now that against the smug complacency of his time that believed itself Christian and did not even know that it was not, Kierkegaard was in the right, and his polemic triumphs. But beyond the historical impact it had upon its own time, *The Attack upon Christendom* broaches the gravest questions about the possibility of religion becoming altogether institutionalized, and thereby brings Kierkegaard to his final statement of what it means to be Christian. Here, it seems to me, he goes against his earlier warning to himself that the Exception, the Single One or extraordinary individual, though he has to follow the law of his own being rather than that of the collective, cannot expect everybody else to follow *his* way. Kierkegaard seems to demand that the average person take up a Christianity as strenuous as his own.

The problem of the institutionalizing of religion was dealt with by another existentialist, Dostoevski, in his tremendous parable of the Grand Inquisitor, and the contrast with Kierkegaard is singularly instructive. Intellectually, to be sure, Dostoevski was on the side of Kierkegaard, and the Grand Inquisitor he intended as a figure of evil, the totalitarian master of men who gives them bread and peace and relieves them from the anguish of being themselves. But Dostoevski *the novelist* was caught up in the toils of a truth different from that of Dostoevski the intellectual: as a novelist he could not create a character without giving himself to it, creating it from the inside out and thereby giving the character its own truth. And as Dostoevski unfolds the parable (told through the mouth of Ivan Karamazov) there is no doubt that the Grand Inquisitor has *his* truth, which Christ Himself, having returned to earth, recognizes by bestowing a final kiss upon the Inquisitor's cheek. But the polemicist, in the necessity of driving a point home, may lose sight of the novelist's truth. Men are sheep, says the Inquisitor, and need to be relieved of the agony of selfhood. It will not do to say, as Kierkegaard does, that he represents not a Christian severity as opposed to a

Christian leniency, but only a Christian honesty; for what is more severe than honesty, and particularly an honesty that would tell the sheep they can only live as sheep? Humankind cannot bear very much reality, says T. S. Eliot; and it is doubtful whether they can even bear the reality of being told so. The Grand Inquisitor, the Pope of Popes, relieves men of the burden of being Christian, but at the same time leaves them the peace of believing they are Christians.

Nietzsche, the passionate and religious atheist, insisted on the necessity of a religious institution, the Church, to keep the sheep in peace, thus putting himself at the opposite extreme from Kierkegaard; Dostoevski in his story of the Grand Inquisitor may be said to embrace dialectically the two extremes of Kierkegaard and Nietzsche. The truth lies in the eternal tension between Christ and the Grand Inquisitor. Without Christ the institution of religion is empty and evil, but without the institution as a means of mitigating it the agony in the desert of selfhood is not viable for most men.

Nietzsche remarked that "the last Christian" died on the Cross. In a somewhat different spirit we might apply the term to Kierkegaard and say that he was the last Christian, or at least the last Christian writer. This may seem paradoxical, in view of the fact that present-day Protestant theology practically lives off Kierkegaard's capital. Theologians like Karl Barth and Emil Brunner stand for a severe as against a liberal Protestantism, and they follow Kierkegaard in stressing the absolute paradox of Faith. But nowhere in the work of these men do we hear the personal accent as we do in Kierkegaard; neither of them raises the question of Christianity, as did their predecessor, as something that in the end concerns only himself, or interrogates himself as to whether or not he can really hope to be a Christian at all. The systematic theology of Paul Tillich could be embraced by any naturalist who was not too obtuse psychologically and was interested in religion as a system of symbols. The theology of Rudolf Bultmann is not much more than the philosophy of Heidegger touched with the emotions of Christianity. The fact is that Kierkegaard stated the question of Christianity so nakedly, made it turn so decisively about the individual and his quest for his own eternal happiness, that all religious writers after him seem by comparison to be symbolical, institutional, or metaphorical—in a word, gnostic. Perhaps the very nakedness of Kierkegaard's statement of faith makes it impossible for Christianity now to go anywhere but in the direction of some kind of gnosticism. The religious Existentialists of this century, such as Berdyaev and Marcel, do not match Kierkegaard's passion or his passionate cleaving to the central issue any more than the Protestant pastors do. The one exception to this would be Miguel Unamuno, whose passion is worthy of Kierkegaard and who in fact makes the whole question of religion hinge on the individual's desire for an eternal happiness—that and nothing less. The question of death is thus central to the whole of religious thought, is that to which everything else in the religious striving is an accessory: "If there is no immortality, what use is God?" Unamuno quotes an old peasant, approvingly. The comparison of these religious writers with Kierkegaard is not meant to disparage the former; they are all subtle, powerful, and profound, within their limits. It is meant rather to call attention to the fact that the quality of these writers' Christianity is historically different from Kierkegaard's. They happen also to be lesser men than Kierkegaard, and therefore perhaps any comparison is unfair. At any rate, it is fitting that the simplest and most profound tribute to Kierkegaard should have come from the pen of Unamuno: "Y que hombre!"—"And what a man!"

If he had been carving the epitaph for his own tombstone, Kierkegaard said, he would have chosen nothing more than the simple phrase: The Individual. We do not yet know, but history may already have dug a grave for that individual for whom he was nearly the last to speak.

NIETZSCHE

Chapter Eight

BY THE middle of the nineteenth century, as we have seen, the problem of man had begun to dawn on certain minds in a new and more radical form: Man, it was seen, is a stranger to himself and must discover, or rediscover, who he is and what his meaning is. Kierkegaard had recommended a rediscovery of the religious center of the Self, which for European man had to mean a return to Christianity, but what he had in mind was a radical return that went back beyond organized Christendom and its churches to a state of contemporaneity with the first disciples of Christ. Nietzsche's solution harked back to an even more remote and archaic past: to the early Greeks, before either Christianity or science had put its blight upon the healthiness of man's instincts.

It was Nietzsche's fate to experience the problem of man in a peculiarly personal and virulent form. At twenty-four, an unheard-of age in the German academic world, he became Professor of Classical Philology at the University of Basel. The letter of recommendation written for him on this occasion by his teacher, Ritschl, is almost one continuous exclamation of awe at the prodigy of culture being sent to Basel. Besides being immensely learned in the classical languages, Nietzsche showed extraordinary literary promise and was also a gifted musician. But this prodigy was also a very delicate and sickly youth, with weak eyesight and a nervous stomach. Nietzsche had undoubtedly inherited this fragile constitution, but in later years he tended to think

resentfully that it had been brought about by the excessive
labors of scholarship. At any rate, intensive study had not
helped his health. He thus knew at first hand the war between culture and vitality: he was himself, in fact, the field
of battle between the two. He had to resign his professor-
ship after ten years because of his poor health. Thereafter
he became the wanderer and his shadow—to use the title
of one of his books, which accurately describes his own life
—traveling all over southern Europe in search of a health
that he never could regain. In those disconsolate and lonely
years all his glittering cultural attributes did not help him
in the least; culture, in fact, was a screen between the wanderer and the natural man that he strove to resurrect. As a
scholarly bookworm he had not even known that he was
unknown to himself, but when his eyesight became too poor
to read books he began at last to read himself: a text that
culture up to that time had obscured.

Nietzsche had originally encountered the god Dionysus
in his studies of Greek tragedy. Dionysus was the patron
deity of the Greek tragic festivals, and so the cult of this
god had received all the blessing of high culture, since it
was associated with the most sublime and formally beautiful products of human art. On the other hand, the Dio-
nysian cult reached back into the most primitive and archaic eras of the Greek race. For Dionysus was the god of
the vine, the god of drunken ecstasy and frenzy, who made
the vine come to life in spring and brought all men together
in the joy of intoxication. This god thus united miraculously
in himself the height of culture with the depth of instinct,
bringing together the warring opposites that divided Nietzsche himself. The problem of reconciling these opposites
was the central theme later of D. H. Lawrence, of Gide in
his *Immoralist* (a fiction based upon Nietzsche's life), and
of Freud in one of his last and most significant works, *Civilization and Its Discontents*. It is still the most formidable
problem of man in our twentieth, the psychoanalytic, century. Dionysus reborn, Nietzsche thought, might become a
savior-god for the whole race, which seemed everywhere
to show symptoms of fatigue and decline. The symbol of

the god became so potent for Nietzsche that it ended—as only symbols can do—by taking possession of his life. He consecrated himself to the service of the god Dionysus.

But Dionysus is a dangerous as well as an ambiguous god. Those in antiquity who meddled with him ended by being torn to pieces. When he took possession of his own followers he drove them to frenzies of destruction. He was called, among other names, "the horned one" and "the bull" by the Greeks, and in one of his cults was worshiped in the form of a bull who was ritually slaughtered and torn to pieces. So Dionysus himself, according to the myth, had been torn to pieces by the Titans, those formless powers of the subterranean world who were always at war with the enlightened gods of Olympus. The fate of his god overtook Nietzsche: he too was torn apart by the dark forces of the underworld, succumbing, at the age of forty-five, to psychosis. It may be a metaphor, but it is certainly not an exaggeration, to say that he perished as a ritual victim slaughtered for the sake of his god.

It is equally true, and perhaps just another way of saying the same thing, that Nietzsche perished for the sake of the problems of life that he set out to solve. The sacrifice of a victim, in the ancient and primitive world, was supposed to bring blessings upon the rest of the tribe, but Nietzsche was one of those who bring not peace but a sword. His works have divided, shocked, and perplexed readers ever since his death, and at the low point of his posthumous fortune his name was polluted by a Nietzschean cult among the Nazis. Nevertheless, the victim did not perish in vain; his sacrifice can be an immense lesson to the rest of the tribe if it is willing to learn from him. Nietzsche's fate is one of the great episodes in man's historic effort to know himself. After him, the problem of man could never quite return to its pre-Nietzschean level. Nietzsche it was who showed in its fullest sense how thoroughly problematical is the nature of man: he can never be understood as an animal species within the zoological order of nature, because he has broken free of nature and has thereby posed the question of his own meaning—and with it the meaning of nature as well—as his destiny. Nietzsche's works are an immense mine of observations on the condition of man, one that we are still in the process of quarrying.

Moreover, Nietzsche's life stands in a double sense as a great warning to mankind, to be heeded lest we too suffer the fate of being torn apart like Dionysus Zagreus. He who would make the descent into the lower regions runs the risk of succumbing to what the primitives call "the perils of the soul"—the unknown Titans that lie within, below the surface of our selves. To ascend again from the darkness of Avernus is, as the Latin poet tells us, the difficult thing, and he who would make the descent had better secure his lines of communication with the surface. Communication means community, and the adventurer into the depths would do well to have roots in a human community and perhaps even the ballast, somewhere in his nature, of a little bit of Philistinism. Nietzsche lacked such lines of communication, for he had cut himself off from the human community; he was one of the loneliest men that ever existed. By comparison, Kierkegaard looks almost like a worldly soul, for he was at least solidly planted in his native Copenhagen, and though he may have been at odds with his fellow citizens, he loved the town, and it was his home. Nietzsche, however, was altogether and utterly homeless. He who descends must keep in touch with the surface, but on the other hand—and this is the other sense of Nietzsche's warning—modern man may also be torn apart by the titanic forces within himself if he does *not* attempt the descent into Avernus. It is no mere matter of psychological curiosity but a question of life and death for man in our time to place himself again in contact with the archaic life of his unconscious. Without such contact he may become the Titan who slays himself. Man, this most dangerous of the animals, as Nietzsche called him, now holds in his hands the dangerous power of blowing himself and his planet to bits; and it is not yet even clear that this problematic and complex being is really sane.

1. ECCE HOMO

"In the end one experiences only oneself," Nietzsche observes in his *Zarathustra*, and elsewhere he remarks, in the same vein, that all the systems of the philosophers are just so many forms of personal confession, if we but had eyes to see it. Following this conviction, that the thinker cannot be separated from his thought, Nietzsche revealed himself in his work more fully than any philosopher before or since. Hence the best introduction to him may be the little autobiographical book *Ecce Homo*, which is his own attempt to take stock of himself and his life. Nietzsche is not the most prepossessing figure, as we are introduced to him here, for in this work he was clearly already in the grip of the psychological malady that three years later was to bring on his breakdown. But he is a great enough figure that he can stand being approached from his weakest side. And did not he himself say we must divest philosophers of their masks, learn to see the thinker's *shadow* in his thought? Paradoxical as it may sound, to praise Nietzsche properly we have also to say the worst possible things about him. This too is in line with his own principle, that good and bad in any individual are inextricably one, all the more so as the opposing qualities become more extreme. All of Nietzsche—in his extremes of good and bad—is summed up in *Ecce Homo*, and it is precisely the *all* that he himself could not see.

An unprejudiced psychological observer is at once fascinated and appalled by what he finds in *Ecce Homo*. The process of ego-inflation has already gone beyond the bounds of what we ordinarily call neurosis. And this inflation is already tinged with curious distortions of the facts: Nietzsche refers to himself swaggeringly as "an old artilleryman" as if he had had a robust military career, though we of course know that his service in the artillery was so brief as to be almost non-existent, and that it terminated with his illness after a fall from his horse. The relation with Lou Salome, which was in fact very slight, is described obliquely in such a fashion as to suggest that Nietzsche was a devil

of a fellow with women. These are not the shallow lies of a
calculating mind, but delusions in the systematic sense of
psychopathology: that is, fantasies in which the man himself has begun to live. He rails against the Germans, yet he
himself is German to the marrow. And while he proclaims
himself above all resentments, we are aware throughout of
a thin skin that is smarting with resentment at his lack of
readers and of recognition in Germany. Nietzsche speaks of
himself as the greatest psychologist who ever lived; and
while there is some basis for so grandiose a boast—he was
indeed a great psychologist—the overwhelming question his
book raises is why this psychologist has so little insight into
himself. The vision of his true self, we suspect, would have
been too terrifying for him to face. The fantasies, the delusions, the grandiose inflation of the ego are only devices
to shield him from the sight of *the other side of himself*
—of Nietzsche the sickly lonely man, emotionally starved,
a ghost flitting from place to place, always without a home
—the dwarf side, that is, of the giant about whom he boasts.
Nietzsche's systematic shielding of himself from the other
side is relevant to his explanation of the death of God: Man
killed God, he says, because he could not bear to have anyone looking at his ugliest side. Man must cease to feel guilt,
he goes on; and yet one senses an enormous hidden guilt
and feeling of inferiority behind his own frantic boasts. Yet,
though the wind of madness may already be blowing
through *Ecce Homo,* at the same time the powers of Nietzsche's mind were never more formidable. The style is as
brisk and incisive as anything he wrote, as he lays before
us in bold and simple outline the guiding pattern of his
ideas. It is this split between madness and coherence that
makes the book so paradoxical. How could the mind of this
man have so split off from the rest of himself—and this in a
thinker who, above all other philosophers, seemed to have
found access to the unconscious?

   The title of the book itself *Ecce Homo*—"Behold the
Man!", the words of Pontius Pilate spoken about Christ—
supplies a very definite clue. The imitation of Christ, in
however remote and unconscious a form, is something that

almost nobody raised a Christian can avoid. ("All my life I have compared myself with Christ," exclaims the tramp in Samuel Beckett's *Waiting For Godot.*) Nietzsche had come from a line of Protestant pastors, had been raised in a very pious atmosphere, and was himself as a boy very devout. The religious influences of childhood are the hardest things to extirpate; the leopard can as easily change his spots. Had Nietzsche merely lost his Christian faith, or even simply attacked it intellectually, these acts would in themselves have been sufficient to create a conflict within him; but he went further by attempting to deny the Christian in himself, and thereby split himself in two. The symbol of Dionysus had possessed him intellectually; he identified with this pagan god (in one place in *Ecce Homo* he actually speaks of himself as Dionysus), and thenceforth, with all the energy of mind that he could summon, he devoted himself to elaborating the opposition between Dionysus and Christ. In the end, however, the symbol of Christ proved the more potent; and when his unconscious finally broke irremediably into the open, it was Christ who took possession of Nietzsche, as is shown by the letters written after his breakdown which he signed "The Crucified One."

In a life so filled with portents and omens it is remarkable that he should have recorded one—in a dream he had when a schoolboy of fifteen, at Pforta—that was prophetic of the central conflict out of which he was to write and live. In the dream he was wandering about in a gloomy wood at night, and after being terrified by "a piercing shriek from a neighboring lunatic asylum," he met with a hunter whose "features were wild and uncanny." In a valley "surrounded by dense undergrowth," the hunter raised his whistle to his lips and blew such "a shrill note" that Nietzsche woke out of his nightmare. Now it is interesting that in this dream he had been on his way to Eisleben, Luther's town; but on meeting the hunter it became a question of going instead to Teutschenthal (which means, German Valley). That is, the two roads diverge, one leading toward Lutheran Christianity, the other toward the primeval pagan German soil. Being a classical scholar, Nietzsche preferred to let his wandering German god assume the Greek guise of Dionysus. It would be farfetched to make much of this dream if it were merely an isolated revelation, but it is in fact of a piece with the other dreams and visions that Nietzsche poured into his writings. Even the frightening prophecy of madness that occurs in the dream is echoed among the images of *Zarathustra*. Nietzsche's life has all the characteristics of a psychological fatality.

Now all these self-revelations that we have been discussing, it might be said, reflect nothing but a pathological process, and therefore had best be left to one side while we discuss the philosophic ideas of this thinker. Unfortunately, nothing in life is *nothing but;* it is always something more. What we have been talking about is indeed a pathological process, but it is also a pathological process taking place in a thinker of genius, from whom the process thereby acquires an immense significance. It is just as much a mistake for interpreters of Nietzsche to cast aside this whole matter of Nietzsche's sickness, as it was for the Philistines, shocked by his ideas, to discount them simply as the ravings of a madman. It may be that genius and neurosis are inextricably linked, as some recent discussions of the subject have held; in any case Nietzsche would be one of the prime examples of the kind of truth neurosis, and even worse than neurosis, can be made to reveal for the rest of mankind. The pathological process in Nietzsche, which we have dealt with only briefly here, is in fact indispensable for an understanding of the philosophic meaning of atheism as he tried to live it. Nietzsche was engaged in a process of tearing himself loose from his psychological roots at the very moment in history that Western man was doing likewise—only the latter did not know it. Up to that time man had lived in the childhood shelter of his gods or of God; now that all the gods were dead he was taking his first step into maturity. This, for Nietzsche, was the most momentous event in modern history, one to which all the social, economic, and military upheavals of the nineteenth and indeed of the coming twentieth century would, as he prophesied, be secondary. Could mankind meet this awful challenge of becoming adult and godless? Yes, said Nietzsche, because man is the most courageous animal and will be able to survive even the death of his gods. The very process of tearing consciousness loose from its roots, which ends inevitably in *Ecce Homo* in the grandiose inflation of the ego, had for Nietzsche himself the significance of a supreme act of courage. Not a day goes by, he wrote in one of his letters, that I do not lop off some comforting belief. Man must live without any religious or metaphysical consolations. And if it was to be humanity's fate to become godless, he, Nietzsche, elected to be the prophet who would give the necessary example of courage. It is in this light that we must look upon Nietzsche as a culture hero: he chose, that is, to suffer the conflict within his culture in its most acute form and was ultimately torn apart by it.

Now, there are atheists and atheists. The urbane atheism of Bertrand Russell, for example, presupposes the existence of believers against whom he can score points in an argument and get off some of his best quips. The atheism of Sartre is a more somber affair, and indeed borrows some of its color from Nietzsche: Sartre relentlessly works out the atheistic conclusion that in a universe without God man is absurd, unjustified, and without reason, as Being itself is. Still, this kind of atheism seems to carry with it the bravado of one who is ranging himself on the side of a less sanguine truth than the rest of mankind. Nietzsche's atheism, however, goes even deeper. He projects himself into the situation where God is really dead for the whole of mankind, and he shares in the common fate, not merely scoring points off the believers. Section 125 of *The Joyful Wisdom*, the passage in which Nietzsche first speaks of the death of God, is one of the most heart-rending things he ever wrote. The man who has seen the death of God, significantly enough, is a madman, and he cries out his vision to the unheeding populace in the market place, asking the question: "Do we not now wander through an endless Nothingness?" Here we are no longer dealing with the abstractions of logical argument, but with a fate that has overtaken mankind. Of course, Nietzsche himself tried elsewhere to assume the

witty mask of the *libre penseur* of the Enlightenment and
to make brilliant aphorisms about God's non-existence. And
in his *Zarathustra* he speaks of "Zarathustra the godless"
and even "the most godless." But godless is one thing Nietzsche certainly was not: he was in the truest sense possessed
by a god, though he could not identify what god it was
and mistakenly took him for Dionysus. In a very early
poem, "To the Unknown God," written when he was only
twenty years old, he speaks about himself as a god-
possessed man, more truthfully than he was later, as a philosopher, to be able to recognize:

> I must know thee, Unknown One,
> Thou who searchest out the depths of my soul,
> And blowest like a storm through my life.
> Thou art inconceivable and yet my kinsman!
> I must know thee and even serve thee.

Had God really died in the depths of Nietzsche's soul or
was it merely that the intellect of the philosopher could not
cope with His presence and His meaning?

If God is taken as a metaphysical object whose existence
has to be proved, then the position held by scientifically-
minded philosophers like Russell must inevitably be valid:
the existence of such an object can never be empirically
proved. Therefore, God must be a superstition held by
primitive and childish minds. But both these alternative
views are abstract, whereas the reality of God is concrete,
a thoroughly autonomous presence that takes hold of men
but of which, of course, some men are more conscious than
others. Nietzsche's atheism reveals the true meaning of God
—and does so, we might add, more effectively than a good
many official forms of theism. He himself scoffs in one place
at his being confused with the ordinary run of freethinkers,
who have not the least understanding of his atheism. And
despite the desperate struggle of the "godless Zarathustra,"
Nietzsche remained in the possession of this Unknown God
to whom he had paid homage in his youth. This possession
is shown in its most violent form in *Zarathustra* (IV, 65),
even though Nietzsche puts the words into the mouth of

the Magician, an aspect of himself that he wishes to exorcise:

Thus do I lie,
Bend myself, twist myself, convulsed
˜˜Vith all eternal torture,
And smitten
By thee, cruelest huntsman,
Thou unfamiliar—GOD

At this point we are ready to see what takes place behind the scenes in *Zarathustra*, where all the aforementioned themes become fully orchestrated.

2. WHAT HAPPENS IN "ZARATHUSTRA"; NIETZSCHE AS MORALIST

No adequate psychological commentary on *Thus Spake Zarathustra* has yet been written, perhaps because the materials in it are so inexhaustible. It is a unique work of self-revelation but not at all on the personal or autobiographical level, and Nietzsche himself ostensibly does not appear in it; it is self-revelation at a greater, more primordial depth, where the stream of the unconscious itself gushes forth from the rock. Perhaps no other book contains such a steady procession of images, symbols, and visions straight out of the unconscious. It was Nietzsche's poetic work and because of this he could allow the unconscious to take over in it, to break through the restraints imposed elsewhere by the philosophic intellect. For this reason it is important beyond any of his strictly philosophic books; its content is actually richer than Nietzsche's own conceptual thought, and its symbols of greater wisdom and significance than he himself was able to grasp.

Nietzsche himself has described the process of inspiration by which he wrote this book, and his description makes it clear beyond question that we are in the presence here of an extraordinary release of and invasion by the unconscious:

> Can any one at the end of this nineteenth century have any distinct notion of what poets of a more vigorous period meant by inspiration? If not, I should like to describe it. . . . The notion of revelation describes the condition quite simply; by which I mean that something profoundly convulsive and disturbing suddenly becomes visible and audible with indescribable definiteness and exactness. . . . There is an ecstasy whose terrific tension is sometimes released by a flood of tears, during which one's progress varies from involuntary impetuosity to involuntary slowness. There is the feeling that one is utterly out of hand. . . . Everything occurs quite without volition, as if in an eruption of freedom, independence, power and divinity. The spontaneity of the images and similes is most remarkable; one loses all perception of what is imagery and simile; everything offers itself as the most immediate, exact, and simple means of expression.

"One loses all perception of what is imagery and simile" —that is to say, the symbol itself supersedes thought, because it is richer in meaning.

His most lyrical book, *Zarathustra* is also the expression of the loneliest Nietzsche. It has about it the icy and arid atmosphere not merely of the symbolic mountaintop on which Zarathustra dwells, but of a real one. Reading it, one sometimes feels almost as if one were watching a film of the ascent of Mount Everest, hearing the climber's sobbing gasp for breath as he struggles slowly to higher and still higher altitudes. Climbing a mountain is the aptest metaphor for getting above ordinary humanity, and this precisely is what Zarathustra-Nietzsche is struggling to do. One hears throughout the book, though, in the gasping breath of the climber, the lament of Nietzsche the man.

The book begins with the recognition of this human relevance as Zarathustra, about to leave his mountain solitude, declares he is going down among men "once again to be a man." The mountain is the solitude of the spirit, the lowlands represent the world of ordinary men. The same symbolic contrast appears in Zarathustra's pet animals, the eagle and the serpent: the one the creature of the upper air, the other the one that moves closest to the earth. Zarathustra, as the third element, symbolizes the union between the two animals, of high and low, heaven and earth. He is going down among men, he says, as the sun sets dipping into the darkness below the horizon. But the sun sets in order to be reborn the next morning as a young and glowing god. The book thus opens with the symbols of rebirth and resurrection, and this is in fact the real theme of *Zarathustra*: how is man to be reborn, like the phoenix, from his own ashes? How is he to become really healthy and whole? Behind this question we see the personal shadow of Nietzsche's own illness and his long struggle to regain health; Zarathustra is at once the idealized image of himself and the symbol of a victory, in the struggle for health and wholeness, that Nietzsche himself was not able to achieve in life.

Despite the intensely personal sources of his theme, Nietzsche was dealing in this work with a problem that had already become central in German culture. Schiller and Goethe had dealt with it—Schiller as early as 1795 in his remarkable *Letters on Aesthetic Education*, and Goethe in his *Faust*. Schiller has given an extraordinarily clear statement of the problem, which was for him identical in all its salient features with the problem later posed by Nietzsche. For man, says Schiller, the problem is one of forming *individuals*. Modern life has departmentalized, specialized, and thereby fragmented the being of man. We now face the problem of putting the fragments together into a whole. In the course of his exposition, Schiller even referred back, as did Nietzsche, to the example of the Greeks, who produced real individuals and not mere learned abstract men like those of the modern age. Goethe was even closer to Nietzsche; *Faust* and *Zarathustra* are in fact brothers among books. Both attempt to elaborate in symbols the process by which the superior individual—whole, intact, and healthy—is to be formed; and both are identically "immoral" in their content, if morality is measured in its usual conventional terms.

Placed within the German cultural context, indeed, Nietzsche's immoralism begins to look less extreme than the popular imagination has taken it to be; it is not even as extreme as he was led to make it appear in some of the bloody creations of his overheated imagination in his last work, *The Will to Power*. Goethe in *Faust* was every bit as much at odds with conventional morality as was Nietzsche, but the old diplomatic fox of Weimar was a more tactful and better-balanced man and knew how to get his point across quietly, without shrieking it from the housetops as Nietzsche did. The Faust of the second part of Goethe's poem is already, as we have seen, something of a Nietzschean Superman, beyond ordinary good and evil. The story of the other, moral Faust is told in the popular sentimental opera of Gounod, in which the character sells himself to the Devil and wrongs a young girl; the whole thing comes to an end with the girl's tragic death. But Goethe could not leave matters at this; the problem that had taken hold of him, through his creation of Faust, led him to look upon Gretchen's tragedy simply as a stage along Faust's way. A process of self-development such as his cannot come to a close because a young girl whom he has seduced goes crazy and dies. The strong man survives such disasters and becomes harder. The Devil, with whom Faust has made a pact, becomes in a real sense his servitor and subordinate, just as our devil, if joined to ourselves, may become a fruitful and positive force; like Blake before him Goethe knew full well the ambiguous power contained in the traditional symbol of the Devil. Nietzsche's immoralism, though stated much more violently, consisted in not much more than the elaboration of Goethe's point: Man must incorporate his devil or, as he put it, man must become better and more evil; the tree that would grow taller must send its roots down deeper.

If Nietzsche was not able to contain himself as tactfully as Goethe, on this point, he nevertheless had something to shriek about: The whole of traditional morality, he believed, had no grasp of psychological reality and was therefore dangerously one-sided and false. To be sure, this had always been known but mankind, spouting ideals, had looked at such realities and winked, or adopted casuistry. But if one is going to live one's life literally and totally by the Sermon on the Mount or Buddha's *Dhammapada*, and one cannot manage to be a saint, one will end by making a sorry mess of oneself. Nietzsche's point has already carried so far that today in our ordinary valuations we are actually living in a post-Nietzschean world, one in which the psychoanalyst sometimes finds it necessary to tell a patient that he *ought* to be more aggressive and more selfish. Besides, what does the whole history of ethics amount to for that half, and more than half, of the human race, women, who deal with moral issues in altogether different terms from men? It amounts to rather a silly man-made affair that has very little to do with the real business of life. On this point Nietzsche has a perfectly sober and straightforward case against all those idealists, from Plato onward, who have set universal ideas over and above the individual's psychological needs. Morality itself is blind to the tangle of its own psychological motives, as Nietzsche showed in one of his most powerful books, *The Genealogy of Morals,* which traces the source of morality back to the drives of power and resentment. There are other motives that Nietzsche did not see, or did not care to honor, but no one can deny that these two, power and resentment, have historically been part of the shadow behind the moralist's severity.

But it is precisely here, in the context of the Faust-Zarathustra parallel, that the chief problem arises for Nietzsche as man and moralist. Suppose the ethical problem becomes the problem of the individual; the ethical question then becomes: How is the individual to nourish himself in order to grow? Once we set ourselves to reclaim that portion of human nature that traditional morality rejected—man's devil, to put it symbolically—we face the immense problem of socializing and taming those impulses. Here the imagination of Faustian man tends to become much too highfalutin. For Western man Faust has become the great symbol of the titanically striving individual, so much so that the historian Spengler could use the term "Faustian culture" to denote the whole modern epoch of our dynamic conquest of nature. In Nietzsche's Superman the spiritual tension would be even greater, for such an individual would be living at a higher level than all of humanity in the past. But what about the individual devil within the Superman? What about Zarathustra's devil? So far as Nietzsche attempts to make the goal of this higher individual the goal of mankind, a fatal ambiguity appears within his ideal itself. Is the Superman to be the extraordinary man, or the complete and whole man? Psychological wholeness does not necessarily coincide with extraordinary powers, and the great genius may be a crippled and maimed figure, as was Nietzsche himself. In our own day, of course, when men tend more and more to be miserable human fragments, the complete man, if such existed, would probably stand out from the others like a sore thumb, but he might not at all be a creature of genius or extraordinary powers. Will the Superman, then, be the titanically striving individual, dwelling on the mountaintop of the spirit, or will he be the man who has realized within the world his own individual capacities for wholeness? The two ideals are in contradiction—a contradiction that is unresolved in Nietzsche and within modern culture itself.

The fact is that Zarathustra-Nietzsche did not come to terms with his own devil, and this is the crucial failure of Zarathustra in the book and of Nietzsche in his life. Consequently, it is also the failure of Nietzsche as a thinker. Not that Zarathustra-Nietzsche does not see his devil; time and again the latter pokes a warning finger at Zarathustra, and like a good devil he knows how to assume many shapes and disguises. He is the clown who leaps over the rope-dancer's head at the beginning of the book, he is the Ugliest Man, who has killed God, and he is the Spirit of Gravity, whom Zarathustra himself names as his devil—the spirit of heaviness which would pull his too high-soaring spirit to earth. Each time Zarathustra thrusts aside the warning finger, finding it merely a reason for climbing a higher mountain to get away from it. The most crucial revelation, however, comes in the chapter "The Vision and the Enigma" (III, 46), in which the warning figure becomes a dwarf sitting on Zarathustra's back as the latter climbs a lonely mountain path. Zarathustra wants to climb upward, but the dwarf wants to pull him back to earth. "O Zarathustra," the dwarf whispers to him, "thou didst throw thyself high, but every stone that is thrown must fall." And then, in a prophecy the more menacing when applied to Nietzsche himself: "O Zarathustra, far indeed didst thou throw thy stone, but upon *thyself* will it recoil!" This is the ancient pattern of the Greek myths: the hero who soars too high crashes to earth; and Nietzsche, as a scholar of Greek tragedy, should have given more respectful ear to the dwarf's warning.

But why a dwarf? The egotism of Zarathustra-Nietzsche rates himself too high; therefore the figure in the vision, to right the balance, shows him to himself as a dwarf. The dwarf is the image of mediocrity that lurks within Zarathustra-Nietzsche, and that mediocrity was the most frightening and distasteful thing that Nietzsche was willing to see in himself. Nietzsche had discovered the shadow, the underside, of human nature, and he had correctly seen it as a side that is present inescapably in every human individual. But he converted this perception into a kind of romantic diabolism; it amused him to play at being wicked and daring. He would have been prepared to meet his own devil if this devil had appeared in some grandiose form. Precisely what is hardest for us to take is the devil as the personification of the pettiest, paltriest, meanest part of our personality. Dostoevski understood this better than Nietzsche, and in that tremendous chapter of *The Brothers Karamazov* where the Devil appears to Ivan, the brilliant literary intellectual nourished on the Romanticism of Schiller, it is not in the guise of a dazzling Miltonic Lucifer or a swaggering operatic Mephistopheles, but rather of a faded, shabby-genteel person, a little out of fashion and ridiculous in his aestheticism—the perfect caricature of Ivan's own aesthetic mind. This figure is *the* Devil for Ivan Karamazov, the one that most cruelly deflates his egotism; and Dostoevski's genius as a psychologist perhaps never hit the nail on the head more accurately than in this passage. Nietzsche himself said of Dostoevski that he was the only psychologist from whom he had had anything to learn; the remark is terribly true, and in a profounder sense than Nietzsche realized.

Zarathustra—to return to him—is too touchy to acknowledge himself as this dwarf. He feels his courage challenged and believes it will be the supreme act of courage, the highest virtue, to get rid of the dwarf. "Courage at last bade me stand still and say: Dwarf! Either thou or I!" It would have been wiser, and even more courageous, to admit who the dwarf really was and to say, not "Either thou or I" but rather "Thou and I (*ego*) are one self."

The vision shifts and pauses for a moment, and Nietzsche now presents us with the idea of the Eternal Return. This idea has an ambiguous status in Nietzsche. He tried to base it rationally and scientifically on the premise that if time were infinite and the particles in the universe finite, then by the laws of probability all combinations must repeat themselves over and over again eternally; and that therefore everything, we ourselves included, must recur again and again down to the last detail But to take this as a purely intellectual hypothesis does not explain why the idea of the Eternal Return had such a powerful hold upon Nietzsche's emotions, and why, particularly. the idea is revealed at this most charged and visionary moment in *Zarathustra*. The circle is a pure archetypal form for the eternal: "I saw Eternity the other night," says the English poet Vaughan, "Like a great ring of pure and endless light." The idea of the Eternal Return thus expresses, as Unamuno has pointed out, Nietzsche's own aspirations toward eternal and immortal life. On the other hand, the notion is a frightening one for a thinker who sees the whole meaning of mankind to lie in the future, in the Superman that man is to become; for if all things repeat themselves in an endless cycle, and if man must come again in the paltry and botched form in which he now exists—then what meaning can man have? For Nietzsche the idea of the Eternal Return becomes the supreme test of courage: If Nietzsche the man must return to life again and again, with the same burden of ill health and suffering, would it not require the greatest affirmation and love of life to say Yes to this absolutely hopeless prospect?

Zarathustra glimpses some of the fearful implications in this vision, for he remarks after expounding the Eternal Return, "So I spoke, and always more softly: for I was afraid of my own thoughts, and afterthoughts." Thereupon, in the dream, he hears a dog howl and sees a shepherd writhing on the ground, with a heavy black reptile hanging from his mouth. "Bite!" cries Zarathustra, and the shepherd bites the serpent's head off and spits it far away. The uncanny vision poses its enigma to Zarathustra:

> Ye daring ones! Ye venturers and adventurers, and whoever of you have embarked with cunning sails on unexplored seas! Ye enjoyers of enigmas!
>
> Solve unto me the enigma that I then beheld, interpret for me the vision of the loneliest one.
>
> For it was a vision and a foresight. *What* did I then behold in parable? And *who* is it that must come some day?
>
> *Who* is the shepherd into whose throat the serpent thus crawled? *Who* is the man into whose throat all the heaviest and blackest will crawl?
>
> —The shepherd bit as my cry had admonished him; he took a good bite, and spit the head of the serpent far away:—and sprang up—
>
> No longer shepherd, no longer man—a transfigured being, a light-surrounded being, that *laughed*. Never on earth laughed a man as *he* laughed!
>
> O my brethren, I heard a laughter which was no human laughter.

"Who is the shepherd into whose throat the serpent thus crawled?" He is Nietzsche himself, and both the serpent and the dwarf set for him the same task: to acknowledge "the heaviest and the blackest in himself." We commonly speak of the truth as a bitter pill that we have to swallow, but the truth about ourselves may take even the more repulsive form of a reptile. Nietzsche does not swallow the serpent's head; he denies his own shadow, and out of it he sees a transfigured being spring up. This being laughs with a laughter that is no longer human. We know this laughter all too well: it is the laughter of insanity. A few years ago André Breton, the surrealist, published an *Anthologie de l'humeur noir,* in which was included one of Nietzsche's letters written after his psychosis. If one did not know who the author was and what his condition was when he wrote it, one could indeed take the letter as a dazzling piece of surrealistic laughter, a high empty mad laughter. This is the laughter Nietzsche hears in his vision, and he speaks like a tragic character ironically ignorant of his own prophecy when he says, "It was a vision and a prevision." This laughter already began to sound eerily in the pages of *Ecce Homo.*

There is an inner coherence in the vision of Zarathustra, in that each of its three parts—the dwarf, the Eternal Return, and the shepherd spitting out the serpent—presents an obstacle and objection to Nietzsche's utopian conception of the Superman. They prefigure his own personal catastrophe; but since he was a thinker who really lived his thought, they indicate the fatal flaw in all such utopian thought. He who would launch the Superman into interstellar space had better recognize that the dwarf goes with him. "Human, all too human!" Nietzsche exclaimed in disgust at mankind as it had hitherto existed. But he who would try to improve man might do well not to make him inhuman but, rather, a little more human. To be a whole man—a round man, as the Chinese say—Western man may have to learn to be less Faustian. A touch of the average, the mediocre, may be necessary ballast for human nature. The antidote to the hysterical, mad laughter of Zarathustra's vision may be a sense of humor, which is something

Nietzsche, despite his brilliant intellectual wit, conspicuously lacked.

The conclusions we have reached here on a psychological level become confirmed when we turn to Nietzsche's systematic philosophy of power.

3. POWER AND NIHILISM

Nietzsche is considered by many philosophers to be an unsystematic thinker. This view, a mistaken one, is based largely on the external form of his writings. He loved to write aphoristically, to attack his subjects indirectly and dramatically rather than in the straightforward solemn form of a pedantic treatise; he was one of the great prose stylists of the German language, and in his writing he could not, or would not, deny the artist in himself. He even went so far as to say that he was viewing science and philosophy through the eyes of art. But beneath and throughout all these belletristic forays a single consuming idea was moving in him toward a systematized development. As thinking gradually took over the whole person, and everything else in his life being starved out, it was inevitable that this thought should tend to close itself off in a system. At the end of his life he was making notes for a great systematic work which would be the complete expression of his philosophy. This work we now have in unfinished form in *The Will to Power*. The increase in systematization in Nietzsche's work is in many ways a psychological loss, since in pursuing his thematic idea he lost sight of the ambiguity in matters of the human psyche. However, there is a gain as well, for by carrying his ideas to the end he lets us see what they finally amount to. Heidegger has, in a recent memorable essay, called attention to the hitherto unrecognized fact that Nietzsche is a thoroughly systematic thinker. Indeed, according to Heidegger, Nietzsche is the last metaphysician in the metaphysical tradition of the West, the thinker who at once completes and destroys that tradition.

We do not know when the idea of the Will to Power first dawned upon Nietzsche, but there is a striking and picturesque incident, which he later told to his sister, that is relevant to it: During the Franco-Prussian War, when Nietzsche was a hospital orderly, he saw one evening his old regiment ride by, going into battle and perhaps to death, and it came to him then that "the strongest and highest will to life does not lie in the puny struggle to exist, but in the Will to war, the Will to Power." But it is a mistake to locate the birth of this idea in any single experience; it was, in fact, fed by a number of tributary streams, by Nietzsche's struggle against ill health and also by his studies in classical antiquity. Nietzsche's greatness as a classical scholar lay in his ability to see plain and simple facts that the genteel tradition among scholars had passed over. The distinguished British classicist F. M. Cornford has said of Nietzsche that he was fifty years ahead of the classical scholarship of his day; the tribute was meant to be generous, but I am not sure that the classical scholarship of our own day has yet caught up with Nietzsche. It requires much more imagination to grasp the obvious than the recondite, and a kind of imagination that Nietzsche had much more of than the classical scholars of his time. Take, for example, the obvious fact that the noble Greeks and Romans owned slaves and thought this quite natural; and that because of this they had a different orientation toward existence than did the Christian civilization that followed them. The humanistic tradition among classical scholars had idealized the ancients, and thereby, as in all idealistic views, falsified the reality. One does not need to be much of a classical specialist to note, on the first page of Julius Caesar's *Gallic Wars*, that the word *virtus*, virtue, means courage and martial valor—just the kind of thing that a military commander would most fear in the enemy and most desire in his own soldiers. (It is one of the odd developments of history—as one philosophical wag put it, making thereby a perfectly Nietzschean joke—that the word "virtue," which originally meant virility in a man, came in Victorian times to mean chastity in a woman.) Nor does it require any greater classical scholarship to recognize in the Greek word that we translate as virtue, *arete*, the clanging tone of Ares, god of battle. Classical civilizations rested on the recognition of power, and the relations of power, as a natural and basic part of life.

Nietzsche's idea also reflected the modern influence of Stendhal and Dostoevski, the two nineteenth-century novelists whom he most admired. Stendhal had shown the components of ego and power mingled in all the exploits of Eros: in the arts of seduction and conquest, in the battle of the sexes. Dostoevski had revealed how the most self-abasing acts of humility could be brutally aggressive. Nietzsche's own psychological acuity, however, once started on this path, did not need much prompting. He was able to see the Will to Power secretly at work everywhere in the history of morals: in the asceticism of the saint and the resentment of the condemning moralist, as well as in the brutality of the primitive legislator. All his separate insights on the theme accumulated finally in a single monolithic idea of all-comprehending universality: the Will to Power was in fact the innermost essence of all beings; the essence of Being itself.

Now, it is one thing to perceive that all the psychological impulses of man are mingled in some way with the impulse to power; it is quite another thing to say that this impulse toward power is *the* basic impulse to which all the others may be reduced. We are faced at once with that problem of reduction which haunts particularly the battle among the modern schools of psychology. As is well known, the individual psychology of Alfred Adler split off from Freudian psychoanalysis over just this point—Adler, who had read Nietzsche, declaring that the Will to Power was basic, Freud maintaining that sexuality and Eros were. But what —to confound matters by speaking paradoxically—if both are right and both wrong? What if the human psyche cannot be carved up into compartments and one compartment wedged in under another as being more basic? What if such dichotomizing really overlooks the organic unity of the human psyche, which is such that a single impulse can be just as much an impulse toward love on the one hand as it is toward power on the other? Dostoevski, at least as a novelist, preserves this sense of duality and ambivalence; and Nietzsche too, where his intuition was functioning as concretely as a novelist's, saw this interplay between power and the other drives. (In *Beyond Good and Evil* he remarked, rather as a good Freudian than an Adlerian, "The degree and nature of a man's sensuality extends to the highest altitudes of his spirit.") But later he had Zarathustra the loveless declare that "Love is the danger of the loneliest one," and suppress love and compassion; and so Nietzsche gave the last word to the Will to Power, making it the basis of every other psychological motive; he became one of the reductive psychologists.

What is most remarkable is that this Will to Power should have been made by him into the essence of Being. Remarkable because Nietzsche had ridiculed the very notion of Being as one of the most deceptive ghosts spawned by the brains of philosophers, the most general and therefore the emptiest of concepts, a thin and impalpable ectoplasm distilled from the concrete realities of the senses. He had perceived correctly that the principal conflict within Western philosophy lay at its very beginning, in Plato's condemnation of the poets and artists as inhabiting the world of the senses rather than the supersensible world of the abstractions, the Ideas, which represent true Being as opposed to the constant flux of Becoming in the world of the senses. Nietzsche took the side of the artist: The real world, he said, than which there is no other, is the world of the senses and of Becoming. Nevertheless, to become a systematic thinker Nietzsche had to become a metaphysician, and the metaphysician is driven to have recourse to the idea of Being. To be sure, Nietzsche's thought preserves his dynamism, for Being is turned into Becoming—becomes, in fact, essentially the Will to Power.

But what is power? It is not, according to Nietzsche, a state of rest or stasis toward which all things tend. On the contrary, power itself is dynamic through and through: power consists in the discharge of power, and this means the exercise of the will to power on ever-ascending levels of power. Power itself is the will to power. And the will to power is the will to will.

It is at this point that Nietzsche's doctrine begins to look rather terrifying to most people, and to seem merely an expression of his own frenetic and unbalanced temperament. Frenetic he had certainly become, in many passages of *The Will to Power,* where indeed he resembles nothing so much as "the pale Criminal" of his own description (in *Zarathustra*), the loveless one who thirsts for blood. But here, as elsewhere, the personal frenzy of Nietzsche had a much more than personal meaning; and precisely in this idea of power he was the philosopher of this present age in history, for he revealed to it its own hidden and fateful being. No wonder, then, that the age should have branded him as a wicked and malevolent spirit.

The fact is that the modern age has prided itself everywhere on its dynamism. In history textbooks we represent the emergence of the modern period out of the Middle Ages as the birth of an energetic and dynamic will to conquer nature and transform the conditions of life, instead of submitting passively to them while waiting to be sent to the next world as medieval man had done. We congratulate ourselves over and over again on all this. But when a thinker comes along who seeks to explore what lies hidden behind all this dynamism, we cry out that we do not recognize ourselves in the image he draws and seek refuge from it by pointing an accusing finger at his derangement. Technology in the twentieth century has taken such enormous strides beyond that of the nineteenth that it now bulks larger as an instrument of naked power than as an instrument for human well-being. Now that we have airplanes that fly faster than the sun, intercontinental missiles, space satellites, and above all atomic explosives, we are aware that technology itself has assumed a power to which politics in any traditional sense is subordinate. If the Russians were to outstrip us decisively in technology, then all ordinary political calculations would have to go by the boards. The classical art of politics, conceived since the Greeks as a thoroughly human art addressed to humans, becomes an out-

moded and fragile thing beside the massive accumulation
of technological power. The fate of the world, it now appears, turns upon sheer mastery over things. All the refinements of politics as a human art—diplomatic tact and
finesse, compromise, an enlightened and liberal policy, good
will—are as little able to avail against technological suprem-
acy as the refinement of a man's dress and person are able
to ward off the blow of a pile driver. The human becomes
subordinated to the machine, even in the traditionally human business of politics.

Here Nietzsche, more acutely than Marx, expresses the
real historical meaning of Communism and especially of the
peculiar attraction Communism holds for the so-called
backward or underdeveloped countries: it is a will to power
on the part of these peoples, a will to take their fate in
their own hands and make their own history. This powerful and secret appeal of Communism is something that our
own statesmen do not seem in the least to understand. And
America itself? Yes, we bear with us still the old liberal
ideals of the individual's right to life, liberty, and the pursuit of happiness; but the actual day-to-day march of our
collective life involves us in a frantic dynamism whose ultimate goals are undefined. Everywhere in the world, men
and nations are behaving precisely in accordance with the
Nietzschean metaphysics: The goal of power need not be
defined, because it is its own goal, and to halt or slacken
speed even for a moment would be to fall behind in achiev-
ing it. Power does not stand still; as we say nowadays in
America, you are either going up or coming down.

But on what, philosophically speaking, does this celebrated dynamism of the modern age rest? The modern era
in philosophy is usually taken to begin with Descartes. The
fundamental feature of Descartes' thought is a dualism between the ego and the external world of nature. The ego
is the subject, essentially a thinking substance; nature is the
world of objects, extended substances. Modern philosophy
thus begins with a radical subjectivism, the subject facing the object in a kind of hidden antagonism. (This subjectivism has nothing to do with Kierkegaard's idea of

"subjective truth"; Kierkegaard simply chose his term unfortunately, for his intention is the very opposite of Cartesianism.) Nature thus appears as a realm to be conquered, and man as the creature who is to be conqueror of it. This is strikingly shown in the remark of Francis Bacon, prophet of the new science, who said that in scientific investigation man must put nature to the rack in order to wring from it an answer to his questions; the metaphor is one of coercion and violent antagonism. A crucial step beyond Descartes was taken when Leibniz declared that material substances are not inert, as Descartes thought, but endowed with a fundamental dynamism: all things have a certain drive (*appetitio*) by which they move forward in time. Here the Cartesian antagonism between man and nature is stepped up by having added to it an intrinsic dynamism on both sides. Nietzsche is the culmination of this whole line of thought: the thinker who brings the seed to its violent fruition. The very extremity of his idea points to a fundamental error at the source of the modern epoch. Whether or not it points beyond that to a fundamental error at the root of the whole Western tradition, as Heidegger holds, is another matter, and one that we shall examine in the context of Heidegger's own philosophy.

Power as the pursuit of more power inevitably founders in the void that lies beyond itself. The Will to Power begets the problem of nihilism. Here again Nietzsche stands as the philosopher of the period, for he prophesied remarkably that nihilism would be the shadow, in many guises and forms, that would haunt the twentieth century. Supposing man does not blow himself and his earth to bits, and that he really becomes the master of this planet. What then? He pushes off into interstellar space. And then? Power for power's sake, no matter how far the power is extended, leaves always the dread of the void beyond. The attempt to stand face to face with that void is the problem of nihilism.

For Nietzsche, the problem of nihilism arose out of the discovery that "God is dead." "God" here means the historical God of the Christian faith. But in a wider philosophical sense it means also the whole realm of supersensi-

ble reality—Platonic Ideas, the Absolute, or what not—that
philosophy has traditionally posited beyond the sensible
realm, and in which it has located man's highest values.
Now that this other, higher, eternal realm is gone, Nietzsche declared, man's highest values lose their value. If man
has lost this anchor to which he has hitherto been moored,
Nietzsche asks, will he not drift in an infinite void? The
only value Nietzsche can set up to take the place of these
highest values that have lost their value for contemporary
man is: Power.

But do we today really have any better answer? An answer, I mean, that we live and not just pay lip service to?
Nietzsche is more truly the philosopher for our age than
we are willing to admit. To the degree that modern life
has become secularized those highest values, anchored in
the eternal, *have* already lost their value. So long as people
are blissfully unaware of this, they of course do not sink
into any despondency and nihilism; they may even be
steady churchgoers. Nihilism, in fact, is the one subject on
which we speak today with the self-complacency of com-
mencement-day orators. We are always ready to invoke the
term against a new book or new play that has anything
"negative" to say, as if nihilism were always to be found in
the other person but never in ourselves. And yet despite
all its apparently cheerful and self-satisfied immersion in
gadgets and refrigerators American life, one suspects, is
nihilistic to its core. Its final "What for?" is not even asked,
let alone answered.

Man, Nietzsche held, is a contradictory and complex being, and he himself is as complex and contradictory an example as one could find. One has the feeling in reading
him that those ultimate problems with which he dealt
would have been enough almost to drive any man mad.
Was it necessary that he be deranged in order to reveal
the secret derangement that lies coiled like a dragon at the
bottom of our epoch? He does not bring us any solutions
that satisfy us to the great questions he raises, but he has
stated the central and crucial problems for man in this pe-

riod, as no one else has, and therein lies at once his greatness and his challenge.

And Nietzsche's fate might very well prefigure our own,
for unless our Faustian civilization can relax its frantic
dynamism at some point, it might very well go psychotic.
To primitives and Orientals, we Western men already seem
half crazy. But it will not do merely to assert blandly that
the tension of this dynamism has to be relaxed somehow
and somewhere; we need to know what in our fundamental
way of thinking needs to be changed so that the frantic
will to power will not appear as the only meaning we can
give to human life. If this moment in Western history is
but the fateful outcome of the fundamental ways of thought
that lie at the very basis of our civilization—and particularly
of that way of thought that sunders man from nature, sees
nature as a realm of objects to be mastered and conquered,
and *can* therefore end only with the exaltation of the will
to power—then we have to find out how this one-sided and
ultimately nihilistic emphasis upon the power over things
may be corrected.

This means that philosophers must take up the task
of rethinking Nietzsche's problems back to their sources,
which happen also to be the sources of our whole Western
tradition. The most thoroughgoing attempt at this, among
philosophers in the twentieth century, has been made by
Heidegger, who is, as we shall now see, engaged in nothing
less than the Herculean task of digging his way patiently
and laboriously out of the Nietzschean ruins, like a survivor
out of a bombed city.

HEIDEGGER

Chapter Nine

WE CANNOT HEAR the cry of Nietzsche, Heidegger tells us, until we ourselves begin to think. And lest we fancy this an easy and obvious thing to do, he adds: *"Thinking only begins at the point where we have come to know that Reason, glorified for centuries, is the most obstinate adversary of thinking."*

This rather sensational opposition of thinking to reason goes against all the catch phrases of our culture. Heidegger is not a rationalist, because reason operates by means of concepts, mental representations, and our existence eludes these. But he is not an irrationalist either. Irrationalism holds that feeling, or will, or instinct are more valuable and indeed more truthful than reason—as in fact, from the point of view of life itself, they are. But irrationalism surrenders the field of thinking to rationalism and thereby secretly comes to share the assumptions of its enemy. What is needed is a more fundamental kind of thinking that will cut under both opposites. Heidegger's statement points backward through the whole philosophic tradition with which his own thought is intended as a decisive break and at the same time forward to a new territory in which, as he says of himself, he is like a wanderer lost in a forest, attempting to mark out trails. And his statement tells us that if we his contemporaries would assimilate his thought, we too must learn to think, even in opposition to all our inherited rigidities of reason; think more rigorously than rationalism ever did.

Kierkegaard and Nietzsche fell like block-busters upon the quiet world of academic philosophy. They were philosophers outside the Academy, a new and revolutionary thing for modern times, and consequently they wrote not as professors but as poets: their books are passionate and colorful, addressed to all men and not merely to the professionals. Heidegger by contrast is a thoroughly academic figure, a professor, and the mark of this is upon all his writings. He never expresses himself with the radical boldness and passion of a Kierkegaard or Nietzsche, but his message swathed though it may be in academic and formal lingo may nevertheless prove in the end to be as dramatic and fateful a bombshell as were those of his two predecessors.

Heidegger clearly belongs—as may be gathered from the statement of his quoted above—to that line of development within modern culture that we discussed earlier (in Chapter 6) as the flight from Laputa. But his escape from the aery realm of pure reason has been planned more systematically and quietly than those of the other antagonists of Laputa, and in carrying it out Heidegger reaches back beyond the situation of modern man into the beginnings of Western thought among the Greeks. Both Kierkegaard and Nietzsche point up a profound dissociation, or split, that has taken place in the being of Western man, which is basically the conflict of reason with the whole man. According to Kierkegaard, reason threatens to swallow up faith; Western man now stands at a crossroads forced to choose either to be religious or to fall into despair. Having chosen the former, he must, being rooted historically in Christianity, enact a radical renewal of the Christian faith. For Nietzsche the era of reason and science raises the question of what is to be done with the primitive instincts and passions of man; in pushing these latter aside the age threatens us with a decline in vitality for the whole species. What lies behind both prophetic messages is the perception that man is estranged from his own being. Now, the estrangement from Being itself is Heidegger's central theme. But he attacks this problem on its own terms and as a systematic thinker, and so his writings do not shine with the bold and striking colors of religious and psychological prophecy. The emotional, vital, and religious regeneration of modern man is something altogether outside his concern as a thinker. The problem as he puts it to himself is quite different: Granted that modern man has torn himself up by his roots, might not the cause of this lie farther back in his past than he thinks? Might it not, in fact, lie in the way in which he thinks about the most fundamental of all things, Being itself? And might not a more rooted kind of thinking—rooted in Being—lead the rootless Laputan back to the earth? Heidegger deals in a radical way with the celebrated alienation of modern man, and indeed with the problem of man generally, by subordinating it to something else, without which man can never regain his roots: to Being itself.

Heidegger's text is on the whole so austerely devoid of metaphor that when one does occur it stands out in our memory like a solitary tree on a plain. In one of his more exoteric messages, the *Letter on Humanism* (1947), Heidegger concludes with an especially memorable figure that describes very aptly the whole direction of his own thought: the thinker, he says, is trying to trace a furrow in human language as the peasant traces a furrow across a field. Heidegger himself is of peasant stock, strongly attached to his native region of southern Germany, and one feels this attachment to the soil in his thinking. "Remain true to the earth," Zarathustra had counseled his followers; and Heidegger as a thinker, despite the apparent abstractness of his themes, comes much closer to obeying this counsel than did the unlucky Nietzsche. The picture of man that emerges from Heidegger's pages is of an earth-bound, time-bound, radically finite creature—precisely the image of man we should expect from a peasant, in this case a peasant who has the whole history of Western philosophy at his fingertips. And for precisely this reason if for no other we today, who have gone so far from the soil, ought to find great significance in this philosophy.

In this same *Letter on Humanism* Heidegger also permits himself a brief personal aside, which is also rare in the scrupulous impersonality of his writings. He is complaining

about some of the misunderstandings of his thought (and
on this score he has good grounds for complaint), and he
remarks: *"Because we hark back to Nietzsche's saying
about the 'death of God,' people take such an enterprise
for atheism. For what is more 'logical' than to consider the
man who has experienced the 'death of God' as a Godless
person."* Even here the personal meaning is oblique; Heidegger refers to himself objectively and in the third person.
Nevertheless, it is the closest he comes in his writings to a
personal spiritual confession. Heidegger has experienced the
death of God, and this death casts a shadow over all his
writings; but he announces it quietly, almost indirectly,
while the madman in Nietzsche's *Joyful Wisdom* shouted
it out in the market place. And this change of tone in itself
shows how far history has moved from Nietzsche's day,
when the discovery of God's death was a rending and
prophetic vision, to our own, when the death of God is admitted calmly and the thinker tries to take sober stock of
the situation. Heidegger's philosophy is neither atheism nor
theism, but a description of the world from which God is
absent. It is now the night of the world, Heidegger says,
quoting the poet Hölderlin; the god has withdrawn himself, as the sun sets below the horizon. And meanwhile the
thinker can only redeem the time by seeking to understand
what is at once nearest and farthest from man: his own
being and Being itself. Heidegger has described Hölderlin's
poetry as a "temple without a shrine," a description which
really fits his own philosophy. If the god, reborn, returns,
his temple will be ready for him, thanks to Heidegger; but
it will take someone else, with a little more fire, to build
the shrine and light the candles. And if the god does not
come back, the temple can be converted into an imposing,
if bleak, secular edifice, as in the case of Sartre, the atheist
engagé. Both atheist and theist have to reckon with Heidegger's thought, for he is dealing with matters with which
both will have to come to terms, if in their separate creeds
they are to measure up to the height of our times. It may
even be that atheism and theism, as public creeds, matter

less than our becoming alive to these things that Heidegger
is struggling to bring to light.

1. BEING

But what about Being, the reader may ask, impatiently.
After so many centuries can we really be told something
new and significant—above all, significant to us as busy
moderns—on this apparently very remote and abstract subject? The impatience itself comes out of a certain attitude
or orientation toward Being, of which we are on the whole
unconscious. We want to know about things, beings, and
particularly we want to have information about definite and
observable traits of these beings; what lies behind this, in
the enveloping background of all beings, seems to have little to do with our practical needs, the bulk of which are
concerned with mastering the things in our environment.
This is nothing less than the endemic positivism of our age;
and there is no doubt that Positivism as a philosophy has
simply given expression to this prevailing attitude toward
Being.

Nevertheless, Being has been the central and dominating
concept of twenty-five hundred years of Western philosophy; and if we are going to jettison all that past, we ought
at least to know what was at stake, intellectually speaking,
in the slow unfolding of those centuries. Some of our
present-day philosophers fortify the prejudice of the age by
telling us that the concern with Being is merely a linguistic
accident, due to the fact that the Indo-European languages
have the copula "to be," whereas other languages have no
such word and consequently no empty verbal battles about
the meaning of Being. But the Indo-European languages
cut a pretty wide swath in history, and it happens to be our
swath, *our* tradition, with which we must come to terms.

That tradition itself, however, is also to blame for our
contemporary indifference to Being. And precisely in this
matter the bold quality of Heidegger's thought shows itself:
he is working within this tradition but he is also seeking to
destroy it—destroy it creatively so that it may surpass itself.

In his greatest book, *Sein und Zeit* (*Being and Time*) published in 1927, which has become a kind of systematic
Bible—sometimes almost an unread Bible—of modern Existentialism, he proposed no less a task than a "repetition"
of the problem of Being: a repetition in the sense of a radical renewal, a fetching back from the oblivion of the past
the problem as the first Greek thinkers confronted it. This
aspect of the book, however, got lost amid the excitement
over Heidegger's dramatic and moving descriptions of human existence—of death, care, anxiety, guilt, and the rest;
and critics have gone so far as to see in his later writings,
which lack such topics of human interest, a break and
change in his thought. This is a mistake, for the singleness
and continuity of Heidegger's thinking is such that all his
later writings can be considered as commentaries and elu-
cidations of what was already in germ in his *Being and
Time*. He has never ceased from that single task, the "repetition" of the problem of Being: the standing face to face
with Being as did the earliest Greeks. And on the very first
pages of *Being and Time* he tells us that this task involves
nothing less than the destruction of the whole history of
Western ontology—that is, of the way the West has thought
about Being.

Why should this be necessary? And, to go back to our
previous point, how has the tradition itself been responsible for our contemporary indifference to Being?

In the first place, the word "being" is ambiguous in English. As a participle, it has at once the characteristics of
verb and noun. As a noun, it is a name for beings, things:
a table is a being, as is the tree outside the window, etc.,
etc. Anything that is is a being. This we can recognize even
though we find the fact that it is a being the most empty
and abstract (and therefore nugatory) characteristic of any
thing. But in its aspect as a verb "being" signifies the "to-be"
of things, and for this we have no single word in English,
perhaps because this is even more difficult to conceive.
Other languages do have a more adequate vocabulary here
and pair off the two meanings neatly: in Greek, *to on* (the
thing which is) and *to einai* (the Being of the thing which

is); in Latin, *ens* and *esse;* in French, *l'étant* and *l'être;* in German, *das Seiende* and *das Sein.* (Heidegger's suggestion is that the best accommodation to this usage we can find in English would be: *beings,* where we mean the things that are, and *Being,* where we mean the to-be of whatever is; and we shall keep to this suggestion in what follows.)

Now, it is Heidegger's contention that the whole history of Western thought has shown an exclusive preoccupation with the first member of these pairs, with the thing-which-is, and has let the second, the to-be of what is, fall into oblivion. Thus that part of philosophy which is supposed to deal with Being is traditionally called *ontology*—the science of the thing-which-is—and not *einai-logy,* which would be the study of the to-be of Being as opposed to beings. This observation may look like a piece of scholarly pettifoggery, but it is not. What it means is nothing less than this: that *from the beginning the thought of Western man has been bound to things, to objects.* The whole history of the West takes its fateful course from this fact, and by starting from it Heidegger is able—simply out of his single-minded preoccupation with Being—to throw new light on that history and thereby on the present situation of the world.

Once Being has been understood solely in terms of beings, things, it becomes the most general and empty of concepts: "The first object of the understanding," says St. Thomas Aquinas, "that which the intellect conceives when it conceives of anything." Thus, a table is an article of furniture; articles of furniture are human artifacts; human artifacts are physical things; and then, with the next jump of generalization, I can say of this table merely that it is a being, a thing. "Being" is the ultimate generalization I can make about the thing, and therefore the most abstract term I can apply to it, and it gives me no useful information about the table at all. Hence the ordinary person's impatience, which we have noted, on hearing any talk about Being at all: it is something that does not concern him or any of his vital needs. But here again Heidegger overturns the traditional applecart: Being is not an empty abstraction but something in which all of us are immersed up to our necks, and indeed over our heads. We all understand the meaning in ordinary life of the word "is," though we are not called upon to give a conceptual explanation of it. Our ordinary human life moves within a *preconceptual* understanding of Being, and it is this everyday understanding of Being in which we live, move, and have our Being that Heidegger wants to get at as a philosopher. Far from being the most remote and abstract of concepts, Being is the most concrete and closest of presences; literally, the concern of every man. This preconceptual understanding of Being is given to most men—I remark to a neighbor, "Today *is* Monday," and there are no questions asked, and none need be asked, about the meaning of "is"; and *without this understanding man could not understand anything else*. But this does not in the least mean that this preconceptual understanding has been brought into the light. On the contrary, it remains in the dark because for most ordinary purposes we need not ask any questions about it. The whole aim of Heidegger's thinking is to bring this sense of Being into the light.

2. PHENOMENOLOGY AND HUMAN EXISTENCE

But how is something so banal, so close and yet so hidden, to be brought into the light? Here Heidegger makes use of an instrument, phenomenology, borrowed from his teacher, Edmund Husserl; but in adopting the instrument he gives it a different sense and direction from Husserl's. The difference is at once a difference of temperament between the two philosophers and a radical difference between their philosophies. For Husserl, phenomenology was a discipline that attempts to describe what is given to us in experience without obscuring preconceptions or hypothetical speculations; his motto was "to the things themselves"—rather than to the prefabricated conceptions we put in their place. As Husserl saw it, this attempt offered the only way out of the impasse into which philosophy had run at the end of the nineteenth century when the realists, who affirmed the independent existence of the object, and the idealists, who affirmed the priority of the subject, had settled down into a stalemated war. Instead of making intellectual speculations about the whole of reality, philosophy must turn, Husserl declared, to a pure description of what is. In taking this position Husserl became the most influential force not only upon Heidegger but upon the whole generation of German philosophers who came to maturity about the time of the First World War.

Heidegger accepts Husserl's definition of phenomenology: he will attempt to describe, he says, and without any obscuring preconceptions, what human existence is. But his imagination could not let the matter go at this, for he noted that the word "phenomenon" comes from the Greek. The etymologies of words, particularly of Greek words, are a passion with Heidegger; in his pursuit of them he has been accused of playing with words, but when one realizes what deposits of truth mankind has let slip into its language as it evolves, Heidegger's perpetual digging at words to get at their hidden nuggets of meaning is one of his most exciting facets. In the matter of Greek particularly—a dead language, whose whole history is now spread out before us— we can see how certain truths are embedded in the language itself: truths that the Greek race later came to *forget* in its thinking. The word "phenomenon"—a word in ordinary usage, by this time, in all modern European languages —means in Greek "that which reveals itself." Phenomenology therefore means for Heidegger the attempt to let the thing speak for itself. It will reveal itself to us, he says, only if we do not attempt to coerce it into one of our readymade conceptual strait jackets. Here we get the beginning of his rejoinder to the Nietzschean view that knowledge is in the end an expression of the Will to Power: according to Heidegger we do not know the object by conquering and subduing it but rather by letting it be what it is and, in letting it be, allowing it to reveal itself as what it is. And our own human existence too, in its most immediate, internal nuances, will reveal itself if we have ears to hear it.

The etymological harvest does not stop with the single

word "phenomenology." Heidegger finds around that word a whole cluster of etymologies, all of them having an internal unity of meaning that brings us to the very center of his thought. The Greek word *phainomenon* is connected with the word *phaos*, light, and also with the word *apophansis*, statement or speech. The sequence of ideas is thus: revelation-light-language. The light is the light of revelation, and language itself is in this light. These may look like mere metaphors, but perhaps they are so only for us, whose understanding is darkened; for early man, at the very dawn of the Greek language, this inner link between light and statement (language) was a simple and profound fact, and it is our sophistication and abstractness that makes it seem to us "merely" metaphorical.

This metaphor of light, as we shall see, opens the way to Heidegger's theory of truth, which is for him one of the most fateful issues in human history and human thought. The etymology of the Greek word for truth, *a-letheia*, is another key to Heidegger's theory: the word means, literally, un-hiddenness, revelation. Truth occurs when what has been hidden is no longer so. If we put this alongside the previous ideas of revelation-light-language, then the importance of the idea Heidegger is getting at may emerge. It is an idea, in fact, that challenges altogether the view of "truth" usually held nowadays, as something to be ascribed only to statements or propositions: a statement is true, for us, when it corresponds to fact. But statements do not exist without the minds that comprehend them; and truth is therefore, in modern usage, to be found in the mind when it has a correct judgment about what is the case. The trouble with this view is that it cannot take account of other manifestations of truth. For example, we speak of the "truth" of a work of art. A work of art in which we find truth may actually have in it no propositions that are true in this literal sense. The truth of the work of art is in its being a revelation, but that revelation does not consist in a statement or group of statements that are intellectually correct. The momentous assertion that Heidegger makes is that truth does not reside primarily in the intellect, but that, on the contrary, intellectual truth is in fact a derivative of a more basic sense of truth.

What this more basic sense of truth is, we shall deal with fully in a moment. We must point out, however, before we do so, that the question of truth arose as soon as we began to outline the Heideggerian view of human existence. Critics have usually got at Heidegger's thought by a more sensational route. The Italian commentator Ruggieri, for example, describes Existentialism with colorful superficiality as "philosophy done in the style of a thriller or crime novel"—no doubt because it scandalizes the academic philosopher to hear talk about such urgent human matters as death, care, anxiety, and the like. Heidegger does discuss these questions; but before we can deal with his attitude to them we must understand his view of man as a being who is situated in a certain relation to truth. Indeed, what man becomes—in his history as well as his thinking—turns upon the decision he makes as to what truth is. Critics who find sensationalism in Heidegger find it because that is what they are looking for.

It is by harking back to the primeval meaning of truth as it became embedded in the Greek language, that Heidegger takes his theory, in a single leap, beyond the boundaries of Husserlian phenomenology. Husserl was still rooted in the point of view of Descartes, which is the prevailing view of the modern epoch in philosophy, while the whole meaning of Heidegger's thought is as an effort to overcome Descartes.

By doubting all things Descartes arrived at a single certainty: the existence of his own consciousness—the famous *Cogito, ergo sum*, "I think, therefore I am." This is the point at which modern philosophy, and with it the modern epoch, begins: man is locked up in his own ego. Outside him is the doubtful world of things, which his science has now taught him are really not the least like their familiar appearances. Descartes got the external world back through a belief in God, who in His goodness would not deceive us into believing that this external world existed if it really did not. But the ghost of subjectivism (and solipsism too) is there and haunts the whole of modern philosophy. David Hume, in a moment of acute skepticism, felt panicky in the solitude of his study and had to go out and join his friends in the billiard room in order to be reassured that the external world was really there. And Leibniz expressed the whole thing in a powerful image when he said of his monads, the ultimate substances of the world, that they had no windows—i.e., did not communicate with each other.

And for Descartes, though he might allow himself moments of doubting the external world, the fact is that the existence of things took priority when it came to understanding the Being of man. What are external things? Bodies, extended substances. In contrast the ego, the I, is an immaterial substance, a thinking substance. And just as various qualities—color, shape, and so on—"inhere" in a physical substance, so what we call psychic states—moods or thoughts—"inhere" in a soul substance. Though man and nature are irremediably split off from each other, secretly what takes place is that the Being of man is always understood in analogy to physical substances. While modern thought has split off man from nature, it has tried nevertheless to understand man in terms of physical realities.

Heidegger destroys the Cartesian picture at one blow: what characterizes man essentially, he says, is that he is Being-in-the-world. Leibniz had said that the monad has no windows; and Heidegger's reply is that man does not look out upon an external world through windows, from the isolation of his ego: he is already out-of-doors. He is in the world because, existing, he is involved in it totally. Existence itself, according to Heidegger, means to stand outside oneself, to be beyond oneself. My Being is not something that takes place inside my skin (or inside an immaterial substance inside that skin); my Being, rather, is spread over a field or region which is the world of its care and concern. Heidegger's theory of man (and of Being) might be called the Field Theory of Man (or the Field Theory of Being) in analogy with Einstein's Field Theory of Matter, provided we take this purely as an analogy; for

Heidegger would hold it a spurious and inauthentic way
to philosophize to derive one's philosophic conclusions from
the highly abstract theories of physics. But in the way that
Einstein took matter to be a field (a magnetic field, say)
—in opposition to the Newtonian conception of a body as
existing inside its surface boundaries—so Heidegger takes
man to be a field or region of Being. Think of a magnetic
field without the solid body of the magnet at its center;
man's Being is such a field, but there is no soul substance
or ego substance at the center from which that field
radiates.

Heidegger calls this field of Being *Dasein. Dasein* (which,
in German, means literally Being-there) is his name for
man. One of the most remarkable things about Heidegger's
description of human existence is that it is made without
his using the term "man" at all! He thereby avoids the assumption that we are dealing with a definite *object* with
a fixed nature—that we already know, in short, what man is.
His analysis of existence also takes place without the use
of the word "consciousness," for this word threatens to
bring us back into the Cartesian dualism. That Heidegger
can say everything he wants to say about human existence
without using either "man" or "consciousness" means that
the gulf between subject and object, or between mind and
body, that has been dug by modern philosophy need not
exist if we do not make it. Far from being arbitrary, his
terminology is extremely deliberate and shrewd.

Now, there is nothing at all remote or abstract about
this idea of man, or *Dasein,* as a field. It checks with our
everyday observation in the case of the child who has just
learned to respond to his own name. He comes promptly
enough at being called by name; but if asked to point out
the person to whom the name belongs, he is just as likely
to point to Mommy or Daddy as to himself—to the frustration of both eager parents. Some months later, asked the
same question, the child will point to himself. But before
he has reached that stage, he has heard his name as naming a field or region of Being with which he is concerned,
and to which he responds, whether the call is to come to

food, to mother, or whatever. And the child is right. His name is not the name of an existence that takes place within the envelope of his skin: that is merely the awfully abstract social convention that has imposed itself not only on his parents but on the history of philosophy. The basic meaning the child's name has for him does not disappear as he grows older; it only becomes covered over by the more abstract social convention. He secretly hears his own name called whenever he hears any region of Being named with which he is vitally involved.

It takes a little time to get used to this Heideggerian notion of a field, but once familiar it is at once inevitable and natural and alters our whole way of looking at the human person. To be sure, this existence is always *mine;* it is not an impersonal fact, as the existence of a table is merely to be an individual case of the class table. Nevertheless, the mine-ness of my existence does not consist in the fact that there is an I-substance at the center of my field, but rather in that this mine-ness permeates the whole field of my Being.

Heidegger has with this notion planted both feet solidly in that banal, public, everyday world of our experience. Philosophers in the past have construed existence from a much different point of view—that of a privileged mode of experience, the solitude of reflection. The thought of a Descartes or Hume smells of this solitude, of the private chamber or study in which a man may toy with the doubt of an external world. In the daylight of everyday experience such doubts become unreal; they do not need to be refuted, they simply fade away, for they do not apply to the existence that we actually live.

In this everyday prephilosophical world in which we live, in which even Descartes and Hume lived though they forgot it, none of us is a private Self confronting a world of external objects. None of us is yet even a Self. We are each simply one among many; a name among the names of our schoolfellows, our fellow citizens, our community. This everyday public quality of our existence Heidegger calls "the One." The One is the impersonal and public

creature whom each of us is even before he is an I, a real
I. One has such-and-such a position in life, one is expected
to behave in such-and-such a manner, one does this, one
does not do that, etc., etc. We exist thus in a state of
"fallen-ness" (*Verfallenheit*), according to Heidegger, in
the sense that we are as yet below the level of existence
to which it is possible for us to rise. So long as we remain
in the womb of this externalized and public existence, we
are spared the terror and the dignity of becoming a Self.
But, as happened to Ivan Ilyich in Tolstoy's story, such
things as death and anxiety intrude upon this fallen state,
destroy our sheltered position of simply being one among
many, and reveal to us our own existence as fearfully and
irremediably our own. Because it is less fearful to be "the
One" than to be a Self, the modern world has wonderfully
multiplied all the devices of self-evasion.

Whether it be fallen or risen, inauthentic or authentic,
counterfeit copy or genuine original, human existence is
marked by three general traits: (1) mood or feeling;
(2) understanding; (3) speech. Heidegger calls these
existentialia and intends them as basic categories of existence. As categories they seem at first glance rather strange,
for other philosophers' categories—quantity, quality, space,
time, etc.—are very different. These latter, which the tradition from Aristotle onward makes the fundamental categories of Being, are all categories of physical objects. But
human existence cannot be understood as a thing, and
therefore cannot be characterized by categories that are
derived from things. This does not mean, however, that
Heidegger intends his three *existentialia* to refer to internal
states of some purely mental entity or soul substance.
Rather, they must be understood in terms of Heidegger's
view of *Dasein,* human existence, as a field.

(1) *Mood.* What is a mood really? We tend to think of
it as an internal state. But when we do so, we are still
thinking of it as inhering in some nuclear substance of ourselves, a soul or ego, as the color of a table inheres in the
table. We do not actually have our moods in this way.
Strictly speaking, we do not "have" them at all as we might

"have" articles of furniture stored away in some interior attic. The mood, rather, penetrates the whole field of Being that we are. The German word for mood, *Stimmung*, has the root sense of being attuned, and in a mood our whole Being is attuned in a certain way. We *are* a certain joy, sadness, dread. It leavens and permeates the whole of our existence.

Moreover, in every mood or feeling I suddenly find myself here and now within my situation, within my world. *Dasein*, as we have seen, means to be there—or perhaps, as we might more commonly say in English, to be here and now—and in every mood I come to myself here and now in a certain way. Whether the mood be slight, almost impalpable, or a volcanic eruption, what always reveals itself if I give it heed is my own Being-there in its world in a certain way. The fundamental mood, according to Heidegger, is anxiety (*Angst*); he does not choose this as primary out of any morbidity of temperament, however, but simply because in anxiety this here-and-now of our existence arises before us in all its precarious and porous contingency.

Notice that Heidegger is talking about moods or feelings as modes of Being. He is propounding not psychology but ontology, but in so doing he is also recasting our whole understanding of psychological matters. Man is illuminated by letting Being reveal itself, and not vice versa. The whole approach is decidedly not anthropocentric.

(2) *Understanding*. The understanding Heidegger refers to here is not abstract or theoretical; it is the understanding of Being in which our existence is rooted, and without which we could not make propositions or theories that can claim to be "true." As such it lies underneath and at the basis of our ordinary conceptual understanding. We open our eyes in the morning, and the world opens before us. We do not reflect enough on what happens in this simple act of seeing—namely, that the world opens around us as we see. This open-ness, or standing open, of the world must always be given, even for the most humble human existent, whose mind might be quite devoid of ideas and who might claim no specifically intellectual understanding

of the world at all. Without this open-ness he could not exist, for to exist means to stand beyond himself in a world that opens before him. In this world that lies before him, open beneath the light, things lie unconcealed (also concealed); but unconcealedness, or un-hiddenness, for Heidegger, is truth; and therefore so far as man exists, he exists "in the truth." (At the same time, because he is finite, he must always exist "in untruth.") Truth and Being are thus inseparable, given always together, in the simple sense that a world with things in it opens up around man the moment he exists. Most of the time, however, man does not let himself see what really happens in seeing.

Here is an example: An intellectual approaches to tell me a new "theory" of his. The theory may be about a new book, another person, or some new twist in psychoanalysis —it does not matter. (Suppose, to make our illustration more concrete at least for some readers, that this intellectual is one of that peculiarly traditionless, deracinated, and therefore cerebral breed, the New York intellectual.) As soon as I hear his theory, I know it to be false. Challenged to give arguments against it, I may stumble inarticulately; in some cases, indeed, I find it not worth while to give a rebuttal, for the ideas ring false the moment they strike my ear. Some dumb inarticulated understanding, some sense of truth planted, as it were, in the marrow of my bones, makes me know that what I am hearing is not true. Whence comes this understanding? It is the understanding that I have by virtue of being rooted in existence. It is the kind of understanding we all have when confronted with ideas that we know to be false even though it may take us a long time to articulate reasons for rejecting them. If we did not have this understanding, we could never utter any propositions as true or false. We become rootless intellectually to the degree that we lose our hold upon this primary form of understanding, which is there in the act of opening our eyes upon the world.

(3) *Speech.* Language, for Heidegger, is not primarily a system of sounds or of marks on paper symbolizing those sounds. Sounds and marks upon paper can become lan-

guage only because man, insofar as he exists, stands within language. This looks very paradoxical; but, as with the rest of Heidegger, to understand what he means we have to cast off our usual habits of thought and let ourselves see what the thing is—i.e., let the thing itself be seen rather than riding roughshod over it with ready-made conceptions.

Two people are talking together. They understand each other, and they fall silent—a long silence. This silence is language; it may speak more eloquently than any words. In their mood they are attuned to each other; they may even reach down into that understanding which, as we have seen above, lies below the level of articulation. The three—mood, understanding, and speech (a speech here that is silence)—thus interweave and are one. This significant, speaking silence shows us that sounds or marks do not constitute the essence of language. Nor is this silence merely a gap in our chatter; it is, rather, the primordial attunement of one existent to another, out of which all language —as sounds, marks, and counters—comes. It is only because man is capable of such silence that he is capable of authentic speech. If he ceases to be rooted in that silence all his talk becomes chatter.

This is an approach to language very different from that of the various forms of semanticism now in vogue in this country and in England. Where the semanticists deal with words as signs or counters, and sometimes systems of such signs as logical calculi, Heidegger points rather to the existential background out of which those signs emerge. The semanticist I. A. Richards once presented a theory of poetry in which the poet became a manipulator of verbal signs—a sort of emotional engineer. But all semantical interpretations of language, however useful they may be, are doomed at the start to be incomplete because they do not get at the roots of language in human existence. Take Richards' series of books, *Basic English*, *Basic German*, etc., which attempt through pictures and words to instruct the pupil in a language he knows nothing of: On the first page of the *Basic English* text I find a picture (supposed to be of a man) pointing to himself and saying, "I am a man," and another of a woman and a child declaring what they are. Suppose I knew no English altogether and picked up the book; I might very well think "I am a man" meant "I am a male ballet dancer," for that is what the man in the little abstract drawing looks like. The point may appear frivolous, but it is not. Such misunderstandings are avoided only because there is an unexpressed context of mutual understanding within which the instructor and pupil in the language communicate. Such a context of understanding is not expressed because all expression takes place within it. The instructor may lengthen his preamble to the linguistic manual, in the hope of eliminating such misunderstandings, but at whatever point he begins there must be, behind and around his words, this context of mutual understanding.

In what does this unexpressed context of understanding consist? As we have seen above, in the understanding in which our existence itself is rooted. We have spoken earlier of Heidegger's Field Theory of Being; we might just as well call it a contextual theory of Being. Being is the context in which all beings come to light—and this means those beings as well that are sounds or marks on paper. Because man stands in this context, this open space of Being, he may communicate with other men. Men exist "within language" prior to their uttering sounds because they exist within a mutual context of understanding, which in the end is nothing but Being itself.

It is a pity that Heidegger's view of language has not become known in this country. It might have spared us many fruitless and self-defeating forays in literary criticism, in which the effort has been to pick poems apart into the words that make them up. And it might illuminate discussions by our logicians of formalized languages and logics, by pointing out that every attempt at formalization must presuppose a context of language within which understanding is already taking place.

3. DEATH, ANXIETY, FINITUDE

Men die. This happens every day in the world. Death is a public event in the world, of which we take notice in obituaries; we pay the necessary social obsequies and are sometimes deeply touched emotionally. But so long as death remains a fact outside ourselves, we have not yet passed from the proposition "Men die" to the proposition "I am to die." The realization of the latter brings with it the shattering experience of Tolstoy's Ivan Ilyich.

Heidegger's analysis of death—one of the most powerful and celebrated passages in *Being and Time*—reveals in thought the truth that the artist Tolstoy had revealed in his story. (Truth in both cases has to be understood basically as revelation.) The authentic meaning of death—"I am to die"—is not as an external and public fact within the world, but as an internal possibility of my own Being. Nor is it a possibility like a point at the end of a road, which I will in time reach. So long as I think in this way, I still hold death at a distance outside myself. The point is that I may die at any moment, and therefore death is my *possibility* now. It is like a precipice at my feet. It is also the most extreme and absolute of my possibilities: extreme, because it is the possibility of not being and hence cuts off all other possibilities; absolute, because man can surmount all other heartbreaks, even the deaths of those he loves, but his own death puts an end to him. Hence, death is the most personal and intimate of possibilities, since it is what I must suffer for myself: nobody else can die for me.

Only by taking my death into myself, according to Heidegger, does an authentic existence become possible for me. Touched by this interior angel of death, I cease to be the impersonal and social One among many, as Ivan Ilyich was, and I am free to become myself. Though terrifying, the taking of death into ourselves is also liberating: It frees us from servitude to the petty cares that threaten to engulf our daily life and thereby opens us to the essential *projects* by which we can make our lives personally and significantly our own. Heidegger calls this the condition of "freedom-toward-death" or "resoluteness."

The acceptance of death, as possible here and now, dis closes the radical finitude of our existence. More than any philosopher before him—more even than Kant, from whom he derived a good deal in this respect—Heidegger has ex plored the depths of human finitude. We tend to think of finitude principally in connection with physical objects: ob jects are finite because they are contained within definite spatial boundaries. They extend so far and no farther. The essential finitude of man, however, is experienced not at his boundaries but, so to speak, at the very center of his Being He is finite because his Being is penetrated by non-Being At first glance, this looks utterly paradoxical; and our rea son, basing itself rigidly upon the law of contradiction, can not comprehend it. But we ourselves, as existing beings comprehend it all too well when we are plunged into the mood of anxiety, when the void of non-Being opens up within our own Being.

Anxiety is not fear, being afraid of this or that definite object, but the uncanny feeling of being afraid of nothing at all. It is precisely Nothingness that makes itself present and felt as the object of our dread. The first time this fun damental human experience was described was by Kierke gaard in his *Concept of Dread*, but there it was done only briefly, in passing Heidegger has greatly expanded and deepened Kierkegaard's insight Significantly enough, the dread described by Kierkegaard was in connection with the theological problem of Original Sin, the sin that comes down to all human beings from the first sin of Adam. Be fore Adam chose to bite the apple, Kierkegaard says, there opened in him a yawning abyss; he saw the possibility of his own freedom in the committing of a future act against the background of Nothingness. This Nothingness is at once fascinating and dreadful. In Heidegger Nothingness is a presence within our own Being always there, in the inner quaking that goes on beneath the calm surface of our pre occupation with things. Anxiety before Nothingness has many modalities and guises: now trembling and creative now panicky and destructive; but always it is as inseparable from ourselves as our own breathing because anxiety is our existence itself in its radical insecurity. In anxiety we both are and are not, at one and the same time, and this is our dread. Our finitude is such that positive and negative interpenetrate our whole existence.

That man is finite is not merely a psychological characteristic of him personally or his species. Nor is he finite merely because his number of allotted years on this earth is limited. He is finite because the "not"—negation—penetrates the very core of his existence. And whence is this "not" derived? From Being itself. *Man is finite because he lives and moves within a finite understanding of Being.* This means, among other things, that human truth too is always penetrated by untruth. And here we have gone as far as possible from Hegel and the philosophers of the Enlightenment, who had hoped to enclose all truth in a system.

4. TIME AND TEMPORALITY; HISTORY

Our finitude discloses itself essentially in time. In existing, to take the word etymologically, we stand outside ourselves at once open to Being and in the open clearing of Being; and this happens temporally as well as spatially. Man, Heidegger says, is a creature of distance: he is perpetually beyond himself, his existence at every moment opening out toward the future. The future is the not-yet, and the past is the no-longer; and these two negatives—the not-yet and the no-longer—penetrate his existence. They *are* his finitude in its temporal manifestation.

We really know time, says Heidegger, because we know we are going to die. Without this passionate realization of our mortality, time would be simply a movement of the clock that we watch passively, calculating its advance—a movement devoid of human meaning. Man is not, strictly speaking, in time as a body is immersed in a river that rushes by. Rather, time is in him; his existence is temporal through and through, from the inside out. His moods, his care and concern, his anxiety, guilt, and conscience—all are saturated with time. Everything that makes up human existence has to be understood in the light of man's temporality: of the not-yet, the no-longer, the here-and-now.

These three tenses of time—future, past, and present—Heidegger calls *ekstasies*, in the literal sense of the Greek *ek-stasis*, a standing outside and beyond oneself. Philosophers before Heidegger had constructed time as a series of "nows"—present moments—following each other like points upon a line. This is what we call clock time—time as measured by chronometers and calendars. But in order to construct time as a sequence of "nows" we have to be able, Heidegger says, to understand what "now" means; and to do this we have to understand it as the moment dividing past and future—that is, we have to understand past and future together in order to understand the present. Hence, every attempt to interpret time as a sequence of present moments, sliding away into the past, presupposes that man already stands beyond himself in one of the three *ek-stases* of time. His existence is thus a field spread out over time as it is over space; his temporality is a basic fact of this existence, one that underlies all his chronometrical measurements of time. Clocks are useful to man only because his existence is rooted in a prior kind of temporality.

Heidegger's theory of time is novel, in that, unlike earlier philosophers with their "nows," he gives priority to the future tense. The future, according to him, is primary because it is the region toward which man projects and in which he defines his own being. "Man never is, but always is to be," to alter slightly the famous line of Pope. Man looks ever forward, toward the open region of the future, and in so looking he takes upon himself the burden of the past (or of what out of the past he selects as his inheritance) and thereby orients himself in a certain way to his present and actual situation in life.

Here time reveals itself for Heidegger as being essentially historical. We are not born at some moment in general, but at *that* particular moment in that particular milieu and in entering the world we also enter, however humbly, into its historical destiny. The more concretely and humanly we grasp the temporal roots of human existence, the more clearly we see that this existence is in and of itself, through and through, historical. As temporality is to time, so is historicity to history; as we make clocks to measure time because our being is essentially temporal, so man writes histories or makes history by his actions because his very being is historical. Heidegger here corrects the historicism of thinkers like Hegel or Marx, to whom man is an historical creature because he takes part in the vast historical process of the world. World history, for Hegel and Marx, is like a mighty river that carries individuals and nations in its flow. But this meaning of history, says Heidegger, really derives from the more basic sense in which man is temporal simply through being a creature whose very existence stands temporally open. Man is an historical creature, true; but not merely because he wears such-and-such clothes at a given period, has such-and-such "historical" customs, or is decisively shaped by the class conflicts of his time. All these things derive their significance from a more basic fact: *namely, that man is the being who, however dimly and half-consciously, always understands, and must understand, his own being historically.*

And a thinker like Heidegger? He too—and indeed he more than all men, if his thought is to be rooted and not rootless—has to understand himself historically. He has to see his own thought as an historical undertaking, an act that projects a certain future and scrupulously relates itself to the whole tradition in which his thinking takes place. More than any other contemporary thinker Heidegger seeks to relate his thought to the history of Western thought and not in an external and merely scholarly sense, but as an event transpiring within that history. Therein his thinking shows itself to be more essentially historical than the thought of any formal historian of philosophy. The final summation of his philosophy has in fact to be given now in terms of the perspective in which it places the whole history of Western thought—and more than thought, the history of the very Being of the West.

This perspective is outlined for us most sharply in two brief but extremely significant essays, *Plato's Theory of Truth* (1942) and *On the Nature of Truth* (1943), and especially in the first of these. Here we come back inevitably to the problem of truth, for that is central to Heidegger's philosophy, as neither time, history, care, anxiety, death, nor any of the other dramatic matters that have caught the attention of critics are. The decision about truth is crucial for Heidegger because it is the decision about the meaning of Being, and hence the pivot on which the history of men and of whole civilizations turns.

The history of Being (for the West), Heidegger says, begins with the fall of Being. In this respect, his view is parallel with the Biblical view which takes Adam's fall to be the beginning of all human history. The fall of Being, for Heidegger, occurred when the Greek thinkers detached things as clear and distinct forms from their encompassing background, in order that they might reckon clearly with them. The terms used in Gestalt psychology—figure and ground—may be helpful here: By detaching the figure from the ground the object could be made to emerge into the daylight of human consciousness; but the sense of the ground, the environing background, could also be lost. The figure comes into sharper focus, that is, but the ground recedes, becomes invisible, is forgotten. The Greeks detached beings from the vast environing ground of Being. This act of detachment was accompanied by a momentous shift in the meaning of truth for the Greeks, a shift which Heidegger pinpoints as taking place in a single passage in Plato's *Republic*, the celebrated allegory of the cave. The quality of *a-letheia, un-hiddenness,* had been considered the mark of truth; but with Plato in that passage truth came to be defined, rather, as the correctness of an intellectual judgment. Truth henceforth resided in the human intellect insofar as that intellect judged truly about things. By adopting this meaning of truth as the primary and essential one, the

Greeks were able to develop science, the unique and distinguishing characteristic of Western civilization.

None of the Oriental civilizations had effected a similar detachment of beings from Being. Though Heidegger makes no reference to these Oriental civilizations—he always takes his data from the West, even while trying to think beyond it—we, in placing his thought, cannot fail to refer to them. In neither India nor China, nor in the philosophies that these civilizations produced, was truth located in the intellect. On the contrary, the Indian and Chinese sages insisted on the very opposite: namely, that man does not attain to truth so long as he remains locked up in his intellect; a man who located his truth in the mind would have struck these sages not merely as mistaken, but as a human psychological aberration. The great historical parting of the ways between Western and Eastern man came about because each made a different decision as to what truth is.

(This should not be interpreted, however—as some of our more glib Orientalizers do interpret it—in any superficial sense as an error into which the West strayed, one which might have been corrected by the exercise of a little more wisdom. History has to be seen as somewhat more fateful than that. The project—to use the word in Heidegger's sense —of the Greeks of defining truth in a certain way was essentially finite like all human projects, and therefore carried within itself its own negative. We cannot define ourselves without negating the alternatives that we do *not* become. If the Greeks had not detached objects from their enveloping ground of Being, what we know as the Western intellect would not have come into existence. The lack of this intellect is the negative, the shadow, in the historical project of the Oriental civilizations. Every light has its shadow.)

The Greeks, however, did not themselves become subjectivists in the modern sense. They philosophized in the market place, in the open air, and they were still close enough to Being, which their thinking had just begun to forget. It remained for modern science, at the beginning of our epoch, to effect a sharper division between man and nature; and the thought of Descartes is the expression of this cleavage. The object which has been detached from the enveloping ground of Being can be measured and calculated, but the essence of this object—the thing-in-itself—becomes more and more remote from man. The subject becomes conscious of himself as cut off from the object even as his power to manipulate the object mounts almost unbelievably. The word "object" is itself instructive here: it is from the Latin *ob-jectum*, that which is thrown or put before—hence, an obstacle that has to be conquered, manipulated, transformed. Man masters beings, but Being—the open region in which both subject and object stand out and are thus not divided—is forgotten. There is left to man nothing but his Will to Power over objects; and Heidegger is right when he says that Nietzsche is in this respect the culmination of Western metaphysics, which metaphysics in turn culminates in the situation of the world today where power rides supreme.

Heidegger here is talking about one of the most pervasive attitudes in the world today, one which shows itself in our fantastic passion for the organization of life in every area. The businessman who flies to the country for a week-end, is whisked off to golf, tennis, sailing, entertains his guests successfully, all on split-second schedule, and at the end of the week-end flies back to the city, but without once having had the occasion or the desire to lose himself walking down a country lane—such a man, we say, is marvelously organized and really knows how to manage things. And, to be sure, he does show an admirable mastery over things; over beings but not Being, with which he never comes in contact. To lose oneself walking down a country lane is, literally, to lose the self that is split off from nature: to enter the region of Being where subject and object no longer confront each other in murderous division. The relation of the poet to Being is not the relation of the busy man of power to beings. The latter goes to the country and returns, but without ever really *being* there. The man of today, technological man, is the final descendant of Cartesian man, but without Descartes' passion for clear and distinct ideas. As Descartes, locked up in his own luminous ego, confronted a world of material objects as thoroughly alien and perhaps unknowable, so technological man faces the objects in his world with no need or capacity for intimacy with them beyond the knowledge of what button has to be pressed in order to control their working.

And it should also be clear by now what Heidegger's final answer to Nietzsche is: it is that Western man has got to fetch Being back from the oblivion into which it has fallen. Man must learn to let Being be, instead of twisting and dislocating it to make it yield up answers to our need for power. A simple example of such twisting occurs in the case of art. Nietzsche, in his compulsion to erect a system, had included even the artist under the Will to Power: Art is the discharge of the artist's vitality and power, he said, and the experience of great art in turn enhances this vitality and power in us. André Malraux in his long essay on the psychology and history of art, *The Voices of Silence*, has given recently the most eloquent expression to this Nietzschean position. Malraux's book abounds in metaphors of struggle, conquest, victory; the world's art is seen as an imaginary museum of images that represents, in perfect Nietzschean style, man's victory over Nothingness. Malraux, a supremely typical figure of the nervousness of our times, is consumed by the Nietzschean demon of the Will to Power. But do all of his military metaphors show us the other side of art? Do they convey to us that the artist, as well as the spectator, must submit patiently and passively to the artistic process, that he must lie in wait for the image to produce itself; that he produces false notes as soon as he tries to force anything; that, in short, he must let the truth of his art happen to him? All of these points are part of what Heidegger means by our letting Being be. Letting it be, the artist lets it speak to him and through him; and so too the thinker must let it be thought.

In thus counseling passivity as against activity—the words are not too precise, but they will do for the moment—Heidegger seems to be directing us once more toward the Orient. When he repeats over and over that the tradition of the West begins with the forgetting of Being, that this

tradition has come to its completion in a dead end, and
that we have now in our thinking to go beyond it to the
source from which it sprang, one is forced to think of the
other great civilization of mankind that arose in the East.
Certainly, there are distinct points of correspondence between Heidegger's thought and that of the East. Western
metaphysics, before Heidegger, had never thought out the
nature of non-Being, but Buddhist metaphysics had; and
Chinese Taoism accepts cheerfully the necessary complementarity of Being and non-Being, where the Western mind
recoils from this with its scandalized cry of "nihilism." Says
Lao-tse:

Thirty spokes unite in one nave,
And because of the part where nothing exists we have
            the use of a carriage wheel.
Clay is molded into vessels,
And because of the space where nothing exists we are able
            to use them as vessels.
Doors and windows are cut out in the walls of a house,
And because they are empty spaces, we are able to use
            them.
Therefore, on the one hand we have the benefit of existence,
            and on the other of non-existence.

I even venture to think that the nearest thing to Heidegger's
notion of Being that we find in the past may be the *Tao*
of Chinese philosophy. But such suggestions prove nothing,
for Heidegger, as we have seen, stays resolutely within the
tradition of the West while thinking beyond it. He is probably right to do so. Aside from the difficulty of the Eastern
languages—and Heidegger proves abundantly that we cannot understand Greek or Latin philosophy apart from the
words in which they were uttered—we cannot even be sure
that we understand the experience out of which Eastern
philosophies grew: it is still too remote from us. If Western
thought moves beyond its present impasse, it may very well
be through orientalizing itself, but what results will be
something very different from anything the Orient knew.

"But what *is* Being?" I imagine the reader asking in perplexity, now that I have given at least the outlines of Heidegger's thought. "We still haven't been told about that." We like the compact formulae that tell us clearly what a thing is. A triangle is a plane figure bounded by three straight lines—well then, we know what a triangle is. We want a concept to go by, and a concept is a representation, or picture, of the thing. But Being, unlike a triangle, is something of which we can have no mental picture or representation. We reach it by a kind of thought other than conceptual reason. "Think" and "thank" are kindred roots, and the German word *an-denken*—literally, "to think on"—means to remember; hence, for Heidegger, think, thank, and remember are kindred notions. Real thinking, thinking that is rooted in Being, is at once an act of thanking and remembrance. When a dear friend says, in parting, "Think of me!" this does not mean "Have a mental picture of me!" but: "Let me (even in my absence) be present with you." So too we must think of Being by letting it be present to us even though we can have no mental picture of it. Being is indeed just this presence, invisible and all-pervasive, which cannot be enclosed in any mental concept. To think it is to thank it, to remember it with gratitude, for our human existence is ultimately rooted in it. And if, just because we cannot represent it in any mental concept, we choose to forget it, then all our human and humanistic enterprises are threatened with the void, since our existence itself would thereby be torn from its root.

Heidegger has not told us in so many words what Being is; but anyone who has read his text through has from it a concrete sense of Being quite different from anything that our philosophic tradition has so far brought to light. One has, from a book like *Being and Time*, a sense of man as a creature transparent and open to Being in every nerve and fiber of his life; and this perhaps is as clear a sense of Being, the unutterable, as any thinker in the West has yet given us. Indeed, that book is so charged and compact, in its analysis of human existence, that the few points from it cited above hardly suffice to give more than a sketchy idea of its real range and depth. In the years when Heidegger was writing it, during the early 1920's when he was a young professor at Marburg, he was thinking at white heat—thinking for a whole lifetime, it would seem, for the rest of his writings are largely elucidation of this monumental book.

The most frequent criticism of Heideggerian man is that he is a creature of solitude rather than community, that his authentic existence is secured in relation to himself alone and not essentially to others. This criticism has been made by Existentialists like Jaspers, Buber, Berdyaev, Marcel—and in a somewhat different form, by Sartre too. Buber's criticism (in *Between Man and Man*) is the most forcefully put and, because Buber is enjoying something of a vogue now in the United States, is likely to be the most influential here. His criticism entirely misses the point, however, that Heideggerian man—or the authentic Heideggerian man—is related not merely to himself but to Being, and that only in virtue of the latter can this creature attain authenticity. Buber, the religious humanist, does not really see that Heidegger is concerned with Being and so is not constructing a philosophical anthropology. Man is for Heidegger merely a means of access, a gateway to the problem of Being; and such a project of thought is not likely to do justice to all the concrete facets of man's existence, psychological and social. Heidegger does not philosophize humanly (he calls it existentielly) as do Jaspers and Buber, who are rather like lyricists of existence, seeking to awaken authentic existence in their hearers. Heidegger is a thinker, no more and no less; and the project that is his life is an austere and somber meditation upon Being.

Still, although formally speaking Buber's objections are beside the point, this old rabbi has wonderful instincts and he has sniffed out where the trouble really lies: namely in that obscure region where the thinker and the man meet and are one. Heidegger seeks only to be a thinker; and as such, he towers above men like Jaspers and Buber: to put it in blunt American, as thinkers they are not even in the same league with Heidegger. But being a thinker (even in the exalted sense in which Heidegger is one) is not enough for being a man. If thinking could give us back our roots, Heidegger's thought would do that, since no thinker has ever been so rooted in the everyday; but it clearly does not. He has led us back, as has no other thinker, to see what is involved in light and vision, but we need to go one step farther and see that all light requires fire. After Heidegger, we feel the need of a new Kierkegaard to pump back living blood into the ontological skeleton of the Heideggerian *Dasein.*

Kierkegaard as against Heidegger—that is the essential opposition to which criticism like Buber's returns us. And the opposition turns, as Heidegger would wish it to, on the two men's varying notions of truth: it lying for Kierkegaard in the ethical and religious passion of the individual, for Heidegger in Being itself, as the open region in which subject and object can be and therefore can meet, and without which there could be neither subject nor object. These two notions of truth have not yet been reconciled by existential philosophy—that is a task for the future. But must not the quest for Being, as the Orient held, be one and the same with the individual's burning thirst for personal salvation? Is not thinking itself incomplete until it unites these—or, rather, ceases to divide them? Does not the Greek word for truth, *a-letheia,* of which Heidegger makes so much, derive after all from the more concrete adjective, *alethes*—meaning, as applied to the individual, a man who is true, open, sincere? Truth comes to be, in short, only with the *man* who is true.

Heidegger is far closer in spirit to Nietzsche than he is to Kierkegaard; and his thinking, though much more in control, breathes the icy superhuman air of solitude of *Zarathustra.* It is no accident that Heidegger finds such an affinity with Hölderlin—the great poet of a loneliness so intense that he too, like Nietzsche, drifted off into schizophrenia. Heidegger acquiesces too calmly in the "death of God." If he has really experienced it, we feel, then his thought should be more tormented—or, on the other hand, more cheerful, since he has survived that death. Hölderlin

and Nietzsche were the great poets of this death of God;
Heidegger has not succumbed to their dire fate—perhaps
because he is not a poet, as Kierkegaard might have put
it, but only a professor.

Nevertheless, German professors are marvelous beings.
Over a century ago there was a German professor named
Hegel whose thought might have looked to an ordinary observer like the veriest academic woolgathering, of no interest to anyone except other professional woolgatherers
And yet, Hegel's thought went far and wide outside the
walls of the Academy and in the end begot Marx and Com
munism. Heidegger may prove equally influential. Already
he is recasting our whole perspective on Western history
the history textbooks of the future may be built on his idea;
of historicity, as in the last few generations they were buil;
on Hegel's. And Finitism is already beginning to triumph
in modern mathematics. In bringing non-Being, or Noth
ingness, into thought. Heidegger points up the possibility
that the West may at long last face the problem of nihilism
without either scandalized rhetoric or complacent self-
deception. And his thought has already touched the world
outside the Academy, since through Sartre he was the prime
mover in French Existentialism. Although in this case, as
we shall see, the child did not remain very true to its parent.

SARTRE

Chapter Ten

WE MAY as well begin with Sartre in a moment of heroism. Much in his writings is distinctly unheroic in nature, but the note of heroism does sound, and here it is in *The Republic of Silence*, where Sartre is describing the life of the French Resistance from 1940 to 1945:

> We were never more free than during the German occupation. We had lost all our rights, beginning with the right to talk. Every day we were insulted to our faces and had to take it in silence. Under one pretext or another, as workers, Jews, or political prisoners, we were deported *en masse*. Everywhere, on billboards, in the newspapers, on the screen, we encountered the revolting and insipid picture of ourselves that our suppressors wanted us to accept. And because of all this we were free. Because the Nazi venom seeped into our thoughts, every accurate thought was a conquest. Because an all-powerful police tried to force us to hold our tongues, every word took on the value of a declaration of principles. Because we were hunted down, every one of our gestures had the weight of a solemn commitment. . . .
>
> Exile, captivity, and especially death (which we usually shrink from facing at all in happier days) became for us the habitual objects of our concern. We learned that they were neither inevitable accidents, nor even constant and inevitable dangers, but they must be considered as our lot itself, our destiny, the profound source of our

reality as men. At every instant we lived up to the full
sense of this commonplace little phrase: "Man is mortal!"
And the choice that each of us made of his life was an
authentic choice because it was made face to face with
death, because it could always have been expressed in
these terms: "Rather death than . . ." And here I am not
speaking of the elite among us who were real Resistants,
but of all Frenchmen who, at every hour of the night and
day throughout four years, answered *No*.

And a few years later (1947), in his *What is Literature?*
he draws another philosophic conclusion from this experience:

> We have been taught to take Evil seriously. It is nei-
> ther our fault nor our merit if we lived in a time when
> torture was a daily fact. Chateaubriand, Oradour, the
> Rue des Saussaies, Dachau, and Auschwitz have all dem-
> onstrated to us that Evil is not an appearance, that know-
> ing its cause does not dispel it, that it is not opposed to
> Good as a confused idea is to a clear one, that it is not
> the effect of passions which might be cured, of a fear
> which might be overcome, of a passing aberration which
> might be excused, of an ignorance which might be en-
> lightened, that it can in no way be diverted, brought
> back, reduced, and incorporated into idealistic human-
> ism, like that shade of which Leibnitz has written that
> it is necessary for the glare of daylight. . . .
>
> Perhaps a day will come when a happy age, looking
> back at the past, will see in this suffering and shame one
> of the paths which led to peace. But we are not on the
> side of history already made. We were, as I have said,
> *situated* in such a way that every lived minute seemed
> to us like something irreducible. Therefore, in spite of
> ourselves, we came to this conclusion, which will seem
> shocking to lofty souls: Evil cannot be redeemed.

It is necessary to emphasize passages like these for American readers who wish to understand Sartre, because Americans have not yet comprehended what the French have

lived through: that we have at last arrived at "the age of
assassins" which the poet Rimbaud predicted. Sartre came
to maturity during the 1930's. The atmosphere of Leftist
politics was over everything, and Sartre has never ceased
politically to be on the Left. But over France also was the
stale and tired atmosphere of a world already doomed to
defeat: The Popular Front government of Léon Blum
drifted, nerveless and flaccid, incapable of meeting the crisis
of the times; the French bourgeoisie hung on, entrenched
and petty, unable even to conceive the possibility of any
great action. "*Les salauds*" became a potent term for Sartre
in those days—the *salauds*, the stinkers, the stuffy and self-
righteous people congealed in the insincerity of their virtues
and vices. This atmosphere of decay breathes through
Sartre's first novel, *Nausea*, and it is no accident that the
quotation on the flyleaf is from Céline, the poet of the abyss,
of the nihilism and disgust of that period. The nausea in
Sartre's book is the nausea of existence itself; and to those
who are ready to use this as an excuse for tossing out the
whole of Sartrian philosophy, we may point out that it is
better to encounter one's existence in disgust than never to
encounter it at all—as the *salaud* in his academic or bourgeois or party-leader strait jacket never does. The Resistance came to Sartre and his generation as a release from
disgust into heroism. It was a call to action, an action that
brought men to the very limits of their being, and in hearing this call man himself was not found wanting. He could
even rediscover his own irreducible liberty in saying No to
the overpowering might of the occupying forces.

The essential freedom, the ultimate and final freedom
that cannot be taken from a man, is to say No. This is the
basic premise in Sartre's view of human freedom: freedom
is in its very essence negative, though this negativity is also
creative. At a certain moment, perhaps, the drug or the pain
inflicted by the torturer may make the victim lose consciousness, and he will confess. But so long as he retains the
lucidity of consciousness, however tiny the area of action
possible for him, he can still say in his own mind: No. Consciousness and freedom are thus given together. Only if

consciousness is blotted out can man be deprived of this residual freedom. Where all the avenues of action are blocked for a man, this freedom may seem a tiny and unimportant thing; but it is in fact total and absolute, and Sartre is right to insist upon it as such, for it affords man his final dignity, that of being man.

The experience of this freedom is not so new in philosophy as it might seem. It is this kind of freedom, in fact, that accompanied Descartes throughout the course of his famous Systematic Doubt, in which he proposed to say *No* to every belief, no matter how plausible, so long as he saw a possibility of doubting it. For the young and brilliant Sartre, teaching philosophy before the Second World War, Descartes was a special hero—a hero of thought if not of the life of action. The experience of the Resistance gave the figure of Descartes even greater importance for Sartre, since in the Resistance Cartesianism could be incarnated in the life of action. As Descartes proposed to say No to that imaginary demon who might seduce him into assenting to a proposition that was not altogether clear and indubitable, though everything in society and nature around him also urged him to assent, so the Resistant could say No to the might of the Occupation.

Sartre is a Cartesian who has read Proust and Heidegger, and whose psychological explorations of man go far beyond those of the seventeenth-century philosopher; more important still, he is a Cartesian who has experienced war and terror in the modern world and who is therefore situated historically in an altogether different relation to the world. But a Cartesian he is, nonetheless, as perhaps no Frenchman—or no French thinker—can help being when the chips are really down. Descartes and the French Resistance— Descartes *in* the French Resistance—these are the simple keys to the whole of Sartre's apparently complicated and involved philosophy.

To see this clearly we need only go back to Descartes at a certain moment in his Systematic Doubt. He proposes to reject all beliefs so long as they can in any way be doubted, to *resist* all temptations to say Yes until his understanding

is convinced according to its own light; so he rejects belief
in the existence of an external world, of minds other than
his own, of his own body, of his memories and sensations.
What he cannot doubt is his own consciousness, for to
doubt is to be conscious, and therefore by doubting its existence he would affirm it. In the dark void in which Des
cartes hovered there shone only the light of his own mind
But before this certitude shone for him (and even after it
before he passed on to other truths), he was a nothingness
a negativity, existing outside of nature and history, for he
had temporarily abolished all belief in a world of bodies
and memories. Thus man cannot be interpreted, Sartre says,
as a solid substantial thing existing amid the plenitude of
things that make up a world; he is beyond nature because
in his negative capability he transcends it. Man's freedom
is to say No, and this means that he is the being by whom
nothingness comes into being. He is able to suspend all of
nature and history in doubt, to bracket it against the back-
drop of nothingness before which the Cartesian doubter
hovers. Sartre here merely draws conclusions from what is
existentially implicit in the Cartesian doubt.

Descartes, of course, was a good Christian and a Catholic, and as a practical matter he had no intention of im-
periling his immortal soul by placing his religious faith in
doubt while he was performing his intellectual gyrations
in the void. As a canny and sagacious Frenchman, he proposed to abide by the customs of his time and place (which
included the practice of religion). Hence, when he launched
himself into the Doubt, he made certain of securing his
lines of communication behind him; he took no chances
when he made the descent into the painful night of the
void. The next step after the certitude of the *Cogito*, the
"I think," thus turns out to be a proof of the existence of
God; and with God as guarantee the whole world of na
ture, the multitude of things with their fixed nature or es
sences that the mind may now know, is re-established
around Descartes. Sartre, however, is the Cartesian doubte
at a different place and time: God is dead, and no longe
guarantees to this passionate and principled atheist that

vast structure of essences, the world, to which his freedom
must give assent. As a modern man, Sartre remains in that
anguish of nothingness in which Descartes floated before
the miraculous light of God shone to lead him out of it.
For Sartre there is no unalterable structure of essences or
values given prior to man's own existence. That existence
has meaning, finally, only as the liberty to say No, and by
saying No to create a world. If we remove God from the
picture, the liberty which reveals itself in the Cartesian
doubt is total and absolute; but thereby also the more an-
guished, and this anguish is the irreducible destiny and dignity of man. Here Cartesianism has become more heroic—
and more demoniacal.

Thus Sartre ends by allotting to man the kind of freedom
that Descartes has ascribed only to God. It is, he says, the
freedom Descartes secretly would have given to man had
he not been limited by the theological convictions of his
time and place. Descartes' God derives from the absolutely
free God of Duns Scotus rather than from the God of St.
Thomas Aquinas, who is bound by the laws of logic. This
Cartesian God, says Sartre, is the freest God that man ever
invented. He is not subordinate to a realm of essences:
rather, He creates essences and causes them to be what
they are. Hence such a God transcends the laws of logic
and mathematics. As His existence precedes all essences, so
man's existence precedes *his* essence; he exists, and out of
the free project which his existence can be he makes himself what he is. When God dies, man takes the place of
God. Such had been the prophecy of Dostoevski and Nietzsche, and Sartre on this point is their heir. The difference,
however, is that Dostoevski and Nietzsche were frenzied
prophets, whereas Sartre advances his view with all the
lucidity of Cartesian reason and advances it, moreover, as
a basis for humanitarian and democratic social action. To
put man in the place of God may seem, to traditionalists,
an unspeakable piece of diabolism; but in Sartre's case it is
done by a thinker who, to judge from his writings, is a man
of overwhelming good will and generosity.

1. BEING-FOR-ITSELF AND
BEING-IN-ITSELF

Sartre's philosophy is based on a dualism which, if not
Cartesian to the letter, is certainly Cartesian in spirit. Being, says Sartre, is divided into two fundamental kinds: (1)
Being-in-itself and (2) *Being-for-itself*. *Being-in-itself* (Sartre's *en-soi*) is the self-contained being of a thing. A stone
is a stone; it is what it is; and in being just what it is, no
more and no less, the being of the thing always coincides
with itself. *Being-for-itself* (*pour-soi*) is coextensive with
the realm of consciousness, and the nature of consciousness
is that it is perpetually beyond itself. Our thought goes beyond itself, toward tomorrow or yesterday, and toward the
outer edges of the world. Human existence is thus a perpetual self-transcendence: in existing we are always beyond
ourselves. Consequently we never possess our being as we
possess a thing. Our existence from moment to moment is a
perpetual flying beyond ourselves, or else a perpetual falling behind our own possibilities; in any case, our being
never exactly coincides with itself. It could do so only if we
sank into the self-contained form of the being of a thing,
and this would be possible only if we ceased to be conscious.

This notion of the For-itself may seem obscure, but we
encounter it on the most ordinary occasions. I have been to
a party; I come away, and with a momentary pang of sadness I say, "I am not myself." It is necessary to take this
proposition quite literally as something that only man can
say of himself, because only man can say it *to* himself. I
have the feeling of coming to myself after having lost or
mislaid my being momentarily in a social encounter that
estranged me from myself. This is the first and immediate
level on which the term yields its meaning. But the next
and deeper level of meaning occurs when the feeling of sadness leads me to think in a spirit of self-reproach that I am
not myself in a still more fundamental sense: I have not
realized so many of the plans or projects that make up my
being; I am not myself because I do not measure up to

myself. Beneath this level too there is still another and deeper meaning, rooted in the very nature of my being: I am not myself, and I can never be myself, because my being stretching out beyond itself at any given moment exceeds itself. I am always simultaneously more and less than I am.

Herein lies the fundamental uneasiness, or anxiety, of the human condition, for Sartre. Because we are perpetually flitting beyond ourselves, or falling behind our possibilities, we seek to ground our existence, to make it more secure. In seeking for security we seek to give our existence the self-contained being of a thing. The For-itself struggles to become the In-itself, to attain the rocklike and unshakable solidity of a thing. But this it can never do so long as it is conscious and alive. Man is doomed to the radical insecurity and contingency of his being; for without it he would not be man but merely a thing and would not have the human capacity for transcendence of his given situation. There is a curious dialectical interplay here: that which constitutes man's power and glory, that which lies at the very heart of his power to be lord over things, namely his capacity to transcend himself and his immediate situation, is at one and the same time that which causes the fragility, the wavering and flight, the anguish of our human lot.

With enormous ingenuity and virtuosity Sartre interweaves these two notions—Being-in-itself and Being-for-itself—to elucidate the complexities of human psychology. The principal work in which he does this is *L'être et le néant* (*Being and Nothingness*), a great, uneven, brilliant and verbose tome which he worked on during the Resistance and which appeared in 1944. Sartre's debt to Heidegger is great, but his own originality is unquestionable. He is one of the most brilliant minds alive—sometimes we feel too brilliant, for the greatest mind needs a little saving streak of earth-bound stupidity somewhere, so the feet can be planted mulishly on the soil of some unshakable fact. Sartre has learned all the dialectical tricks of Hegel, and he can trot them out as he chooses with a virtuosity that is at times excessive. It is a use of Hegel's means toward an existential rather than an idealistic end, of course, for Sartre

can never go the way of Hegel: he believes, in opposition
to the idealist, that Evil is real and cannot be redeemed,
that the negative can never be sublimated in the pure positive being of the Absolute. Dachau and Belsen have taught
him that. Where Sartre goes beyond Heidegger is in giving
a more detailed elaboration of the negative side of human
existence. For Heidegger the essentially temporal being of
man is pervaded by the negatives of the *not*-yet and *no*-
longer; but Sartre does much more with this, nosing out all
the sordid and seedy strands of nothingness that haunt our
human condition like a bad breath or body odor. Never in
the thought of the West has the Self been so pervaded by
negation. One would have to go to the East, to the Buddhist philosopher Nagarjuna (*circa* 200 A.D.), with his
doctrine of *Anatman,* the insubstantiality of the Self, to
meet as awesome a list of negations as Sartre draws up.
The Self, indeed, is in Sartre's treatment, as in Buddhism,
a bubble, and a bubble has nothing at its center.

But neither in Buddhism nor in Sartre is the Self riddled
with negations to the end that we should, humanly speaking, collapse into the negative, into a purely passive nihilism. In Buddhism the recognition of the nothingness of ourselves is intended to lead into a striving for holiness and
compassion—the recognition that in the end there is nothing
that sustains us should lead us to love one another, as sur-
vivors on a life raft, at the moment they grasp that the
ocean is shoreless and that no rescue ship is coming, can
only have compassion on one another. For Sartre, on the
other hand, the nothingness of the Self is the basis for the
will to action: the bubble is empty and will collapse, and
so what is left us but the energy and passion to spin that
bubble out? Man's existence is absurd in the midst of a
cosmos that knows him not; the only meaning he can give
himself is through the free project that he launches out of
his own nothingness. Sartre turns from nothingness not to
compassion or holiness, but to human freedom as realized
in revolutionary activity. In this final appeal to the will to
action there is a secret kinship with Nietzsche; and nothing
justifies more fully Heidegger's contention that Nietzsche is

the secret master of Western metaphysics in its final stage than the way in which Sartre's thinking comes around in the end to join Nietzsche's.

However great his initial dependence upon Heidegger, Sartre's philosophy moves finally in an altogether opposite direction. He misses the very root of all of Heidegger's thinking, which is Being itself. There is, in Sartre, Being-for-itself and Being-in-itself but there is no Being. How can the For-itself and In-itself meet unless both stand out in the open space of Being? We have here, in Sartre, the world cleft once again into the Cartesian dualism of subject and object, the world of consciousness and the world of things. Sartre has advanced as the fundamental thesis of his Existentialism the proposition that existence precedes essence. This thesis is true for Heidegger as well, in the historical, social, and biographical sense that man comes into existence and makes himself to be what he is. But for Heidegger another proposition is even more basic than this: namely, Being precedes existence. For without the open clearing of Being into which man can transcend himself, he could not ex-sist, i.e., stand out beyond himself. Man can make himself be what he is only because all his projects are revealed to him as taking place within the open field or region of Being. This is why Heidegger has declared, "I am not an Existentialist"—because the Existentialists of the Sartrian school do not grasp this priority of Being, and so their thinking remains, like that of Descartes, locked up in the human subject.

To be sure, Sartre has gone a considerable step beyond Descartes by making the essence of human consciousness to be transcendence: that is, to be conscious is, immediately and as such, to point beyond that isolated act of consciousness and therefore to be beyond or above it. Descartes, at the extreme point of his thought, had envisaged consciousness as absolutely enclosed in itself, with the world of external objects shut out, and all the past and future suspended. But this step forward by Sartre is not so considerable if the transcending subject has nowhere to transcend himself: if there is not an open field or region of Being in which the fateful dualism of subject and object ceases to be. Modern philosophy from Descartes onward has asked itself the question: How can the subject really know the object? By the time of Kant (and despite all the advances in physical knowledge since Descartes) the human mind felt itself so estranged from nature that Kant's answer was that the subject can never know the object-in-itself. And from there it is but a short step to Nietzsche, who declares that knowledge of the object-in-itself is unnecessary—all we need is to be able to master it, and hence the Will to Power becomes primary. (In Sartre what becomes primary is rather the will to action.)

Now, Heidegger's reversal of this development in modern philosophy is radical and goes to the root of the matter; and I do not think Sartre has seen this aspect of Heidegger's thought. For what Heidegger proposes is a more basic question than that of Descartes and Kant: namely, how is it possible for the subject to *be*? and for the object to *be*? And his answer is: Because both stand out in the truth, or un-hiddenness, of Being. This notion of the truth of Being is absent from the philosophy of Sartre; indeed, nowhere in his vast *Being and Nothingness* does he deal with the problem of truth in a radical and existential way: so far as he understands truth at all, he takes it in the ordinary intellectualistic sense that has been traditional with non-existential philosophers. In the end (as well as at his very beginning) Sartre turns out thus to be a Cartesian rationalist—one, to be sure, whose material is impassioned and existential, but for all that not any the less a Cartesian in his ultimate dualism between the For-itself and the In-itself. And the curious irony about this is that Sartre, whose name the general public has come to take as synonymous with Existentialism, is the one existential philosopher who does not deal with the prime question that has been the central passion of nearly all the Existentialists—the question, namely, of a truth for man that is more than a truth of the intellect.

It is altogether consistent therefore that Sartre should advertise his brand of Existentialism to the public as a new humanism. Like every humanism, it teaches that the proper study of mankind is man, or, as Marx put it, that the root of mankind is man. But, again like every humanism, it leaves unasked the question: What is the root of man? In this search for roots for man—a search that has, as we have seen, absorbed thinkers and caused the malaise of poets for the last hundred and fifty years—Sartre does not participate. He leaves man rootless. This may be because Sartre himself is the quintessence of the urban intellectual—perhaps the most brilliant urban intellectual of our time, but still with the inevitable alienation of this type. He seems to breathe the air of the modern city, of its cafés, faubourgs, and streets, as if there were no other home for man.

2. LITERATURE AS A MODE OF ACTION

Such too is the impression with which his more strictly literary works leave us. It is a paradox that although the Existentialists have often been accused of really being literary men or poets rather than philosophers (in the strict academic sense), Sartre, the one Existentialist who has fulfilled himself as a literary man, pouring out novels, plays, and literary essays, and who indeed earns his living now as a professional writer, is in his philosophy the most intellectualistic of all the Existentialists. The fact is that despite Sartre's enormous strictly literary output, men like Kierkegaard and Nietzsche had more of the artist in them. They were poets, and not only is there nothing of the poet in Sartre, but he even shows little real feeling for poetry when he talks about it. His conception of literature is a thoroughly intellectual one: in his *What is Literature* (1947), a long and brilliant essay in critical theory, he develops the fundamental view that literature is a mode of action, an act of the writer's freedom that seeks to appeal to the freedom of other individuals and eventually to the total free collective of mankind. Stripped of its metaphysical language, his theory leads him to espouse a kind of social realism in literature. Thus the greatest living writer, he tells us, is John Dos Passos. Such a judgment is rather shocking

as evidence of Sartre's literary taste—or lack of it. But the
philosopher is really responding to the *idea* of Dos Passos'
fiction, not to the novels as works of art. Dos Passos is, for
Sartre, the perfect example of what he believes a writer
should do and what he himself tries to do in his own later
fiction: that is, grapple with the problems of man in his
time and milieu. Sartre's novels are a technically dazzling,
streamlined variety of social realism. It is always to the
idea, and particularly the idea as it leads to social action,
that Sartre responds. Hence he cannot do justice, either in
his critical theory or in his actual practice of literary criticism, to poetry, which is precisely that form of human expression in which the poet—and the reader who would enter the poet's world—must let Being be, to use Heidegger's
phrase, and not attempt to coerce it by the will to action
or the will to intellectualization. The absence of the poet
in Sartre, as a literary man, is thus another evidence of
what, on the philosophical level, leads to a deficiency in
his theory of Being.

Sartre is a writer of very powerful gifts, nevertheless,
who succeeds in his effects whenever the idea itself is able
to generate artistic passion and life. His first novel, *Nausea*
(1938), may well be his best book for the very reason that
in it the intellectual and the creative artist come closest to
being joined. Much as ideas and the elaboration of ideas
figure in the book, the author has not shirked the novelist's
tasks, and the remarkable thing is the life with which the
ideas are invested, which forms the intimate texture of the
hero's experience and sensibility. The mood of this life is
disgust, which can as well as any other mood become the
occasion of discovery, a radical plunge into one's own existence. It is authentically human, this disgust, and turns
out to be novelistically exciting, though it has nothing like
the grand scope and implications of Céline's disgust. Sartre's treatment is more self-conscious and more subtle,
philosophically, but also more static; his disgust is not embodied, as Céline's is, in the desperate picaresque of common life and the anonymous depths of street characters.
Nausea is not so much a full novel as an extraordinary frag-

ment of one. In his later fiction Sartre has turned away from the narrow and intense form of the early book to a broader panorama, and not always with entirely happy results.

These later novels—originally a trilogy, *Les Chemins de la Liberté* (*The Roads to Liberty*) and now a tetralogy—may go on being issued as endlessly as the *roman fleuve* of Jules Romains, if Sartre's volcanic activity as a writer continues. One does wish that Sartre would pause for a while and regroup his forces. The man really writes too much. Perhaps if literature becomes a mode of action one gets so caught up in it that one cannot stop the action. These later novels of his contain remarkable things—great scenes and passages—and their theme is the central Sartrian one of the search for liberty, or rather for the realization in life of that liberty that we always and essentially are, sometimes even in spite of ourselves. Yet they are so uneven in achievement, one regrets to see Sartre's great talents wandering and thinning out like spilt milk.

Of his plays too, it may be said that his two earlier and shorter ones—*Les Mouches* (*The Flies*) and *Huis Clos* (*No Exit*)—are his best. They are at any rate the things to recommend to the reader who wishes to get the concrete drift of Sartre's philosophy but has no stomach for the elaborate dialectic of *Being and Nothingness*.

The Flies, first produced while the Resistance was still going on, is in form something of a set piece, since it deals with the myth of Orestes and the Furies; but it is charged throughout with a passion and eloquence born of Sartre's own personal convictions. Orestes is the spokesman for the Sartrian view of liberty. The solution of the play is not at all like that in Aeschylus, for here there are no supernatural agencies that can deliver Orestes from his guilt. He has to take that guilt upon himself, and he does so at the end of the play in a superbly defiant speech before the cosmic Gestapo chief Jupiter; he accepts his guilt, he exclaims, knowing that to do so is absurd because he is a man and therefore free. In discharging his freedom man also wills to accept the responsibility of it, thus becoming heavy with his own guilt. Conscience, Heidegger has said, is the will to be guilty—that is, to accept the guilt that we know will be ours whatever course of action we take.

No Exit, the most sensational of Sartre's dramatic successes, displays perhaps to their best advantage his real talents as a writer: the intense driving energy of the play, the passion of the ideas expressed, we can recognize as authentically his. The three characters of *No Exit* are planted in Hell; they are being punished, rather in the manner of Dante, by being given exactly the fruit of their evil itself. Having practiced "bad faith" in life—which, in Sartre's terms, is the surrendering of one's human liberty in order to possess, or try to possess, one's being as a *thing*—the three characters now have what they had sought to surrender themselves to. Having died, they cannot change anything in their past lives, which are exactly what they are, no more and no less, just like the static being of things. These three persons have no being other than that each has in the eyes of the others; they exist in each other's gaze, in fact. But this is exactly what they longed for in life—to lose their own subjective being by identifying themselves with what they were in the eyes of other people. It is a torment that people do in fact choose on earth; the bourgeois *salaud* and the anti-Semite, Sartre says, have chosen as themselves their public stance or role, and thus really exist not as free beings for themselves but as beings in the eyes of others.

Despite the excitement and intensity of *No Exit* as theater, the distinctly intellectual nature of Sartre's gifts once again reveals itself. The three characters are thinly blocked out, hardly more than single intense curves of action, illustrating the three evils of cowardice, Lesbianism, infanticide. Beyond a certain point they hold no surprises for us, they are without contingency—and this from an author who denies the existence of "character" as a fixed thing. The same is true here as we observed earlier of *Nausea:* Sartre succeeds most surely where the fusion of intellectual with creative writer is most intimate and passionate. But this is always achieved by the writer's drawing secret drafts on the philosopher's credit. As a writer Sartre is always the impassioned rhetorician of the idea; and the rhetorician, no matter how great and how eloquent his rhetoric, never has the full being of the artist. If Sartre were really a poet and an artist, we would have from him a different philosophy, as we shall see from turning back now to that philosophy.

3. AN EXISTENTIAL PSYCHOLOGY

One would expect that Being-in-itself, as the realm of self-identical objects, would be invested by Sartre with imagery suggesting stiffness and rigidity. Quite the contrary: this vast realm is associated for him with images of softness, stickiness, viscosity, corpulence, flabbiness. There is too much of it, and it is heavy, like a fat lady in the circus. In the famous episode in *Nausea* where the hero, Roquentin, discovers existence in the experience of disgust, he is looking at a chestnut tree in a provincial park: the roots are tangled and excessive; the tree itself is *de trop*, too much, excessive. Since it has no ultimate reason for existing, Being-in-itself is absurd: its existence is a kind of superfetation. Its softness has the quality of the feminine. Behind all Sartre's intellectual dialectic we perceive that the In-itself is for him the archetype of nature: excessive, fruitful, blooming nature—the woman, the female.

The For-itself, by contrast, is for Sartre the masculine aspect of human psychology: it is that in virtue of which man chooses himself in his radical liberty, makes projects, and thereby gives his life what strictly human meaning it has.

It is necessary to call attention to these feminine and masculine images that circulate in the background of Sartre's more formal concepts because in *Being and Nothingness* and certain other writings he has attempted to sketch a new and radical type of psychology. He calls it "existential psychoanalysis," and it has already caught on somewhat in Europe; a group of psychiatrists there has espoused it, and even in this country it has its professional adherents. This new type of psychoanalysis, Sartre says, will replace or at least supplement the older forms. The essence of man, according to the French thinker, lies not in the Oedipus complex (as Freud held) nor in the inferiority complex (as Adler maintained); it lies rather in the radical liberty of man's existence by which he chooses himself and so makes himself what he is. Man is not to be seen as the passive plaything of unconscious forces, which determine what he is to be. In fact, Sartre denies the existence of an unconscious mind altogether; wherever the mind manifests itself, he holds, it is conscious. A human personality or human life is not to be understood in terms of some hypothetical unconscious at work behind the scenes and pulling all the wires that manipulate the puppet of consciousness. A man *is* his life, says Sartre; which means that he is nothing more nor less than the totality of acts that make up that life. And to understand truly a man's life we have simply to grasp the structure, at once single and complex, that binds together all those overt acts—this structure being, in fact, just the unique and irreplaceable project that *is* that individual's life.

Sartre has given his theory a remarkably concrete application in a biographical study, *Baudelaire*, published here in 1950. We cannot, according to Sartre, understand Baudelaire's life—his poetry, his ideas, his quarrels—by relating all these things to his sexuality; on the contrary, the sexuality must be seen to take its place in the whole life, and indeed to take its form and direction from the total project that is that life. The choice of himself that made Baudelaire's life what it was occurred, says Sartre, when he was sent off to school as a boy and thus for the first time was separated from his mother: alienated and intimidated by his schoolfellows, he withdrew into himself, and there the choice of himself as solitary and different began. Sartre shows how this choice radiates, like the ripple from a stone, through the whole life that followed: the cultivation of the poet's mind as a mirror of his solitude; his withdrawal from the fatness and lubricity of nature in visions of a completely inorganic world, a city of metals without a single tree, etc., etc. Sartre assembles a great number of details and correlates them well, so that we are left with a powerful and unified image of Baudelaire's life. But how convincing is his picture as rendering the total truth about Baudelaire? And how convincing is this new psychoanalysis he has here put to the test?

In the first place, the choice of himself that Baudelaire is supposed to have made at around the age of twelve hardly appears to have been a conscious and resolute project, elected then and there for a whole lifetime. If it was *not* conscious, then Sartre would be forced to admit the existence of an unconscious; for if Baudelaire's life was a single project—that is, a choice of himself as the being he was to be—reflected in all the myriad details of his life, the way in which it was to be reflected was unknown to him at twelve, and therefore the project itself, as a totality, was in good part unconscious. If a human life is a concrete liberty radiating outward into all the details of our actions, some people may indeed know what their project is, what their life means, but at any one time a vast portion of this project as manifested in all our actions must be hidden from us. Sartre does not admit this, but if he did he would be compelled to take refuge in the notion of an unconscious project. In any case, the unconscious has to be reintroduced as soon as we seek to apply existential psychoanalysis concretely.

The merits of Sartre's theory as psychology we leave to the psychologists to determine; what concerns us here is the philosophic thought that lies at the root of the psychology. And once again the root is Cartesianism: the identification of mind with consciousness, with the *Cogito,* is a Cartesian identification. When Descartes said "I think, therefore I am," the statement—apart from its merely functional usage as marking a certain stage in his reasoning—was, humanly speaking, the statement of a man who identifies his own reality with his thought. The unconscious is something alien and opposite: Consciousness is a realm of clear and distinct ideas, but the world of the unconscious is the fat, formless, fructifying domain of the In-itself of nature. This latter world can be forgotten and finally denied to exist. A Cartesian subjectivity (which is what Sartre's is) *cannot* admit the existence of the unconscious because the unconscious is the Other in oneself; and the glance of the

Other, in Sartre, is always like the stare of Medusa, fearful
and petrifying.

This relation to the Other is one of the most sensational
and best-known aspects of Sartre's psychology. To the other
person, who looks at me from the outside, I seem an object,
a thing; my subjectivity with its inner freedom escapes his
gaze. Hence his tendency is always to convert me into the
object he sees. The gaze of the Other penetrates to the
depths of my existence, freezes and congeals it. It is this,
according to Sartre, that turns love and particularly sexual
love into a perpetual tension and indeed warfare. The lover
wishes to possess the beloved, but the freedom of the beloved (which is his or her human essence) cannot be possessed; hence, the lover tends to reduce the beloved to an
object for the sake of possessing it. Love is menaced always
by a perpetual oscillation between sadism and masochism:
In sadism I reduce the other to a mere lump, to be beaten
and manipulated as I choose, while in masochism I offer
myself as an object, but in an attempt to entrap the other
and undermine his freedom. With a dialectical ingenuity
that is almost fiendish Sartre exposes the interplay between
the two tendencies. There is no doubt that he sheds light
on a tension that must be perpetually present when two
persons love each other; but there does seem to be doubt,
after we have got through all his pulverizing analysis, that
the very excess of his dialectic may not actually make disappear the very possibility of love, as love sometimes (despite him) does really occur in our day-to-day life. What
has happened here is simply that Sartre has fallen victim
to his own philosophic principles: As he can find in his philosophy no field or region of Being in which the subject,
Being-for-itself, and the object, Being-in-itself, really meet,
so when he comes to psychology the self must remain irremediably opposed to the Other, and there is no area between in which I may genuinely say Thou to the Other. A
Cartesian subjectivity, which Sartre's fundamentally is,
must work itself out into just such a psychological theory
of the emotions as Sartre has given us.

What he is describing is at bottom the eternal war be-

tween the sexes, of which Adler spoke. In fact, if we strip
Sartre's psychology of its particular philosophical terminology, it turns out to be fundamentally an Adlerian psychology. Adler, following Nietzsche, based his psychology on
the Will to Power, and this, as we see from the endless cycle
of sadism-masochism to which he condemns love, is true of
Sartre too. Eros disappears before the Will to Power. Sartre
is driven once again into the Nietzschean camp: where Being is lost—the Being that would unite the For-itself, the
subject, with the In-itself, the object—man is left to find his
meaning only in his mastery over objects. What is the Sartrian project that makes up our very being but a confirma-
tion of the Adlerian notion of a "guiding thread or motive"
by which we try to unify and give meaning to our whole
life? Like Adler's, Sartre's is fundamentally a masculine psychology; it misunderstands or disparages the psychology of
woman. The humanity of man consists in the For-itself, the
masculine component by which we choose, make projects,
and generally commit ourselves to the life of action. The element of masculine protest, to use Adler's term, is strong
throughout Sartre's writings—whether it be the disgust of
Mathieu (in *Roads to Liberty*) at his pregnant mistress, or
the disgust (it is fundamentally the same disgust) of
Roquentin, in *Nausea*, at the bloated roots of the chestnut
tree; or Sartre's philosophical analysis (in *Being and Nothingness*) of the viscous, the thick, sticky substance that
would entrap his liberty like the soft threat of the body of
a woman. And the woman is a threat, for the woman is
nature and Sartrian man exists in the liberty of his project,
which, since it is ultimately unjustified and unjustifiable, in
effect sunders him totally from nature. The whole of Sartre's
psychology is thus the Cartesian dualism given a new and
startling modern content.

We are now in a better position to assess Sartre's fundamental notion of liberty. He is right to make the liberty of
choice, which is the liberty of a conscious action, total and
absolute, no matter how small the area of our power: in
choosing, I have to say No somewhere, and this No, which
is total and totally exclusive of other alternatives, is dread-

ful; but only by shutting myself up in it is any resoluteness
of action possible. A friend of mine, a very intelligent and
sensitive man, was over a long period in the grip of a neurosis that took the form of indecision in the face of almost
every occasion of life; sitting in a restaurant, he could not
look at the printed menu to choose his lunch without seeing the abyss of the negative open before his eyes, on the
page, and so falling into a sweat. (He was not a Sartrian,
and had not even read Sartre; but his description of his own
experience was exactly in terms of this abyss of Nothing
opening before his eyes on the page.) Critics may make
the superficial observation that this only shows how silly
and neurotic Sartre's view of freedom is. But, on the contrary, it confirms Sartre's analysis of freedom, for only because freedom is what he says it is could this man have
been frightened by it and have retreated into the anxiety
of indecision. The neurosis consisted in the fact that freedom, that total and absolute thing, could cause the abyss
to open on such trifling occasions. But the example points
up also where Sartre's theory is decidedly lacking: it does
not show us the kind of *objects* in relation to which our
human subjectivity can define itself in a free choice that is
meaningful and not neurotic. This is so because Sartre's
doctrine of liberty was developed out of the experience of
extreme situations: the victim says to his totalitarian oppressor, No, even if you kill me; and he shuts himself up in this
No and will not be shaken from it. Our resoluteness in any
choice exacts from us something as total as this, although
it need not be exacted from us in so violent and extreme a
situation. But he who shuts himself up in the No can be
demoniacal, as Kierkegaard pointed out; he can say No
against himself, against his own nature. Sartre's doctrine of
freedom does not really comprehend the concrete man who
is an undivided totality of body and mind, at once, and
without division, both In-itself and For-itself; but rather an
isolated aspect of this total condition, the aspect of man always at the margin of his existence.

Thus the crucial question, Sartre tells us, is this: Under
what *exceptional* conditions does a man really experience

his freedom? Notice the word "exceptional" here. Why not ask instead: Under what ordinary, average, everyday conditions does a man experience his freedom? An artist—and particularly not an intellectual artist like Sartre—when the work is going well experiences his freedom as just that effortless burgeoning, swelling, flowing, which has for him the quality of the inevitable flow of nature. It is like that pear tree blooming there in the yard—very different from the nauseating chestnut tree of Roquentin—effortlessly and beautifully bringing forth its fruit into the sunlight. Because Sartre's psychology recognizes only the conscious, it cannot comprehend a form of freedom that operates in that zone of the human personality where conscious and unconscious flow into each other. Being limited to the conscious, it inevitably becomes an ego psychology; hence freedom is understood only as the resolute project of the conscious ego.

Under what day-to-day conditions does the religious man —to take another example—experience his freedom? That, from Sartre's thoroughly secular point of view, the beliefs of religion are absurd does not enter into this question; for the religious psychology does in fact exist, and any psychological theory that failed to cover it would be inadequate. How does a St. Paul experience his freedom? He has died the death, cast off the bondage of an old self, and now he lives and energetically organizes a church: "And yet not *I* live, but Christ liveth in me." His freedom is the surrender to the redeeming image of something greater than himself. This is the freedom of spiritual man, not Cartesian man. The project that is the life of a St. Paul is not primarily a conscious choice of himself, but is the result of a conversion that arose out of the depths of his unconscious. Cartesian man knows neither the freedom of spirit nor of nature, for in both of these the dualism of the In-itself and the For-itself breaks down.

Or, to take a third example, consider the psychology of the ordinary woman. Not of the women one meets in Sartre's novels or plays; nor of that woman, his friend, who wrote a book of feminine protest, *The Second Sex*, which is in reality the protest against being feminine. No, take a totally ordinary woman, one of that great number whose being is the involvement with family and children, and some of whom are happy at it, or at least as humanly fulfilled by it as the male by his own essentially masculine projects. What sense does it make to say that such a woman's identity is constituted by her project? Her project is family and children, and these do in fact make up a total human commitment; but it is hardly a project that has issued out of the conscious ego. Her whole life, with whatever freedom it reveals, is rather the unfolding of nature through her. As soon as we begin to think about the psychology of women, Sartre's psychology shows itself indeed to be exclusively a masculine affair; but the masculine that —alone, unjustified, and on the very margins of existence— has sundered itself from nature.

No doubt all of Sartre's theory is, as perhaps every psychological theory must be, a projection of his own personal psychology; there are plenty of signs of this in the novels and plays, where he reveals himself copiously. But he is also a thinker passionately identified with his ideas; and for us the significance of his complicated and often brilliant exploration of human psychology lies in the fact that it stems ultimately from Cartesian dualism, and brings to completion that sundering of man from nature with which Descartes initiated the modern epoch. Sartre is certainly right in insisting that man comes to exist only by sundering himself from nature—that this is his human fate in a universe that knows him not; but it is a question of how far this sundering can go without the human project becoming demoniacal, insane, or simply too brittle to have any human substance. In our own lives, when they are going at their best, the In-itself, the unconscious—or nature—is perpetually flowing through and sustaining the For-itself of our consciousness.

Sartre's freedom *is* demoniacal. It is rootless freedom. This doctrine happens, of course, to be maintained by a man of great good will, generosity, and courage; and the project he has chosen as his own, in which he has chosen himself, is the humanitarian and liberal one of revolutionary action. Sartre's long and checkered relations with the Communists would be a matter of high comedy if they were not so clearly a part of the general contemporary tragedy. Sartre believed that the Communist Party was truly the party of the working class, and he was willing therefore to cast his lot with that party in the field of practical politics. Meanwhile, in philosophy, he intended to retain his own freedom, including his doctrine of freedom. He came to the Communists, offering them all his talents and energy—and was rebuffed. In practical politics Sartre has shown himself very naïve, but in the course of his philosophical quarrels with the Communists he has produced some of the best intellectual polemic of our time. It was a case, in these polemics, of Cartesian man against the Communist robot; and whatever reservations we may have about Cartesian man, he is in part human and dwarfs the party robot. Besides, Sartre is a man of surpassing intelligence, which his opponents among the Communist intellectuals certainly were not. What lay behind the entire controversy was the shadow that Marxist man does not face: Sartre based his revolutionary activity upon a free choice, the Marxist upon an objective historic process, the former recognizing the inalienable subjectivity of man, the latter reducing man to an object in a process. Moreover, Sartre's atheism states candidly what the Philistine atheism of Communism (and all other Philistine forms of atheism) does not have enough imagination or courage to say: that man is an alien in the universe, unjustified and unjustifiable, absurd in the simple sense that there is no Leibnitzian reason sufficient to explain why he or his universe exists. Sartre's atheism—the way in which he exists in it—does not lose its grasp of the essentially problematic nature of man. And therein Sartre points the way to the question Marxist man will have to ask, the devil he will have to face, if and when the classless society should ever be achieved.

It has been remarked that Kierkegaard's statement of the religious position is so severe that it has turned many people who thought themselves religious to atheism. Analogously, Sartre's view of atheism is so stark and bleak that it seems to turn many people toward religion. This is exactly as it should be. The choice must be hard either way; for man, a problematic being to his depths, cannot lay hold of his ultimate commitments with a smug and easy security.

It may be that, as the modern world moves on, the Sartrian kind of freedom will be more and more the only kind man can experience. As society becomes more totalitarian, the islands of freedom get smaller and more cut off from the mainland and from each other—which is to say from any spontaneous interchange with nature or the community of other human beings. Sartre's Orestes says to his celestial oppressor, "I am a man, Jupiter." One imagines the last Resistant of the last Resistance saying No in a prison cell in the Lubianka; saying No without any motive of self-advantage and without any hope that future humans will take up his cause, but saying No nonetheless simply because he is a man and his liberty cannot be taken from him. This last man would exist in a night darker than that into which the great Descartes cast himself, in that historic inn in Holland, when he paused to think and said No to the demon. It cannot be said that Sartre has not given us good warning.

INTEGRAL VS.
RATIONAL MAN

Part Four

THE PLACE OF THE FURIES

Chapter Eleven

THIS BOOK began with a look at the present situation of man and of philosophy; then outlined the historical background against which this situation must be understood; and moved on to a view of four philosophers who have given explicit formulation to the issues implicit in that history. Now, at the end, we come back to our beginning: to the situation of the world here and now, from which all understanding must start and to which it must return. In all existential thinking it is we ourselves, the questioners, who are ultimately in question.

The four philosophers whom we have considered—Kierkegaard, Nietzsche, Heidegger, and Sartre—do not in any way represent all the facets of Existentialism; there may even be, among the Existentialists whom we have not treated at length, figures that would prove more humanly appealing to the individual reader. These four, however, seem to me to be, intellectually speaking, the most considerable figures that the movement has yet brought forward. In any case they pose, for me, the chief questions that stand at issue for philosophy, and indeed for man himself, at this point in Western history. The fact that certain of these thinkers—Heidegger in particular—have disclaimed the label of Existentialist should not deter us from recognizing in them a well-defined movement. We may remember that Kant once protested against the term "idealist" as applied to himself—and with good reason; but history in its rough-and-ready need for groupings overrode his protest, and as

an idealist he now stands classified in all the textbooks—
and with equally good reason. Perhaps the ungentle hand
of history is guided by a keener sense of reality than is
possessed by philosophers themselves, as they squabble
over the niceties of how they are to be labeled. History
senses—beneath and beyond all the differences and squabbles—the unity of source, of influence, and of milieu; just
as the reader of this book will sense, I hope, by this time
that there are certain clearly defined themes and even some
definite and agreed-upon theses common to all the figures
we have called Existentialists, and to something that can
be called existential philosophy.

The four figures we have considered are, in any case,
sufficient for our purposes here, where the aim has been
not to provide a survey or compendium of Existentialism
but rather to deal with the more central question: What is
the *meaning* of Existentialism? Here we are using "meaning" not in its external sense, as a body of more or less organized information on what these philosophers are talking
about, but in a more internal sense: What, we have asked,
is really happening in our own historical existence that it
should come to expression in this way and in these philosophers? Or—in terms that echo Heidegger—what is happening within the Being of the West?

This has been our single theme and subject throughout;
and it brings us back now to the point from which we
started, the present situation.

1. THE CRYSTAL PALACE UNMANNED

It may seem strange, particularly to American readers, that rationalism has been made so much of a target
throughout this book. As a teacher of philosophy, a very
dubious profession in this country, I am in a position to observe how precarious a hold the intellect has upon American life; and this is not true merely of the great majority
of students but of cultured people, of intellectuals, to whom
here in America a philosophical idea is an alien and embarrassing thing. In their actual life Americans are not

only a non-intellectual but an anti-intellectual people. The charm of the American as a new human type, his rough-and-ready pragmatism, his spontaneity and openness to experience are true of him only because he is unreflective by nature. The two greatest American writers of the present day—Hemingway and Faulkner—are superior artists because of their power over physical fact, not because of their grasp of ideas or of the subtleties of psychology. What point, then, do the various animadversions upon rationalism —as put forth by Kierkegaard, Nietzsche, Heidegger—have for Americans today? Americans are not likely at this point to swallow a classical Platonism—to become the dedicated priests of godlike reason as philosophers in the tradition of Plato became.

The fact is that a good dose of intellectualism—genuine intellectualism—would be a very helpful thing in American life. But the essence of the existential protest is that rationalism can pervade a whole civilization, to the point where the individuals in that civilization do less and less thinking, and perhaps wind up doing none at all. It can bring this about by dictating the fundamental ways and routines by which life itself moves. Technology is one material incarnation of rationalism, since it derives from science; bureaucracy is another, since it aims at the rational control and ordering of social life; and the two—technology and bureaucracy—have come more and more to rule our lives.

But it is not so much rationalism as *abstractness* that is the existentialists' target; and the abstractness of life in this technological and bureaucratic age is now indeed something to reckon with. The last gigantic step forward in the spread of technologism has been the development of mass art and mass media of communication: the machine no longer fabricates only material products; it also makes minds. Millions of people live by the stereotypes of mass art, the most virulent form of abstractness, and their capacity for any kind of human reality is fast disappearing. If here and there in the lonely crowd (discovered by Kierkegaard long before David Riesman) a face is lit by a human gleam, it quickly goes vacant again in the hypnotized stare

at the TV screen. When an eclipse of the moon was tele-
vised some years ago, E. B. White wrote in *The New Yorker*
that he felt some drastic turning point in history had arrived: people could have seen the real thing by looking out
of their windows, but instead they preferred looking at the
reflection of it on the screen. Kierkegaard condemned the
abstractness of his time, calling it an Age of Reflection, but
what he seems chiefly to have had in mind was the abstractness of the professorial intellectual, seeing not real life
but the reflection of it in his own mind. We, however, have
fabricated for our time a new kind of abstractness, on a
mass scale; through our extraordinary mastery of technique
we provide a ready-made reflection in place of the real, and
not for university dons but for the millions. Our journey
into untruth has gone farther than Kierkegaard could have
imagined.

To be rational is not the same as to be reasonable. In my
time I have heard the most hair-raising and crazy things
from very rational men, advanced in a perfectly rational
way; no insight or feelings had been used to check the reasoning at any point. Nowadays, we accept in our public and
political life the most humanly unreasonable behavior, provided it wears a rational mask and speaks in officialese,
which is the rhetoric of rationality itself. Witness the recent
announcement that science had been able to perfect a
"clean" hydrogen bomb—to be sure, not perfectly "clean"
yet, but "95 per cent clean" or even "96 per cent clean."
Of course the quantitative measurement makes the matter
sound so scientific and rational that people no longer bother
to ask themselves the human meaning of the whole thing.
No doubt, they tell themselves, there must be a perfectly rational chain of arguments which, starting from the premise
that there must be hydrogen bombs, leads to the conclusion
that there must be "clean" hydrogen bombs—otherwise war
itself would become impossible! The incident makes us suspect that, despite the increase in the rational ordering of
life in modern times, men have not become the least bit
more reasonable in the human sense of the word. A perfect

rationality might not even be incompatible with psychosis; it might, in fact, even lead to the latter.

It may be objected that the fear of what may happen to mankind in our time—the specific fear, today, of atomic extermination—is a recurrent thing; man has such fears in every age, and yet has managed to survive all his presentiments of disaster. Karl Jaspers cites the complaint of an Egyptian of four thousand years ago that things are going to rack and ruin in his time: "Robbers abound. . . . No one ploughs the land. People are saying: We do not know what will happen from day to day." And Ortega y Gasset quotes the lament of the Latin poet Horace, uttered when the Roman Empire was at its very height. "We [Horace and his contemporaries] are the degenerate descendants of fathers who in their turn were degenerate from their forebears." The harking back to an earlier and better state of mankind, to some golden age of the past, is indeed a perpetual tendency of human nature. The present situation must always, when we come to see it fully, appear threatening: it is a situation, we think, that has to be transformed or redeemed. Today is always and for all men the digging of one's way out of the ruins of yesterday. However, it is not a question of rating our own age lower—or higher—than the past; as we have indicated throughout this book, ours is an age of unparalleled achievements and power, and in a variety of fields. The question, rather, is one of assessing the present in all its uniqueness. If, as the Existentialists hold, an authentic life is not handed to us on a platter but involves our own act of self-determination (self-finitization) within our time and place, then we have got to know and face up to that time, both in its threats and its promises. It will not do to say that every age has been like this, that man has always felt threatened and yet managed to survive. The point is precisely that every age is different: each time has been unique, both in what it promised and what it threatened; and sometimes the catastrophe has occurred. It is the very uniqueness of the present in which we live that affords man his unprecedented *power*—including ultimately the power to blow himself and his planet to bits. But the law

of opposites, the oldest tragic wisdom of the race, suggests
that at the very height of his power man is bound to experience, as Oedipus did, his absolute impotence. There are
a good many straws in the wind today that point in that
direction, including the testimony of modern art, as we have
seen. I for one am personally convinced that man will not
take his next great step forward until he has drained to the
lees the bitter cup of his own powerlessness. The trouble
is, however, that this chastening experience may come only
with the destruction of his world—a calamity in which the
tragic hero also destroys himself. That is why all the
politics-as-usual of today seems so terribly antiquated; it
lags so sadly behind the actual situation of man—and behind even our present knowledge of man.

The two chief contestants in the present international situation are both rooted in the Enlightenment, so far at any
rate as their respective civilizations reflect any general conception of man. The uniqueness of the United States is that
it is a nation that was founded at a certain time in history
in the full light of historical consciousness; it did not grow
out of the soil of its own prehistory. Moreover, it was
founded in the eighteenth century in the very heyday of
the Enlightenment, and by men who participated in the
clear rationality of that period. The soil of America appeared to the American as an alien wilderness to be conquered, something inimical, set over against himself, not as
something out of which he himself and his institutions had,
so to speak, grown. Lacking the roots the European has, in
prehistory and the chthonic unconscious, the American
shows an admirable freedom and flexibility in consciousness, particularly of a practical kind. But with this goes also
that celebrated American "innocence"—a quality which in
philosophical terms is simply an ignorance of how questionable a being man really is and which strikes the European
as alien and possibly even somewhat disingenuous. Hence,
the ineptness of the American in handling the human side
of foreign politics, and his inability to understand why his
European allies should look at him askance and question
his generosity and good will. Sartre recounts a conversation

he had with an American while visiting in this country. The American insisted that all international problems could be solved if men would just get together and be rational; Sartre disagreed and after a while discussion between them became impossible. "I believe in the existence of evil," says Sartre, "and he does not." What the American has not yet become aware of is the shadow that surrounds all human Enlightenment.

The philosophy of the other contestant—to look on its best and most "idealistic" side, a side that still enlists the enthusiasm of millions of men—is Marxist humanism. This humanism harks back to the justly celebrated statement of Marx: *"To be radical is to go to the root of the question. Now the root of mankind is man."* Marx here speaks as a member of the generation of Feuerbach and the young Hegelians, those who turned against Hegel and his Idea of the State and toward the concrete man, the historical creature of flesh and blood. This actual and historical man, they said, is to be the root of mankind, the root of society and the state. But there is a further question that this leaves unasked: In what is the individual man to be rooted? The thoroughly problematic nature of man, this highly questionable and self-questioning animal, is conveniently and fatefully dropped out of sight. Marx turned his attention to the social problem, assuming that the only thing in the way of man's coming into his full humanity was the capitalist system. In this he was simply echoing the Enlightenment's optimistic assumption that, since man is a rational animal, the only obstacles to his fulfillment must be objective and social ones. Communism, following Marx, has thus always exhibited a strange ambivalence: the most naïvely optimistic view of human nature in theory, and in practice the most brutal and cynical attitude toward human beings.

Marxism is the ideology of Communism; but in fact and in its actual historical unfolding, the real philosopher of Communism, or what Communism has become, is Nietzsche, as we have seen. The question of power has become paramount; it usurps everything else, as is shown in the recent remarkable book by Milovan Djilas, *The New Class.*

The collective effort to master nature, to have power over things, requires that men have power over other men; and the movement ends by thinking of the men underneath merely as things, for its thinking has long since discarded all the categories that recognize the humanity of the person and his subjectivity. The historical turning point in this case was Lenin, the practical genius and the St. Paul of the Communist movement. Before returning from exile in 1917, Lenin had written a little pamphlet, *State and Revolution,* in which he dealt with human nature in terms of the most naïve and utopian rationalism; but as soon as he was back in Russia and engaged in actual politics there was one, and only one, question before his mind as an active politician: power. Marxist manuals of philosophy refer to all philosophies that deal with the human subject as forms of "irrationalism." *Their* rationalism, of course, consists in technical intelligence, in the power over things (and over men considered simply as things); and this exalting of the technical intelligence over every other human attribute becomes demoniacal in action, as recent history has shown.

Behind the problem of politics, in the present age, lies the problem of man, and this is what makes all thinking about contemporary problems so thorny and difficult. The intellectual collapse that occurred in this country after the decade of the 1930's, when our intellectuals had been able to submerge themselves totally in a program of political action, shows that philosophy can no longer be considered a mere appendage to politics. On the contrary, anyone who wishes to meddle in politics today had better come to some prior conclusions as to what man is and what, in the end, human life is all about. I say "in the end" deliberately because the neglect of first and of last things does not—as so-called "practical" people hope—go unpunished, but has a disastrous way of coming in the back door and upsetting everything. The speeches of our politicians show no recognition of this; and yet in the hands of these men, on both sides of the Atlantic, lies the catastrophic power of atomic energy.

Existentialism is the counter-Enlightenment come at last

to philosophic expression; and it demonstrates beyond anything else that the ideology of the Enlightenment is thin, abstract, and therefore dangerous. (I say its "ideology," for the practical task of the Enlightenment is still with us: In everyday life we must continue to be critics of a social order that is still based everywhere on oppression, injustice, and even savagery—such being the peculiar tension of mind that we as responsible human beings have to maintain today.) The finitude of man, as established by Heidegger, is perhaps the death blow to the ideology of the Enlightenment, for to recognize this finitude is to acknowledge that man will always exist in untruth as well as truth. Utopians who still look forward to a future when all shadows will be dispersed and mankind will dwell in a resplendent Crystal Palace will find this recognition disheartening. But on second thought, it may not be such a bad thing to free ourselves once and for all from the worship of the idol of progress; for utopianism—whether the brand of Marx or of Nietzsche —by locating the meaning of man in the future leaves human beings here and now, as well as all mankind up to this point, without their own meaning. If man is to be given meaning, the Existentialists have shown us, it must be here and now; and to think this insight through is to recast the whole tradition of Western thought. The realization that all human truth must not only shine against an enveloping darkness, but that such truth is even shot through with its own darkness may be depressing, and not only to utopians. But it has the virtue of restoring to man his sense of the primal mystery surrounding all things, a sense of mystery from which the glittering world of his technology estranges him, but without which he is not truly human.

2. THE FURIES

In comparison with traditional philosophy, or with other contemporary schools of philosophy, Existentialism, as we have seen, seeks to bring the whole man—the concrete individual in the whole context of his everyday life, and in his total mystery and questionableness—into philosophy.

This is attempted with varying degrees of success by the different Existentialists; but the attempt itself, even if it did not succeed at all, would be necessary and valuable for our time. In modern philosophy particularly (philosophy since Descartes), man has figured almost exclusively as an epistemological subject—as an intellect that registers sense-data, makes propositions, reasons, and seeks the certainty of intellectual knowledge, but not as the man underneath all this, who is born, suffers, and dies. Naturally, the attempt to see the whole or integral man, in place of the rational or epistemological fragment of him, involves our taking a look at some unpleasant things. Nowadays there is much glib talk, particularly in this country, about "the whole man," or "the well-rounded individual," the terms evoking, in this context, only the pleasant prospect of graciously enlarging the Self by taking extension courses, developing constructive hobbies, or taking an active part in social movements. But the whole man is not whole without such unpleasant things as death, anxiety, guilt, fear and trembling, and despair, even though journalists and the populace have shown what they think of these things by labeling any philosophy that looks at such aspects of human life as "gloomy" or "merely a mood of despair." We are still so rooted in the Enlightenment—or *up*rooted in it—that these unpleasant aspects of life are like the Furies for us: hostile forces from which we would escape. And of course the easiest way to escape the Furies, we think, is to deny that they exist. It seems to me no accident at all that modern depth psychology has come into prominence in the same period as Existentialism and for the same reason: namely, that certain unpleasant things the Enlightenment had dropped into the limbo of the unconscious have begun to backfire and have forced themselves finally upon the attention of modern man.

This is not the first time man has been faced with the problem of placating the Furies. At the very dawn of Western history the Greeks went through a similar experience, the record of which has been left us in the great *Oresteia* trilogy of Aeschylus; a record in which we can also read a prophecy of our own conflict (with differences) as well as the only reasonable proposal for its solution (with differences).

Clytemnestra, in the tragedy, has killed her husband Agamemnon; and Orestes, their son, is directed by Apollo, an extremely promasculine deity, to avenge his father's murder. Orestes kills his mother and is immediately set upon by the Furies, the old goddesses of night and earth who were responsible for the protection of the lines of blood and who therefore must punish the son who murders his mother, as the perpetrator of the most horrible crime man can imagine. Up to a point the drama revolves around human beings, with the gods of course always in the background; but when we come to the last play of the trilogy, the *Eumenides*, in which Orestes meets his final ordeal, the gods themselves take the center of the stage, and Orestes, the human bearer of the conflict, is dwarfed in their shadow. The conflict is now between Apollo, the new god—and *the* god of the Enlightenment—on the one hand and the Furies, the old matriarchal goddesses of the family and the soil, on the other. Apollo is protecting Orestes, and the Furies seek his destruction. There ensues a trial between the rival deities on the hill of the Acropolis at Athens; the verdict of the jury, comprised of citizens, will set Orestes free or hand him over irremediably to the Furies.

The modern reader who skims the play too hastily may get the impression that this trial is a rather prosaic piece of legalism, hardly worthy of the sublime drama that has preceded it; but for the Greek this trial was as intense and dramatic as the more sensational scene in which Orestes murders his mother—was, in fact, the nub of the whole matter. Aeschylus' tragedy records the moment in Greek history at which the old matriarchal deities were superseded by the new patriarchal gods of Olympus; but the average Greek citizen still remembered the older deities and he was still a little bit uneasy forced to choose between old and new. Thus at the very beginning of the *Eumenides* we are told by the Pythian priestess that the first prophetess or seer among the gods was old Mother Earth herself; it was only very lately that Apollo had come to occupy the temples of the oracles throughout Greece. This development from the old matriarchal to the new patriarchal deities parallels the development of Greek consciousness itself, as it advanced in civilization and enlightenment. The question of the play, thus interpreted, becomes: What kind of tribute will this advanced consciousness have to pay to the old earth-bound unconscious?

The vote of the citizen jurors is a tie; and Orestes (as was the Greek rule) is allowed to go free. The tying vote has been cast by Athena herself, an ambiguous female deity, in spirit halfway between man and woman. The Furies wail disconsolately and threaten all kinds of destruction on the land. They are placated, however, by being told that they shall not be entirely displaced by this new upstart of enlightenment, Apollo; they are to be given a revered place, a sanctuary, and every child born of woman shall be born into their protection. The goddess Athena, who was born out of the brain of Zeus, in allotting this final justice to the Furies, acknowledges that they are older and wiser than she.

It would be a mistake to take this as merely a cool barter, a *quid pro quo*. Greek religion was in deadly earnest here, and perhaps it was never wiser. The Furies are really to be revered and not simply bought off; in fact, they cannot be bought off (not even by our modern tranquilizers and sleeping pills) but are to be placated only through being given their just and due respect. They are the darker side of life, but in their own way as holy as the rest. Indeed, without them there would be no experience of the holy at all. Without the shudder of fear or the trembling of dread man would never be brought to stand face to face with himself or his life; he would only drift aimlessly off into the insubstantial realm of Laputa.

Aeschylus' tragedy speaks to us in an archaic language, but it does speak, and directly. We are the children of an enlightenment, one which we would like to preserve; but we can do so only by making a pact with the old goddesses. The centuries-long evolution of human reason is one of man's greatest triumphs, but it is still in process, still incomplete, still to be. Contrary to the rationalist tradition, we now know that it is not his reason that makes man man, but rather that reason is a consequence of that which really makes him man. For it is man's existence as a self-transcending self that has forged and formed reason as one of its projects. As such, man's reason is specifically human (but no more and no less than his art and his religion) and to be revered. All the values that have been produced in the course of the long evolution of reason—everything that goes under the heading of liberalism, intelligence, a decent and reasonable view of life—we wish desperately to preserve and enlarge, in the turmoil of modern life. But do we need to be persuaded now, after all that has happened in this twentieth century, how precariously situated these reasonable ideals are in relation to the subterranean forces of life, and how small a segment of the whole and concrete man they actually represent? We have to establish a working pact between that segment and the whole of us; but a pact requires compromise, in which both sides concede something, and in this case particularly the rationalism of the Enlightenment will have to recognize that at the very heart of its light there is also a darkness.

It would be the final error of reason—the point at which it succumbs to its own *hubris* and passes over into its demoniacal opposite, unreason—to deny that the Furies exist, or to strive to manipulate them out of existence. Nothing can be accomplished by denying that man is an essentially troubled being, except to make more trouble. We may, of course, be able to buy off the Furies for a while; being of the earth and ancient, they have been around much longer than the rational consciousness that would entirely supplant them, and so they can afford to wait. And when they strike, more likely than not it will be through the offending faculty itself. It is notorious that brilliant people are often the most dense about their own human blind spot, precisely because their intelligence, so clever in other things, conceals it from them; multiply this situation a thousandfold, and you have a brilliant scientific and technological civilization that could run amuck out of its own sheer uprooted cleverness. The solution proposed by Greek tragic wisdom through the drama of Aeschylus may not, then, be as frightening as we imagine: in giving the Furies their place, we may come to recognize that they are not such alien presences as we think in our moments of evading them. In fact, far from being alien, they are part of ourselves, like all gods and demons. The conspiracy to forget them, or to deny that they exist, thus turns out to be only one more contrivance in that vast and organized effort by modern society to flee from the self.

Appendices

NEGATION, FINITUDE, AND
THE NATURE OF MAN*

Appendix I

> Nothing is more real than nothing.
> SAMUEL BECKETT

IN Ernest Hemingway's *Winner Take Nothing* (1933) there is one story, "A Clean, Well-Lighted Place," that could be meditated on very profitably by contemporary philosophers. Toward the end of it Hemingway gives the interior monologue of his hero, a waiter in a café somewhere in Spain, in these words:

> Turning off the electric light he continued the conversation with himself . . . what did he fear? It was not fear or dread. It was a nothing that he knew too well. It was all a nothing and a man was nothing too. It was only that and light was all it needed and a certain cleanness and order. Some lived in it and never felt it but he knew it all was nada y pues nada y nada y pues nada. Our nada, who are in nada, nada be thy name thy kingdom nada thy will be nada in nada as it is nada. Give us this nada our daily nada and nada us our nada as we nada our nadas and nada us not into nada but deliver us from nada; pues nada.

* This paper was read at a meeting of the American Philosophical Association, December 29, 1957. It deals, independently of Heidegger, with the meaning of the negative in experience, and can thus be taken as further elucidation of the matters discussed in Chapter 9.

Hail nothing, full of nothing, nothing is with
thee. . . .

The almost antiphonal repetition of "*nada*," the Spanish
word for nothing, and the blasphemous transformation of
two traditional Christian prayers into invocations to this
Nothing may make the ordinary reader gag. Indeed the passage usually provokes the stock cry of "Nihilism!"—the label
by which we seek to dismiss out of hand the kind of experience Hemingway is reporting. But in its context the passage is in no way sensational; in rhythm and tone it fits in
perfectly with the whole story, which though brief (eight
pages) is one of Hemingway's best and one of his most
courageous too, for in it he names the presence that had
circulated, unnamed and unconfronted, through and behind much of his earlier writing. The passage itself only
names what the story as a whole work of art reveals: the
presence that Hemingway and his hero experience—a presence that is fully as real as the lights and shadows of the
café, and the solid objects in it, tables, chairs, and human
bodies—is Nothing.

It is at this that the philosophic reader is likely to gag.
Can this Nothing really be a datum? The question of what
is and what is not given in experience is a thorny one; and
though philosophers today may admit it is thornier than
they used to imagine, they are likely to slam the door pretty
sharply against the kind of datum Hemingway is trying to
present. Sense-data are given, some philosophers say; per-
ceptual objects are given, say others; but however they may
squabble among themselves over such matters, they will
end up joining forces against such a strange negative entity
as that to which Hemingway testifies here.

He is a pretty lucid witness too. His words undercut the
common objection that all that is involved here is a "mere
mood" (as if moods were mere *passiones animae*, modifica-
tions inhering in a psychic substance, in the Cartesian
sense). "It was not fear or dread," he tells us. "It was a
nothing that he knew too well." Fear and dread are moods;
but what is in question for the character in the story is

not a mood, but a presence that he knows and knows all too well. So far as the mood of Hemingway's story is concerned, it is in no way frantic, despairing, or "nihilistic." Rather, its tone is one of somber and clear courage.

As a matter of fact, human moods and reactions to the encounter with Nothingness vary considerably from person to person, and from culture to culture. The Chinese Taoists found the Great Void tranquilizing, peaceful, even joyful. For the Buddhists in India, the idea of Nothing evoked a mood of universal compassion for all creatures caught in the toils of an existence that is ultimately groundless. In the traditional culture of Japan the idea of Nothingness pervades the exquisite modes of aesthetic feeling displayed in painting, architecture, and even the ceremonial rituals of daily life. But Western man, up to his neck in *things*, objects, and the business of mastering them, recoils with anxiety from any possible encounter with Nothingness and labels talk of it as "negative"—which is to say, morally reprehensible. Clearly, then, the moods with which men react to this Nothing vary according to time, place, and cultural conditioning; but what is at issue here is not the mood with which one ought to confront such a presence, but the reality of the presence itself.

It is now a good many years since Husserl set forth the motto, *"Zu den Sachen selbst,"* "To the things themselves," as an exhortation to philosophers to bring themselves closer to the sources of experience. To do so is very hard for philosophers: they come to experience with too many intellectual preconceptions. Artists are better at it. It is, after all, what the artist is paid to do: to be attentive to experience. If Hemingway had read Heidegger, or if he were Jean-Paul Sartre, writing his story out of some intellectual *parti pris*, then his testimony in this case would be suspect, at least initially. But Hemingway is not an intellectual, far from it; and the unique style he has forged for himself—a style which at the period of this story had not yet begun to parody itself—sprang from an urge to report truly, to set things straight for the reader, to get, in Husserl's phrase, to the things themselves. He is at the outset a credible witness.

Artist and thinker have stood in hidden opposition since the very dawn of Western philosophy. Plato's condemnation of Homer was, in the end, not so much moral as metaphysical, as Plato himself acknowledged. The truth the artist reveals eludes the conceptual structure of the philosopher. Hence it is no truth, for the latter, but *untruth*. (In the very late dialogue, *The Sophist*, Plato, as we may remember, classes the poets with the Sophists as merchants of non-Being.) There is, however, another approach open to the philosopher: In the face of the recalcitrant data set forth by the artist, the thinker may choose to let thought rethink itself, to let it stand in more open and living contact with what is given. Hemingway's story may seem a tiny thing to pit against the central tradition of Western thought, but one has to take the experience of the real where one finds it; genuine witnesses to experience are so few and far between that we cannot afford not to listen to one, even at the discomfort of having to think in a way that is unfamiliar to us. And a breach anywhere in the traditional way of thinking, in this case about the negative, may lead us to re-examine that tradition wholly.

1.

In *Metaphysics*, Delta, 7, Aristotle lists, among others, the following meanings of Being, *to on*, that-which-is:

(1) Being is that which is divided by the ten categories [i.e., that which is is either a substance, or a quality (of a substance), or a quantity (of a substance), or a relation (of substances), etc.].
(2) Being is that which signifies the truth of a proposition.

Medieval thinkers (and I believe they were quite accurate in their reading of Aristotle) made this passage the basis for a distinction between (1) *ens reale*, real Being, and (2) *ens rationis*, conceptual Being. (1) The first term defines a real entity as that which has actual and positive existence as an object in the world—ultimately, a primary substance or one of its attributes or relations. (2) The second sense includes entities that do not have real and positive existence in the first sense. Thus, if I can assert a true proposition about a non-existing thing, then in some sense it has Being, since it is not a pure non-entity. "A centaur is half man, half horse" is a true proposition; and obviously a centaur is an entity of some kind, though not a really existent one. A centaur is an entity about which at least one true proposition may be uttered. Since propositions do not exist without minds to interpret them, the centaur is an *ens rationis*—a conceptual or mental entity.

In the light of this distinction, the medieval tradition treats all negative entities (including privations) as *entia rationis*, conceptual entities. The example of a privation used by St. Thomas is blindness. Blindness is not an *ens reale;* the eye is real, and the cataract or other substance that may grow over it to cause blindness is real; but the blindness itself, the not-seeing, is an entity only in the sense that the proposition "The eye does not see" is true—that is, asserts what is the case if we happen to be talking about a blind man.

Perhaps the cogency of this position may be made clearer by another illustration. I remove everything from my table top except a stone paperweight. Both the table and the stone are real entities, things that have actual and positive existence. Now, the following is true:

(1) There is a stone on the table.

If I now remove the stone from the table, the following becomes true:

(2) The stone is not on the table,
or:
(2') The stone is absent from the table.

The absence of the stone is a fact; but this means nothing more than that the preceding propositions (2) and (2') are true. If I took to groping around on the table to lay hold of this absence-of-stone, I would be making a fool of myself both practically and intellectually. The absence-of-the-stone-from-the-table is an entity that exists only in the mind: I have seen the stone on the table, I expect it to be there and it is not, and I think: The stone is not now on the table.

Here common sense speaks in all its luminous simplicity. This way of thought, laid down by Aristotle in his *Metaphysics* and continued by the Schoolmen, was the framework within which the seventeenth-century founders of modern philosophy still thought. It is today the persistent and consistent tradition within which Western man thinks about Being and its negatives. It is remarkable that Carnap, in an essay published in *Erkennis* in 1931 ("The Conquest of Metaphysics Through the Logical Analysis of Language"), seeking to show that Heidegger's conception of *Das Nichts,* Nothing, follows from a misuse of language, still follows the argument of the preceding paragraph. Carnap makes use of the logistical apparatus, but the essential direction of his thinking is the same as that of St. Thomas in the opening pages of *De Ente et Essentia.* At first glance, Carnap and St. Thomas may seem very strange bedfellows, but on second thought we should not be surprised; Positivism belongs, after all, to the Western tradition, and when it thinks about Being, or systematically avoids thinking about it, both the thinking and the avoidance of thinking take place wholly within this tradition. But by keeping its gaze riveted on minute logical matters that lie in the foreground, Positivism can let these preconceptions sink so far into the background that they can be forgotten and even denied to be there.

But common sense, however logical and sound, is after all only one human attitude among many others; and like everything human it may have its limitations—or *negative* side. No matter how massive this tradition that locates real Being exclusively in the positively existing object, we must be ready to put it to the phenomenological test of our own experience, however humble or grubby.

Let us see, then, about this blindness:

One fine morning a man wakes up blind. One day we are born, one day we die; one day, for some people, we go blind. Perhaps, in fact, we should not say "a man." The term removes this man, at the outset, into a more remote realm of objects, where his personal being is shed drop by drop like a face losing contour at a distance. I, you, go— *this* man goes blind. That is better, for it suggests a little more that this is happening to some single human person. Well, then, this man has suddenly gone blind. He has fallen into a great black pit, his whole life has been swallowed up in a darkness. Non-seeing, a privation, has descended on him with more crushing effect than a brick from a rooftop. Roaring with anguish, he crashes and stumbles about his room. A doctor arrives and examines his eyes. If the doctor philosophizes in the manner of Aristotle, St. Thomas, or Carnap, he will observe: the eyes are real, and the growth over the eyes is a real substance, but the non-seeing of the eye is itself not an object and therefore not an *ens reale*, a real entity. And if doctors still know Latin or if this one has a slight touch of Molière, he may even pompously and soothingly quote St. Thomas: *"Caecitas non habet esse in rebus"* (Blindness has no being in things). For my part, I rather hope this doctor is *not* able to get out of the room fast enough to avoid the blind man's fury. His language, for all its Latin gravity, is humanly frivolous; and what is humanly frivolous ought to be somehow and somewhere philosophically wrong too.

What, so far as philosophy is concerned, is happening in this situation? Nothing less than this: In the traditional way of thought a chasm has opened between subject and object, between Being considered as that-which-is, a positively existing object, and Being as the mode of being of a subject; blindness observed from without and blindness experienced from within. For the man who has gone blind his blindness may very well be the *ens realissimum*—or, more accurately, the *esse* or *non-esse realissimum*—of his life.

Here, in the tradition, two notions—negativity and subjectivity—have become essentially linked, with the latter accorded at most a derivative and questionable status. That mode of thought which perpetually stands outside and looks for the object can*not* bring into thought the *subjectivity of the subject*. This subjectivity of the subject has nothing to do with "subjectivism" in any of the skeptical forms that have bedeviled modern philosophy since Descartes. The subjectivity of the subject is a reality within the world. The world contains stones, plants, animals, planets, stars—and also subjects living out their own subjectivity.

Human finitude is the presence of the *not* in the being of man. That mode of thought which cannot understand negative existence cannot fully understand human finitude. Finitude is a matter of human limitations, and limitations involve what we can*not* do or can*not* be. Our finitude, however, is not the mere sum of our limitations; rather, the fact of human finitude brings us to the center of man, where positive and negative existence coincide and interpenetrate to such an extent that a man's strength coincides with his pathos, his vision with his blindness, his truth with his untruth, his being with his non-being. And if human finitude is not understood, neither is the nature of man.

2.

Traditional ontology has always been carried out in connection with theology, and in the actual systems in the West this has always meant theodicy, a justification of the perfection of God and His universe. The classical theory of privations fits into this historical frame. It was in fact linked with the effort to solve the problem of evil, which is why, though the theory exists in germ in Aristotle, it was elaborated fully only by the later Christian Aristotelians. If evil is essentially negative in nature, a *privatio boni* or privation of the good, and if privations have only mental and not real being, then evil becomes an illusory shadow, expunged from the perfection of God's universe. So the seed was planted from which grew the tradition of making negative existence into a reality that is sublimated, mediated, *aufgehoben,* or otherwise made to disappear by a metaphysical trick of *passe-passe*. The human motives for the ontological prejudice are thus abundantly clear.

But this prejudice was, in turn, to provide the main outline for the theory of human nature. If we take as representative of this tradition Aristotle's treatment of man in the *Ethics* (and elsewhere in his works), St. Thomas' *De Homine*, Descartes' *Treatise on the Passions*, Spinoza on the emotions, then the unity of these thinkers begins to appear, to us today, much more significant than their divergences, however considerable. For all of them, man is an object, one object amid that hierarchy of objects that is nature; an object, moreover, with a fixed nature or essence that assigns him his precise place in that hierarchy, which latter, perfect though it may be, depends in turn upon the plenitude of God's being. Whatever any of these thinkers wrote about man was, then, simply the product of an exceptional intelligence reasoning about the essence of an object; none of this reasoning required—and indeed showed no trace of—that fateful and sometimes dreadful experience which we know as the encounter with the Self. Each of them could have written exactly as he did if he had only thought and never lived. This, at least, cannot be said against Kierkegaard and Nietzsche—which may be one very good reason why contemporary thinking about man will have to start from these two.

Idealism might seem to have been a great exception to this general tradition, since it brought subjectivity into philosophy, giving it a role that it had not previously had in Western thought. But the "subject" that idealism introduced into philosophy was only the epistemological subject, not the concrete human subject: it was the mind, that is, with its restrictive conditions for the formation of concepts and systems, not the concrete person in the radical finitude of his existence. And idealism ended by becoming *objective idealism*, the adjective revealing that the ultimate concern was once again with the nature of the object, with *ens* rather than with *esse*. The root of idealism's difference with materialism remained unchanged; it was content merely with turning the tables on its adversary and finding the nature of the object to be mind-stuff rather than matter-stuff. Hegel appears to be dealing with negativity and finitude, to a greater extent than any philosopher before him; certainly he flaunts the terms, at least. But it was only flaunting. Hegel was in the end the most arrogant spokesman for the classical tradition, since everything negative, fragmentary, incomplete, partial—in a word, human—gets transfigured in his System and is absorbed into the plenitude of the Absolute. The image of man that Hegel projects is a glorified one, perhaps, but it is also a travesty of our actual human experience, and therefore, finally, insulting.

But surely, it may be said, this tradition is no longer powerful or operative; we live in a non-metaphysical, or even anti-metaphysical age, and there is no need to expend energy flogging a dead horse. Habits of thought are persistent things, however, and retain their identity through many strange metamorphoses. Those who would interpret man as an object of one kind or another seem to find a kinship that crosses all philosophical boundaries. Thus it is reported that some Jesuits have got together with Communist philosophers on the other side of the Iron Curtain, to seek a *rapprochement* between Marxism and Thomism. No doubt, each side secretly thinks it will devour the other; but it is significant that St. Thomas may be digestible to Communism where Kierkegaard would be absolute anathema; these Communist philosophers repudiate any attempt to deal philosophically with human subjectivity, as being a symptom of bourgeois decadence. On this side of the Curtain, in America, the vogue is rather to interpret man from the point of view of the behavioral sciences, in the light of *scientific objectivity*: man is no longer reduced to a metaphysical object, as in the classical tradition, but to a scientific object. Nineteenth-century naturalism attempted to give us man as a physicochemical object; and as naturalistic thought has become more flexible and subtle, in this century, we have had successively man as a biological object, as a biologicosocial object, as an anthropological object, and now, with some of the younger generation of naturalists, man as a psychoanalytic object.

There seem to me two objections—one practical, one in principle—to the attempt to interpret man in his totality from the point of view of the behavioral sciences. First, these sciences are as yet very youthful, and very poorly provided with reliable general conclusions. If, honoring the requirements of the severely scientific conscience, we restrict ourselves to the *reliable* results now afforded by these sciences, we shall have a picture of only a tiny fragment of man. And while we wish very much that these sciences may develop, in the meantime we have to live, and this means that we must be guided by some general idea of what man is all about. Every age, as André Malraux has shown, projects its own image of man in its art; and even if it has no art, it will live by such an image, sometimes expressed but more often veiled. If the philosopher hands over to the behavioral sciences the task of philosophical anthropology, it does not mean that he is without any total image of man, but only that the image is more likely to be unconscious. When philosophers today deal with human matters, as in ethics, even though they are apparently only doing so through the logical analysis of value statements, I think it can always be shown that there are, concealed within the analysis, presuppositions as to the nature of man.

The second objection—one of principle—to the view of the behavioral sciences is that they must be perpetually incomplete. From what has been established in our time about the incompleteness of mathematics, the most rigorous of all the sciences, we know that such vague and complex amalgams (not yet systems) as the behavioral sciences can never even pretend to completeness; consequently man as a totality will always elude their grasp. Any attempt to interpret man *completely* from the view of these sciences is bound to be reductive in nature.

Indeed, it is hard for even the most well-intentioned of sociologists and anthropologists to avoid slipping into such a reduction—as we can see whenever they are led to generalize about more complex social entities, such as, say, American civilization, whose meaning is part of our own subjectivity. The primitives, if they could read what the anthropologists say about them, might have the same difficulty in recognizing themselves. The problem is especially acute, in fact, when the behavioral scientists are dealing with primitives who have risen to the level of producing great art, such as Benin and Bantu sculpture. These primitive artists already occupy a domain of being that we can enter only as art, and whose meaning we cannot grasp so long as we stand outside it and systematically catalogue objects, artifacts, and materials. The one science of man that has attempted anything like an understanding of the total human personality is psychoanalysis, a field that must be distinguished from its suspicious neighbor, academic psychology, which restricts itself to a relatively tiny part of man's being. But it is psychoanalysis that has undergone violent cleavages into schools and is currently experiencing the deepest crisis over fundamentals, a crisis that has in the end to be evaluated by philosophy since its issues are philosophical, a principal one—that between Freud, Adler, and Jung—being precisely the nature and scope of human subjectivity.

More important, however, than any of the theories of man held by philosophers is the actual image of man in terms of which the historical epoch lives and plays out its destiny. Such an image of man may be derived in part from the theories of philosophers, but more often than not it is the product of historical forces that tend to be unconscious because they are so massive. The phenomena of mass society and the collectivization of man are facts so decisive for our age that all conflicts among political forms and among leaders take place upon and within this basis. Collectivization proceeds by reducing man to an object in functional interplay with other objects (men), returning him ironically enough in some sense to his primitive status as a natural object in use, from which history long ago disentangled him. Collective being is becoming the style of our epoch, despite our Sunday-morning lip service to the ideals of the dignity and value of the individual. Subjectivity is already considered a criminal offense under totalitarianism, a morbid excrescence by our own Philistinism. Against such threatening historical weather, that subjectivity takes on the human dignity of revolt; the reality of the negative shows itself in man's power to say *No*.

EXISTENCE AND ANALYTIC
PHILOSOPHERS

Appendix II

THAT existence is not a genuine predicate has been one of the more entrenched dogmas of Positivism and Analytic Philosophy; yet in some quarters recently the question seems to have been reopened. The question indeed deserves a fresh look on the part of analytic philosophers; and for this purpose we may as well begin with the classical statement on the matter given by Kant in his *Critique of Pure Reason*—a statement that has seemed decisive for most modern philosophers after him.

"Being," Kant says, "is evidently not a real predicate, or a concept of something that can be added to the concept of a thing." That is: if I think of a thing and then think of that same thing as existing, my second concept does not add any observable property to the first, and therefore—so far as its conceptual or strictly representative content is concerned—I am thinking the same thought in both cases. The existing thing and the merely possible thing are, *qua* thing, one and the same. And Kant's example here has become quite as famous as his declaration of general principle: the concept of a hundred real dollars, he tells us, and of a hundred merely possible dollars are, as concepts, one and the same—there is not one cent more or less in the one than the other. The concept, as such, is existentially neutral.

It is worth while to pause for a moment over this rather remarkable example, which is quite typical of the candor with which this great thinker is often likely to bring up as

examples just those that are most embarrassing to the case
he would like to establish. For here he has chosen a most
pointedly existential illustration—at least for most of us who
at one time or another have felt the abysmal difference between real and merely possible dollars when we have put
our hand into our pocket to find it unexpectedly and em-
barrassingly empty. Kant is candid enough to admit this
fact: "In my financial position," he says, "no doubt there
exists more by one hundred dollars than by their concept
only." But why this grudging concession to the earthy fact
of one's financial position, almost by way of incidental
footnote, as if money were something that had only a very
accidental relation to one's financial position and were not
essentially something that has to do with making us richer
or poorer—richer by its existence in our pockets and poorer
by its absence? The ordinary citizen, who feels the pinch
of meeting bills and knows very well the difference between
a hundred merely possible dollars (of which he may
dream) and a hundred real dollars (which he is hard put
to scrape together), might be provoked—and just by the
very homeliness of Kant's example—to exclaim that if the
concepts of philosophers allow no difference between a hundred real dollars and a hundred merely possible dollars,
then so much the worse for the concepts of philosophers! A
human retort which would also seem to be not without its
own philosophic depth.

Kant's contention, however, is readily understandable in
terms of his general doctrine in the *Critique* as to what is
required of a really legitimate concept. Such a concept
must be capable of being represented according to some
schema of the imagination: the concept (if it is not to be
empty) must bind together a series of mental images, thus
ultimately of sensory data which are the sources of those
images. In his doctrine of the schemata Kant was systema-
tizing the view of the nature of the concept which had
appeared in british Empiricism with Berkeley's famous objection to "abstract ideas" and from there had passed down
to Kant through Hume. The concept here is, ultimately,
a mental picture of a sensory datum—either directly or

through a logical chain of concepts constructed from other concepts which are such mental pictures. In this sense, surely, we have to agree with Kant that we can have no mental picture of the existence of a thing. In forming the concept of a table, I can represent to myself its color, size, shape, etc., but not its existence. All of these—color, size, shape, etc.—are what philosophers nowadays call observable properties; and the existence of the table is not one of these properties. To be sure, if there were not actually existing tables, we would not be able to sense these observable properties, and from there proceed to form a mental picture of a table that is indifferently an actual or a possible table. However, this fact is allowed to lurk like an unmentioned and unpleasant ghost in the background of the whole Kantian discussion, turning up some very pretty puzzles elsewhere in the *Critique*, and eventually landing him in that impasse—the scandal of philosophy, as he himself calls it—of being unable to provide any proof of the reality of the external world.

Thus Kant's position that existence is not a predicate belongs to the more explicitly empiricist side of his philosophy, a very considerable side too of Kantianism in which it has shaped later Positivism and Pragmatism much more than Positivists and Pragmatists sometimes seem to remember. His target here, moreover, is perfectly clear—and in philosophical disputes it is imperative for the philosopher to know what he is really after if the dispute is not to lose itself in the bewildering detail of perfectly pointless dialectic: Kant wants to get rid of existence as a predicate in order to demolish the arguments for the existence of God. Later Empiricists and analysts who have followed him in this point have been concerned with a similar, but more general, aim: that of undermining metaphysics altogether; for if existence is an empty concept, then metaphysicians who have talked about it have been talking nonsense. Of course, philosophers have talked a great deal of nonsense about existence, and to expose this nonsense is a laudable aim. But one need not therefore go to the extreme of taking one's revenge on ordinary language and the plain man by casting out the word "exists" from his permissible vocabulary.

More than this: the Kantian position might be accepted, but then put to a very different use from that of the Empiricists. And this is exactly what takes place with Kierkegaard, who agrees with Kant that existence is not a concept (or predicate) but from a diametrically opposite point of view from that of the Empiricists. For the Positivist, existence is not a concept because it is too empty, thin, and therefore ultimately meaningless; for Kierkegaard, my existence is not a concept because it is too dense, rich, and concrete to be represented adequately in any mental picture. My existence is not a mental representation but a fact in which I am plunged up to the ears, and indeed over the head. In that great hall of mirrors—the Kantian mind with all its representations—the image of my existence never appears adequately in any one of those conceptual mirrors simply because it is the enveloping presence surrounding all those mirrors, without which they would not be at all. Men—actual and not merely possible men—are related to their own existence in a quite different way from that of the understanding seeking to secure a mental representation: in moods of joy, or of despair, they may bless or curse their own existence. When Hamlet in his ultimate anxiety puts the question "To be or not to be," the way in which, in this question itself, he relates himself to his own existence is not at all that of the understanding to one of its concepts. Kierkegaard's aim here is as perfectly definite as Kant's, though altogether different in its implications for philosophy: *if existence cannot be a concept, then quite clearly it cannot be reduced to essence, nor can priority for essence over existence be claimed.* Kierkegaard's immediate target, of course, was the Hegelian attempt to reduce existence to essence by showing the former as one stage in the unfolding of the Dialectic; but his protest against essence in the name of existence goes quite beyond this immediate target, and in fact brings into question the whole Platonic tradition within Western philosophy that has always attempted to treat existence as a copy, imitation,

participation in, or even a fall or descent of essence. Here
Kierkegaard points to what is really the significant issue
behind the debate about existence's being a predicate:
what matters in the end is not whether we rig up our language so that "exists" is a permissible predicate or not (and
in fact it can be rigged either way); what does matter is
what we make of existence: whether we give it its due as
a primal and irreducible fact, or somehow convert it into
a shadowy stand-in for essence.

1.

On this point the Platonic inheritance is so subtly and
deeply entrenched in Western thought that its presence is
likely to be potent even where it is unconscious; a rather
striking instance of which is provided by Bertrand Russell
even in a phase of his thought when he had purportedly
thrown over his earlier Platonism. Russell sharpens the
Kantian position considerably: the proposition "Socrates exists" becomes, for him, nonsensical because in the formal
language of his *Principia Mathematica* an expression of this
form is syntactically impossible. The fact that in ordinary
language the statement "Socrates exists" is perfectly understandable, and indeed everybody not only understands its
meaning but knows it to be false since 399 B.C. (when
Socrates drank the hemlock), is something of an obstacle,
nevertheless, that Russell has to get around. Accordingly,
he would permit the surrogate statement "(Ex) (x=Socra-
tes)," which may be translated, "There is an individual
whose proper name is Socrates." Here, in the effort to
get rid of existence as a predicate, we are left with the
suspiciously kindred expression, "There is." Existence, apparently, is a rather sticky and clinging presence. Russell's feat begins to look a little bit like that old comic
routine of the comedian who tries frantically to throw off
a piece of flypaper from his right hand, fails, then sits down
and patiently peels it off with his left hand; at last, holds
up his empty right hand while a look of childish glee
spreads over his face; meanwhile the audience sees the

paper sticking now to the left hand. The early Wittgenstein was one of the first to call attention to the fact that the flypaper was still there.

Since "There is" remains in his language, Russell has to provide an interpretation of what it means to exist; and this he proceeds to do with great boldness, dispatch—and simple-mindedness. Eliminating the details of symbolism, we can boil it down to this: To exist is to satisfy a propositional function, where "satisfy" has the same meaning as when we say in mathematics that the roots of an equation exist—i.e., satisfy the equation. And this is not proposed as a mere illustrative model; on the contrary, Russell tells us, "This is the fundamental meaning of 'existence.' Other meanings are either derived from this, or embody mere confusion of thought." Did Bertrand Russell, the man, ever believe that he existed in the same sense in which the root of an equation exists? I hardly think so; but the fact that probably the most widely known philosopher of our time can advance this view (and get away with it in philosophic circles) would seem to indicate how far into the Kingdom of Laputa the age itself, at any rate its analytic philosophers, have insensibly slipped.

Russell's language here is altered from Plato, but the line of thought is exactly the same. To exist, Plato said, is to be a copy or likeness of the Idea, or essence. Particular things exist to the degree that they fulfill, or *satisfy*, the archetypal pattern of the Idea. To exist, says Russell, is to satisfy a propositional function, just as a certain number may satisfy a given equation. In both cases existence is understood as derivative from essence. Existents exist in virtue of essence.

Wittgenstein, following Russell, was at once bolder and more stringent in his thinking when he protested that the language of Russell's *Principia Mathematica* did not properly get existence out of logic. Not only does this language permit unrestricted existential operators, but in it the proposition "(Ex) (x=x)"—"There is an individual identical with itself"—is an analytic truth. Wittgenstein felt that logic should not even be able to make a statement like this—let alone its being an analytic truth. Speaking as the purist of logic, for whom logic, pure logic, must have nothing to do with existence and the real world, Wittgenstein was undoubtedly justified in this contention. But he was then forced to desperate measures to get the "There is" out of logic. If one had a world where all the atomic facts were properly itemized, so he contended, one could simply say "a is P" or "b is P" or "c is P," etc., etc. (where a, b, and c are proper names, and P is an observable property), without having to stoop to saying "There is an x that is P," which is only a vague and indefinite makeshift for one or the other definite statement. Unfortunately—though perhaps fortunately for us as existing humans—a world of such clear-cut atomic facts, where each individual entity is neatly itemized under its proper name, is but the dream of the logician, with no resemblance to the real world in which we do exist. (Even in mathematics there are compelling reasons why Wittgenstein's proposal could not be adopted.) These early proposals of Wittgenstein have by this time pretty well gone by the boards among analytic philosophers; but the fact that he was forced to such extreme measures to conjure "There is" out of logic serves to suggest again what we have seen in the case of Russell: that existence is indeed a sticky thing, from which even the pure logician finds it difficult to disentangle himself.

2.

At this point we have to compound Kant's original difficulty, or rather push it to its root, by turning from the "There is" to the simple copula "is," and by asking whether this simple verb itself, merely as copula, does not have some existential import. Kant would have the expression "S is" be nonsense, but would find "S is P" acceptable. But what if the "is" in "S is P" were more than a mere sign of the joining of predicate to subject, but also signified existence in some way or other? This aspect of the problem Kant did not at all develop. Modern mathematical logic dispenses with the "is" of predication, usually employing

parentheses for the job—thus "a is P" becomes "P(a)"—
and this latter syntactical form suggests that the "is" of
ordinary language is no more than an auxiliary symbol with
no more meaning than the parentheses used as the formal
sign of predication. Still, it is not quite certain that the "is"
of ordinary language has only this sense; and indeed if we
consult the Oxford Dictionary, we find that it lists six senses
of the verb "to be" before it arrives at its meaning as a
simple copula! No doubt, for the formal logician this is
merely a grubby and earth-bound fact of historical usage,
and of no particular significance for philosophic understanding; but since we happen also to be dealing here with
the grubby and earth-bound fact of existence, we might at
least let this fact of historical usage cut as much weight, at
least *prima facie,* as the formal constructions of logicians.

One effort to dispense with the copula occurred in the
famous episode in earlier Positivism about protocol sentences (here again the original impetus came from Wittgenstein): if instead of "This table is brown" we report
the supposedly more basic datum "Here now a brown
patch," we have got rid of the copula "is." And with an
ample class of such protocol statements, together with the
apparatus of formal logic, which does not employ the copula "is," we should be able to deal with the world of our
experience without any of that metaphysical nonsense that
in the past has attached itself to the verb "to be" and has
made the sheer accident of its usage an occasion for
philosophers to expatiate on the meaning of existence. So,
at any rate, earlier Positivism proposed.

Now, the issue is not the sacrosanct character of the verb
"to be," and we would be quite content to jettison it if that
would help matters; but in appearing to jettison it we have
to be sure that we do not make another verbal form do its
work. And in this last respect, "Here now" is an extremely
suspicious expression; for one could hardly find another in
the language that more vividly signifies the immediate,
actual, enveloping present state of affairs—existence, in
short. Where the temporal reference is thus insisted upon
there certainly something is said about existence. To elim-

inate any existential reference one would have to eliminate the tense of the verb. Thus in the logical form "P(a)"—to be read, "P of a"—the assertion is temporally neutral, or timeless; "Brown (this table)"—"Brown of this table"—does not tell me when it is, was, or will be brown; whereas, "This table *is* brown" indicates that this brown table is a present existing fact. So, too, in languages like Russian and Greek the verb for "to be" can be omitted as a copula in the present tense; but the omission is possible because the tense is clearly understood; when other tenses are signified, the verb for "to be" has to be used.

It might seem possible to eliminate present-past-future by signifying time through some numerical designation that would be temporally neutral. To say "at ten o'clock" is not to say that ten o'clock is past, present, or future. Thus the next step of Positivism beyond its earlier stage of protocol sentences was to assign predicates to space-time co-ordinates: instead of "Here now a a brown patch," with its obvious present and existential reference, we have "Brown (x,y)"—"A brown patch at space-time point x,y." A numerical designation of time abstracts from the tense of the verb. Thus we would seem to arrive at a perfectly non-existential language of pure nouns and adjectives without any verbs.

But this proposal would work only if there were fixed points in an absolute Newtonian space and time that could be known independently of the events or actual bodies that are found at those space-time points. In fact, however, we always have to set up physical space co-ordinates in relation to some existing body (the earth, sun, or what not); and time co-ordinates in relation to some actual event, which as actual was once present, or is so now, or will be. A language purely of nouns and adjectives would thus borrow whatever temporal meanings it still preserves from a language which had genuine verbs. But a genuine verb is one with tenses, and therefore with an essential reference to time; and with time, there is an inexpugnable reference to existence.

3.

To sum up: The question—debated by modern philosophers since Kant—whether existence is or is not a predicate conceals another and historically more momentous question for philosophy: the question namely of existence and essence, and their relation. The denial of existence as a genuine predicate belongs—in the case of most philosophers—to that impulse of the philosophic mind which loves the static and timeless self-identity of essence, and would construe existence as some kind of shadowy derivative of these latter. The effort to transcend the primary fact of existence takes, as we have seen, three forms, of which the denial of existence is perhaps least radical: the second is to cast out the existential operator, "There is," from a properly logical language; the third, to reduce the meaning of the verb "to be" to a mere copula, an auxiliary symbol signifying that predicate and subject are somehow joined. And it has been this last that brought us to the hidden root of the whole question: the meaning of "to be."

The verb with its tense retains an essential reference to the existential. In this respect, "to be" is the verb of verbs, since it expresses the primary fact that makes a verb a verb and not some other part of speech: the pure fact of being present, or of having been past, or of going to be future —and without any accompanying secondary and observable action. The paradoxical fact, however, is that in one range of usage "to be" is precisely the verb that can lose its essential temporality. We say "7 is a prime number"; and it is nonsense to say "7 was a prime number," or "7 will be a prime number." The present tense figures here as a degenerate case of temporality. But it is just this degenerate case—where "is" loses all temporal sense and serves as mere copula—that the logician is apt to take as the primary case, from which all other meanings of "to be" are then to be understood.

That our argument has come finally to turn on the tense of the verb, and therefore on time and the temporal as the inexpugnable feature of existence, is no novelty but in fact returns us to the original source of this problem in history: returns us to Plato, for whom the derivation of existence from essence was the human project of an escape from the temporal into the timeless. To be sure, modern analytic philosophers—since they are anti-metaphysicians—have no Platonic realm of essences. But Platonism—as that fundamental mode of thought which is compelled always to rate essence over existence—may be ejected with great show from the front door only to creep back invisibly by the rear. So long as logic is given absolute pre-eminence in philosophy, and the logical mind placed first in the hierarchy of human functions, reason seems inevitably caught up in the fascination of static and self-identical essence, and existence tends to become an elusive and shadowy matter, as the history of philosophy abundantly confirms. So far as he logicizes, man tends to forget existence. It happens, however, that he must first exist in order to logicize.

INDEX